Issues in Interpretation Theory

Issues in Interpretation Theory

Edited by

Pol Vandevelde

MARQUETTE
UNIVERSITY
PRESS

Marquette Studies in Philosophy
No. 49
Andrew Tallon, Series Editor

Library of Congress Cataloging-in-Publication Data

Issues in interpretation theory / edited by Pol Vandevelde.
        p. cm. — (Marquette studies in philosophy ; no. 49)
Includes bibliographical references and index.
ISBN-13: 978-0-87462-672-8 (pbk. : alk. paper)
ISBN-10: 0-87462-672-2 (pbk. : alk. paper)
1. Hermeneutics. I. Vandevelde, Pol.
BD241.I87 2006
121'.686—dc22

                                    2006031621

Cover photo by Bobbi Timberlake.

♾ The paper used in this publication meets the minimum requirements of the
American National Standard for Information Sciences—
Permanence of Paper for Printed Library Materials, ANSI Z39.48-1992.

MARQUETTE UNIVERSITY PRESS
MILWAUKEE

The Association of Jesuit University Presses

CONTENTS

FOREWORD

This volume contains a selection of the contributions made by the scholars who participated in the Seminar on Phenomenology and Hermeneutics organized at Marquette University since 2002. The Seminar originates from the needs manifested by faculty and graduate students from philosophy and theology at Marquette University to have a forum in which they could exchange the results of their research and interact with prominent scholars in the fields of phenomenology and hermeneutics.

The confluence of interests between philosophy and theology has a long history. While hermeneutics was traditionally a dominion of theology as the main field of investigation of the Bible, philosophy came to recognize its interpretive nature especially with the different brands of existentialism. Karl-Otto Apel claims that we are now in a paradigm where language has taken the role of first philosophy. The complexity of issues related to how an object of investigation is chosen, delimited, and approached, as well as the slew of questions linked to how a subject forms and how far the historical or social boundaries of a subject reach have made the reflection on the mediation between subject and object a task of intellectual necessity.

It is possible and in some instances, for example in processes of justification, valid to pursue the model of methodological solipsism that assumes the subject of knowledge to be a normal adult person exercising her faculty of knowledge independently of other subjects of knowledge. However, for many issues the question regarding the genesis of the subject (how the subject formed) and the social and historical influences on such a subject is directly linked to the choice of the objects of investigation, the methods of investigations, the determination of the utility of the investigation, and the allocation of resources.

These questions in turn can be treated in a causal model, events or other people's behaviors causing individuals to form certain beliefs. However, the causal model eliminates the need for meaning more than it explains what the meaning is, and some, like Donald Davidson, rejoice in this elimination. Phenomenology and hermeneutics have opted for a non-causal model of explanation, still enlivened by the hope expressed by Husserl to bring the still mute experience to expression.

When Friedrich Schlegel along with Schleiermacher, the founder of Romantic hermeneutics, worked toward a fusion of philosophy and poetry, what they had in view was an articulation of that fascinating mystery of a nature that seems amenable to intelligibility and the capacity of the human mind to bring order into the world. This was also Aristotle's key concept of logos—reason, discourse, language—something like understanding. But the notion of understanding cannot be limited to an epistemological notion, as already recognized by Schleiermacher and Dilthey. It is also an ontological component of human existence, and Heidegger and Gadamer expanded much effort in articulating the ontological face of understanding. What was brought to the fore was the identity between what is described by phenomenology—the susceptibility to make sense both of things and human beings—and what makes human beings who they are—their capacity to understand themselves and things around them.

If objects of investigation cannot be neatly disentangled from the framework in which they are represented as objects or appear as objects, the discourse that attempts to render these objects in context or to tell the prose of the world, to borrow Merleau-Ponty's expression, cannot afford to pursue clarity at any cost. It is no easy task to do justice to the complexity of what gravitates around the objective hard core of things or the many perspectives through which a thing gives itself or the hue of shades through which something lets itself become visible or the nuances of what it means that something is. But there may be virtue in complexity.

Disciplines that have reflected on what interpretation is, like phenomenology and hermeneutics, have also developed the conceptual tools as well as the methods suited to various objects of interpretation. They have the means to explain why the way knowledge is structured and things organized in objects of knowledge affects how human beings understand themselves. Yorck von Wartenburg wrote to Dilthey in 1889 that "the 'modern human being,' i.e., the human being since the Renaissance, is ready to be buried."[1] Less than a century later Michel Foucault was predicting another death of human being: "Ought we

---

1   *Briefwechsel zwischen Wilhelm Dilthey und dem Grafen Paul Yorck v. Wart-enburg. 1887-1897.* Hrsg. Sigfrid v.d. Schulenburg. Halle, 1923, 83, quoted in Martin Heidegger, *Les conférences de Cassel (1925) précédées de la Correspondance Dilthey-Husserl* (1911), bilingual edition by Jean-Claude Gens. Paris: Vrin, 2003, 208.

not... give up thinking of man, or, to be more strict, to think of this disappearance of man—and the ground of possibility of all the sciences of man—as closely as possible in correlation with our concern with language? Ought we not to admit that, since language is here once more, man will return to that serene non-existence in which he was formerly maintained by the imperious unity of Discourse?"[2] This interaction between epistemology, history, and ontology has been at the heart the research in phenomenology and hermeneutics.

The essays gathered here testify to the broad range of issues and the variety of methods typical of these disciplines. The quality of the essays presented in this volume also testifies to the lively and fruitful exchanges of ideas made possible by Marquette University. I want to acknowledge the strong support of Dr. Michael McKinney, Dean of the Klingler College of Arts and Sciences, Drs. John Jones and James South, chairs of the department of philosophy, and Frs. Philip Rossi and John Laurance, chairs of the department of theology, who all made possible the establishment of the Seminar on Phenomenology and Hermeneutics. I also want to acknowledge the contribution from faculty and students who lend life to the Seminar.

Pol Vandevelde

---

2 Michel Foucault, *The Order of Things. An Archaeology of the Human Sciences.* New York: Vintage Books, 1994 [1970], 386.

I

THE GENESIS OF THE HEIDEGGERIAN INTERROGATION ON THE ORIGIN OF THE WORK OF ART

JACQUES TAMINIAUX

The text that can be rightly considered the most evident testimony to Heidegger's involvement with the "national-socialist revolution" is the famous Rectorate Address that he pronounced in Freiburg in 1933 under the title *The Self-Affirmation of the German University* (Heidegger 2000, 109 ff).

However it is striking to note that, far from being a summary of the ideological slogans used by the regime now establishing itself, this text is meant to be essentially philosophical in its language and themes. More precisely, the ambition it manifests is to bring the German university, and consequently the German existence in its entirety, to the level of what the Greek beginning of philosophy had been, as it was illustrated by Plato when he celebrated in his works the way of life supposedly the highest accomplishment of the human condition: the *bios theoretikos*, dedicated to the contemplation of the ultimate ontological principles of what is. The Rectorate Address does not use the terms of the current racist ideology, but the key-words of the Platonic dialogues—*theoria, energeia, techne, praxis*. In passing, this speech skillfully subverts the themes these Greek words referred to in their original text and casts them in some of the key-words of the Nazi slogans—*Kampf, Volk, Führung, Sturm*. In its conclusion it is in the shadow of Plato's *Republic* that it evokes the articulation of the State ontologically justified, organized into a hierarchy of levels of activity: the satisfaction of the needs, the defense of the community, under the command of those who are dedicated to science, above whom are the philosophers.

Therefore, it is as if, according to the Rectorate Address, Germany in 1933 was on the verge of ensuring the return of the Greek beginning.

In the following pages, I propose to examine the stakes of the Heideggerian problematic of the return of Greece on the basis of the texts he devoted to the question of the origin of the work of art. This attention to art followed the Rectorate Address and developed in the mid-1930s.

In order to determine these stakes, these texts have to be considered in combining two perspectives: an *ontogenetic* perspective consisting in considering their relationship to Heidegger's previous works, starting with the most famous of them all, *Being and Time*, and a *phylogenetic* perspective consisting in determining the extent to which they draw their inspiration from other philosophers, ancient or modern. A careful reading of the Rectorate Address demonstrates that Heidegger mixes an ontogenetic and phylogenetic thread, in the sense that, on the one hand, he mobilizes some of the central themes of *Being and Time*—Dasein's existence for the sake of oneself, its temporality, its resolution, its unveiling capacity—whereas, on the other hand, he appeals to Plato in the case of Ancient philosophy and both Hegel and Nietzsche in the case of Modern philosophy. This second inspiration is linked to the theme of the return since we know that the nostalgia for Greece played a determining role in the genesis of Hegel's thought and in the work of his long-time friend Hölderlin; we also know that, starting with the first book on *The Birth of Tragedy*, Nietzsche wanted to be the most Greek of his contemporaries.

It could be claimed that these two paths form the fabric of the texts in which Heidegger articulated his questioning on the origin of the work of art. These texts are three and follow each other by a few months between the summer of 1935 and the beginning of the winter of 1936. Before proposing some elements for a genetic analysis of these texts by concentrating on the earliest one with respect to the theme of the return of Greece, it is not superfluous to ask whether, in spite of the fact that it is only in the mid 1930s that the philosophical interest in art suddenly took center stage, this interest does not have some roots in Heidegger's works preceding the time of his involvement with Nazism.

To such a question, it is tempting to oppose immediately a point-blank denial. One can search in vain for the words "art" and "work of art" in the very meticulous index of the English translation of *Sein und Zeit*, published in 1962 (Heidegger 1962). These words do not appear either in the equally meticulous index of Theodore Kisiel's great book on the genesis of *Being and Time* in the lecture courses that Heidegger gave first in Freiburg, when he was Husserl's assistant, then in Marburg

(Kisiel 1995). However, it would be a mistake to conclude that nothing was anticipating the problematic of the origin of the work of art in Heidegger's previous works.

1. The Ontogenesis of a problematic

1.1 *The re-appropriation of the Greeks in the fundamental ontology*

Being and Time is a work that implements a theoretical project to which Heidegger gave the name of fundamental ontology. He was thereby aiming at a discipline centered not on beings and their properties, but on Being in the verbal sense. As it is proper for the question of Being, in this sense, to concern intimately the one who asks it, and thus to bear on him in return, *Being and Time* claimed that a rigorous and synthetic questioning on the diverse meanings of the word "Being" requires first a transcendental analysis, or an analytic of the mode of being of the human being. This mode of being is called *Dasein*, the substantive form of a verb that means, in everyday German "to exist" (the proofs of God's existence, in Kant, are the proofs of God's *Dasein*). Heidegger calls human being Dasein precisely because being and having to be form a stake that concerns him intimately. As is well known, this analytic, after isolating a certain number of intrinsic conditions for the possibility of human existence, factors called existentials, gathers them into a synthetic structure that is called Care—*Sorge*. In Heidegger's vocabulary, this word designates a condition consisting, for Dasein, in finding itself at the same time thrown in its being among other beings, and projecting always anew a possibility of being which is proper to it and only belongs to it. Let us note that Dasein is not a generic title; it is always someone who exists factually at a given moment and can say: my existence; someone who responds to the question *who?*, and not the question *what?* Such Care, according to Heidegger, is finite in the sense that its own end—its death—determines it intrinsically. It is also fundamentally temporal, but of a temporality that, far from being an infinite series of instants in which it would be possible for it to stand, is rather fundamentally ecstatic, i.e., open to a limited future that it must face, while taking over the past this temporality is already. The fundamental ontology has the ambition of showing that this ecstatic and finite temporality of the thrown project characteristic of any Dasein is the only transcendental horizon of intelligibility of the sense of being. Hence the title: *Sein und Zeit* (*Being and Time*).

In spite of the fact that the work of art does not appear among the themes of *Being and Time*, the roots of Heidegger's questioning on that topic can be found in the works preparing the analytic of Dasein and, more generally, fundamental ontology. As it is well known, fundamental ontology constantly puts the emphasis on the oscillation in human existence between two poles: on the one hand, the authenticity which is Dasein's resoluteness of its finite capacity to be and thus of its mortality, and, on the other hand, the everyday inauthenticity which for Dasein consists in being preoccupied by possibilities to be actualized in a world it shares with others, with whom it can be substituted, and to focus on goals to reach, tasks to accomplish, effects or works to produce.

Thanks to the publication starting some years ago of the lecture courses Heidegger gave during the gestation of *Being and Time*, it now appears that the polarity between resolute authenticity and the inauthenticity of everyday concerns was articulated along a patient analysis of Greek philosophical texts: Plato's dialogues as well as the Aristotelian corpus in which the young professor of Marburg enjoyed putting to the fore the *Nicomachean Ethics*, which he regarded as a true ontology of Dasein. Now, art appears among the themes of Aristotle's treatise.

The Greeks had only one word: *techne*, which can be translated as "knowing-how," in order to designate the art of painters, sculptors, tragic poets, as well as the know-how of craftsmen such as potters, carpenters and shoemakers, etc., and the competence of experts such as physicians and strategists. They subsumed under a unique word, *technites*, all those who owned a knowing-how, no matter how diverse the activity their *techne* ruled could be. And this activity itself is of a considerable variety, since it can produce effects such as victory for the art of the strategist, healing for the art of the physician, tools for the art of the blacksmith, tragedies for the art of the dramaturgist. This activity was also subsumed under one single word, *poiesis*, which can be translated as "production." It turns out that art, in this broad sense of a knowing-how ruling some *poiesis*, counts among the topics Aristotle treats in the *Nicomachean Ethics*, in particular in book VI.

Aristotle's treatise investigates the levels of *arete*, that is to say: of virtue or excellence of which human life is capable. Art in the sense of a know-ing-how overseeing a production is one of those excellences. It appears among the dianoetic or intellectual excellences which are analyzed in book VI of the treatise through the establishment of a hierarchy among them into two levels: the level of excellences which involve a deliberation and the higher level of excellences which reach a science and are thus called epistemonic. These epistemonic excellences oversee a *theoria* or contemplation the referent of which in Aristotle—on this point in agreement with Plato—is characterized as being imperishable and inalterable, as forever being and ever since being what it is. *Theoria*, the referent of which has this characteristic, is itself divided into two levels: the level of *episteme* in the narrow sense, which only deals with beings of a determinate type (for example geometrical figures) and the higher level of *sophia*, which bears according to Aristotle on the principles of the whole of nature. Art does not appear among these higher dianoetic excellences. It appears in the lower level of deliberative excellences, those which do not oversee contemplation but a productive activity and which have as referents something perishable and alterable. To be more precise, art is at the lowest level of deliberative excellences. Considered as excellence, *techne*, i.e., the know-how of a good *technites*, is inferior to what Aristotle calls *phronesis* (generally translated by practical wisdom or prudence), which does not oversee the production of effects or works but what Aristotle calls praxis, a word he understands as simply meaning how to conduct one's life. *Praxis* is the way people behave. *Phronesis* is the aptitude to discern in changing circumstances what is propitious to conducting one's life in the right way.

The analysis of the lecture courses Heidegger devoted to book VI of the *Nicomachean Ethics* before *Being and Time* shows that the articulation of his future analytic of Dasein between two poles—inauthenticity and authenticity—is to a very large extent inspired from the distinction Aristotle draws between the activity of *poiesis* enlightened by *techne* and the activity of *praxis* enlightened by *phronesis*. The latter according to Aristotle is for the sake of itself (*ou eneka*) to the extent that what matters for it is precisely the good conduct of life and not the production of this or that effect.

Once reappropriated in a perspective which is no longer ethical but strictly ontological and centered on Dasein, the Aristotelian distinction is metamorphosed in Heidegger in the dichotomy between, on the one hand, Dasein's inauthentic character of everyday concern in productive preoccupations which he shares with others, and, on the other, authenticity, which consists for the individual to assume properly and resolutely his mortal existence for the sake of himself.

The examination of Heidegger's interpretation of book VI of the *Nichomachean Ethics*, precisely because it is thus oriented, also reveals that within the framework of Dasein's ontology, art in general belongs to the level of the inauthentic and could thus not have a fundamental and originary status. However, despite the confinement of art in inauthenticity, a major theme of Heidegger's later meditation on the origin of art is already brought to light in these Marburg lectures. This theme is *truth*, understood not in the traditional sense of an adequacy between intellect and thing which would have its site in judgment, but in the initial sense of *aletheia*, understood as a disclosure which has its site in Dasein's concrete intentionality, its relationship to the world. The Heideggerian reading of Aristotle in these lecture courses stresses that *techne* owes its dignity as dianoetic excellence to its capacity to disclose in the environing world materials, means and ways which are necessary for the bringing into work of the model that any good *technites* considers at the beginning of his activity of production. And since any disclosure according to Heidegger has its site in Dasein's being-in-the-world, art thus understood, even at a lower level, has the status of being a modality of the capacity to disclose in which Dasein dwells and which permeates his whole relation to the world. It is in direct continuation of this reading of Aristotle that Heidegger claims when reflecting on the origin of the work of art that the origin of the work of art is art understood as the event of truth and that, in this event, a disclosure of a world occurs.

This is what is already in seed, but at the lower level of everydayness, in the works preparing *Being and Time*. However, before the questioning on the origin of the work of art could grant this event of truth through art a completely eminent ontological rank as Heidegger did in the mid 1930s, he had in the meantime to introduce a sharp distinction between, on the one hand, ordinary *techne* and *poiesis*, which are strictly bound to everydayness and thus submitted to the realm of the "they" (of anybody) and in the position of fall compared to authenticity, and, on the other, of a *techne* and a *poeisis* of higher rank freed from any kind of inauthenticity. This distinction was absent from *Being and Time* which overall brought all *techne*, know-how of experts and art of artists, back to the inferior level of a pragmatic circumspection dealing with a daily environment.

By contrast, this distinction is present in the famous Rectorate Address of 1933. Since this discourse clearly takes its inspiration from Plato's *Republic*, it thereby invites those who investigate the ontogenesis of the problematics of the origin of the work of art, which was going to be developed soon after, to wonder what this questioning, however dated it is, owes to Heidegger's long familiarity with Plato's text. It is significant that the most detailed reappropriation of Aristotle Heidegger made during his teaching at Marburg was a prelude to an analysis of Plato's *Sophistes* which was centered on the mode of life of the philosopher, the *bios theoretikos*.

Hence the question of what Heidegger took over from Plato at the time of the gestation of his fundamental ontology.

Considered from this angle, the ontogenesis of Heidegger's question on the origin of the work of art forces us to recognize that all the works gravitating around *Being and Time*, either preparing it or immediately furthering it, tend not only to erase any kind of divergence—and they are perceivable—between Aristotle and Plato, but also to keep from Aristotle only what is susceptible to illuminate and confirm in existential terms the absolute precedence Plato grants to contemplative life, i.e., *bios theoretikos*, and the pursuit through this *bios* of an ultimate ontological insight.

As mentioned above Aristotle's mention of dianoetic excellences contains a hierarchy. One can rightly claim to admit that Aristotle follows Plato when he attributes to *sophia*, which concerns the being of the whole, a rank superior to *episteme*, which is always limited to determinate beings such as geometric figures. And *a fortiori* a higher dignity than *phronesis*, which is the highest deliberative excellence, but which always remains bound to particular circumstances. However, different from Plato, Aristotle is careful not to claim that *sophia*—with which only philosophers are concerned—renders null and void *phronesis*, i.e., the practical perspicacity available to anyone in the conduct of one's existence. Shared by a plurality of individuals who interact and speak with each other, *phronesis* according to Aristotle is understood as a practical wisdom in situation and keeps all its dignity. Consequently, it is hard to see how the Platonic thesis that philosophers are exceptionally gifted to rule human affairs can be attributed to Aristotle. This is a Platonic, not an Aristotelian thesis. The corollary of this thesis, which Heidegger reappropriates, is also not Aristotelian: that a valuable city should be organized like a vast workshop where each would be a technician endowed with a strictly limited and definite expertise. This principle is totally opposed to the democratic way of life to which Aristotle granted a real dignity, since he presented Pericles as a model of *phronesis*.

One has to acknowledge that there are not many echoes in Heidegger's lecture courses of Marburg of these Aristotelian reservations toward Plato. This can be seen through some revealing quotations. At the opening of the first paragraph of his course on the *Sophistes*, Heidegger warns his audience that his recourse to Aristotle aims at preparing them for Plato, and more precisely for what is the true theme of the dialogue they will study: "Plato considers human Dasein in one of its most extreme possibilities, namely philosophical existence" (Heidegger 1992, 12; 1997a, 8). Some months earlier in a lecture course dedicated to *Fundamental Concepts of Aristotelian Philosophy*, Heidegger wrote about the Aristotelian definition of human being as "a living being endowed with speech" that the *logos* in Aristotle's sense is accomplished in the delimitation of the essence of what is, of the *ousia*. He added: "existence, the radical fundamental possibility of Dasein, is for the Greeks *bios theoretikos*, life spent in pure contemplation" (Heidegger 2002, 44).

For the Greeks! The shortcut is extremely significant if one considers that at that time Plato and Aristotle were practically alone among the Greeks to mobilize Heidegger's attention and if it is accepted that Plato is at the origin of the attempt to demonstrate the precedence of *bios theoretikos* over any other way of life, and especially over the political way of life. Of itself, the formula "The Greeks" would be sufficient to prove that Heidegger at that time did not perceive any solution of continuity between Plato and Aristotle. And this is confirmed by the interpretation he gave of the other Aristotelian definition of human being: the human being is a *zoon politikon*.

Heidegger takes into account this other definition and acknowledges that in Aristotle the political living being is a living being endowed with language. But when he does it, he is in strict conformity with Plato's views, and not at all with the very text of Aristotle; for Heidegger is careful to claim that for Aristotle as for Plato the *bios politikos* where the living being, which speaks, moves and acts does not exceed the level of everyday concern and of what such a concern generates in terms of inauthenticity, i.e., the leveling realm of *das Man*, of the "they." When a political agent—of course in Athenian democracy each citizen is a political agent—speaks in order to express his opinion on the decisions to be made for the sake of the community, it is not he who speaks but *das Man*, the "they" which speaks through him. Heidegger goes so far as to say that Aristotle, as well as Plato, was "in the most extreme opposition to what was going on around him," (Heidegger 2002, 109) and considered that the speech expressed in the public space of the *agora* was trapped by "the immediate, fashion, idle talk and rumor" (Heidegger 2002, 108).

One could ask how the radical ontological precedence Heidegger attributes to the *bios theoretikos* is compatible with the importance he granted to the Aristotelian analysis of *praxis*. To this, one has to answer that, aside from the relevance of Heidegger's Platonization of the Aristotelian text, the incompatibility is only apparent and vanishes as soon as it is seen that it is one and the same existential ontologization which presides in Heidegger to his interpretation of contemplative life as the accomplishment of the most authentic possibility of Dasein's existence and to his interpretation of *praxis*, in terms of a resolute existence for the sake of oneself. This ontologization of a particular type means that *theoria*, in the sense Plato and Aristotle gave it when they saw its culmination in the contemplative wisdom of the totality of the real, was insufficiently radical to the extent that, bearing on the immutable, the imperishable and the eternal, it moved away from mortality which is intrinsic to Dasein and thus sunk into inauthenticity.

This ontologization also means that *praxis* in Aristotle's sense was in fact insufficiently radical to the extent that it remained bound to interaction and dialogue in which mortals engage in everydayness. By claiming to overcome these insufficiencies Heidegger's ontologization consists in collapsing the sight inherent to the highest contemplation on the exclusive axis of *praxis* now also reinterpreted in terms of existence as Dasein's possibility to be for the sake of itself. This sight inherent to this existence for the sake of itself is the sight Heidegger will grant to *Gewissen*, understood as the most authentic intimate knowledge of Dasein. When Heidegger claimed in his Marburg lectures that the Aristotelian *phronesis* came close to this *Gewissen*, he was careful to add that the *Gewissen* should no longer be considered in ethical terms, i.e., as a moral consciousness in situation caring for good action with regard to this or that circumstance; *Gewissen* was to be ontologically purified. Thus purified, *phronesis* metamorphosed into *Gewissen* ceases to be the prudential and situated sight of the best decision to take: *phronesis* becomes the solitary silent sight by Dasein of the fact that its being is a radically mortal thrown project he alone has to assume resolutely.

All this existential metamorphosis of the Platonic precedence of the sight of being allows us to understand that Heidegger could, some years after the publication of *Being and Time* but before his involvement with Nazism, expound his own conception of the essence of truth through a detailed analysis of the cave myth, which is the key text of the *Republic*. This analysis, which takes the essential of the first part of the lecture course of 1931-32 on "*The Essence of Truth*" (Heidegger 1997), interprets the stages of the Platonic narrative as successive phases of liberation toward the sight of light that the being of beings is. This sight is reappropriated in existential terms since the ultimate meaning of being is eventually the finite temporality which constitutes us. With regard to the ontogenesis of my problem, this lecture course represents an important stage in the putting into place of some central notions which Heidegger will use in his questioning on the origin of the work of art some years later. These central notions all gravitate around the principle that the essence of freedom consists in dedicating oneself to the sight of light, a sight which is itself inseparable from a project or a projection of being of which only Dasein, the human existent, is capable.

What are these central notions? There is first the notion of *origin* which will take center stage in the questioning on the work of art. Pursuing the process of ontologization mentioned above, Heidegger writes:

> To become free means to understand Being as such and such an understanding lets first of all beings be as beings.

> It depends on human freedom whether beings become more beings or more unbeings and freedom measures its extent according to the original character, the breadth and the decisiveness of the tie to beings as they are and to the sight of the Being of these beings as it is, what understands itself only as Dasein, moved back in the isolation and thrownness of his historical provenance and future. The more original the tie [to this sight of the Being of beings] the greater the proximity to beings (Heidegger 1997b, 60).

The second important notion introduced by this text is the explicit reformulation in existential terms of the Platonic concept of the *philosopher-king*. Commenting on the passage of the *Republic*, where Plato deals with the return to the cave of those who have contemplated light, Heidegger writes:

> The authentic guardians of the *Miteinandersein* of human beings in
> the unity of the *polis* must of necessity be people who philosophize...
> The dominating of the state and the ordering of this domination must
> be governed by people who philosophize and who, on the basis of
> the deepest and widest knowledge—a knowledge which freely ques-
> tions—, establish the measure and the rule... As philosophizing they
> must of necessity be in a position of knowing with clarity and rigor
> what human being is and how it is about this Being and capacity to
> be (1997b, 100).

The third notion concerns the *ontological status of the work of art*. In the
context of his commentary on Plato, Heidegger for the first time grants
art, more precisely what he calls "great poetry"—Sophocles' poetry in
particular—the power to manifest "the internal power of the human
understanding of Being, of the sight of light." He adds that in order to
understand this, one has to cease "considering the problem of art as a
problem of aesthetics" (1997b, 64).

It is remarkable that, in this twofold gesture of the ontological
celebration of "great art" and of the overcoming of aesthetics, Plato is
here again the one who inspires Heidegger: in the second part of the
course (dedicated to *Theaetetus*), Heidegger connects the beautiful
in the Platonic sense to Dasein's aptitude of "making being manifest,
discovering it and thus letting the truth happen." In the same context
Heidegger writes that the beautiful as understood by the Greeks does
not pertain to aesthetic enjoyment. It is rather, he says, a determination
concerning the Dasein of human beings. To this Dasein, unquietness
(*Unheimlichkeit*) also belongs, of which Sophocles speaks at the beginning of the second chorus of *Antigone*: "There are many things which
are *deina* [worth admiring, but at the same time worth fearing], but
nothing is more uncanny than human beings" (1997b, 198).

According to Heidegger, human condition in its authenticity is disquieting or uncanny to the extent that it leaves the securing quietness
of daily concerns in order to confront its most proper, i.e., its own mortality. Besides expressing without any echo of the Aristotelian reading
of the Tragics a blunt amalgamation of the Platonic and Sophoclean
texts, these statements suggest that Plato's diatribes against artists and
spectators of their works result not from a recusation of "great art," but
on the contrary, from the rejection in the name of an eminent *techne*
granted to the unconcealment of being of what in the artist's works
appeals to aesthetic enjoyment.

1.2 The Reappropriation of the Greeks in the
Fundamental Ontology Broadened to the Dasein of a People

Two years later, the Rectorate Address puts this eminent *techne*, this great art, at the center stage of the ontological disclosure. In the steps of Heidegger's existential reformulation of the Platonic precedence of *theoria*, this discourse starts by reminding us that the Greeks understood *theoria* as "the highest accomplishment of genuine praxis." Heidegger introduces a significant innovation when in one gesture he closely connects this *theoria* understood as a sight of being by Dasein with a *techne* of Promethean size. Heidegger quotes a verse from Aeschylus' *Prometheus*: "*techne* is much weaker than necessity." Whereas in the context of Aeschylus' tragedy this means that any human know-how has its limits, Heidegger does not hesitate to translate the term *techne* by the German word *Wissen* and to read in Aeschylus' verse not an appeal to moderation but a celebration of the challenge imposed by the overpower of destiny and by the ontological concealment involved in this overpower. Thus *techne*, which has become now Promethean, is put to the level of the highest *theoria*, the one to which the metaphysician dedicates himself, and is called to preside to a setting into work of the same rank: the setting into work of a State of a new type, the description of which in the Rectorate Address is clearly inspired by Plato's *Republic* and in no way, as one can surmise, by Pericles' democratic City.

This Promethean *techne* constitutes the dominating tone of Heidegger's philosophical remarks on art which will appear in the first lecture course on Hölderlin and his course *Introduction to Metaphysics* before the three texts on the origin of the work of art.

I have shown elsewhere (Taminiaux 1989, 255-278) that the articulation of Heidegger's first interpretation of Hölderlin focused on the poems *The Rhine* and *Germania* derives, in its structure, from fundamental ontology and thus from the theoretical project to which *Sein und Zeit* belongs, in the sense that this first reading emphasizes the contrast between falling everydayness and Dasein's resolute authenticity. However, fundamental ontology initially was centered on one individual who is the Dasein always mine. Hence the major question: "who is Dasein?" By contrast, in 1933, the question becomes: "Who are we?" The "we" is the German people to whom the poet Hölderlin is supposed to speak. From the Dasein always mine, from any single existent who can say "I" and who has his own temporality, we have moved to the *unicity* of the

Dasein of a people and the central question now is: "How is it about the Being of this people itself?" (Heidegger 1999, 22). According to this expansion of the notion of Dasein to the existence of a people, we see in Heidegger's reading a semantic modification of the existentials which the existential analytics had isolated some years before. The fundamental *Stimmung* (attunement) in *Being and Time* is anxiety. Now, since the Dasein in question in this reading is the Dasein of the German people, the *Grundstimmung* suited to the being of this people must be different from the attunement which was suited to the being of each individual, while keeping the same function of ontological revelator as anxiety. Heidegger claims that Hölderlin's poems are carried by a fundamental tone suited to the being of the Dasein of the German people and which is the mourning for the sacred: gods have fled. Heidegger grants this *Grundstimmung* the function of revealing ontologically the Dasein of the German people. It reveals its truth to this people and it opens for it the "disposition to be ready" (*Bereitschaft*) to accept the return of the divine (Heidegger 1999, 103). Consequently, the emphasis shifts from the finite historicity of the individual toward the destiny of a single people: "The being of fatherland, i.e., the historial Dasein of the people, experienced as the authentic and unique Being, from which its fundamental stance toward being in totality grows and conquers its articulation" (Heidegger 1999, 121-22). This is the vocabulary of *Being and Time* but broadened to the Dasein of a people. Now if everyone is capable of his own Dasein as individual, not everyone could be capable of the Dasein of a people! Only a few individuals who are creators are at the level of this broadened Dasein.

This is the reason why Heidegger writes:

> The *Grundstimmung*—and this means the truth of the Dasein of a people—is originally instituted by the poet [Hölderlin for Germany]. But the being so disclosed is understood and articulated and thus open for the first time by the thinker. And the being thus understood is set in the last and first seriousness of beings, i.e., in the *decisive* historical truth through the fact that the people is brought to itself as a people. And this happens through the creation by the creator of state of the state which is decisive for the essence of this people. However, this whole event has its own times and thus its own sequence of times... These three creative forces of the historical Dasein bring about that to which we can ascribe greatness. (Heidegger 1999, 144)

The course of *Introduction to Metaphysics* takes place in the continuation of this broadened fundamental ontology (Heidegger 1953). Heidegger gave this lecture course the same year he drafted the first version of the essay on the origin of the work of art. Furthering the texts mentioned above and as in the course on Hölderlin, the *Introduction to Metaphysics* stresses that there are three modalities in the disclosure of the historial Dasein of a people which are meant for the poet, the creator of a state and the great thinker.

Such is the ontogenesis of the notions which are going to articulate the thematic questioning on the origin of the work of art: the historial Dasein of a people, the struggle at the heart of this broadened Dasein between concealment and disclosure, the setting-into-work which is up to what the people can be and is taken over by the poet, the thinker and the creator of a State. The destiny of this broadened Dasein imposes, according to Heidegger, a decision for the sake of Being and against the appearance in which everydayness remains.

Moreover the very notion of origin plays a determining role in the *Introduction to Metaphysics*. At the beginning of the course, Heidegger reminds his audience of the fundamental question of metaphysics: "why is there being and not rather nothing?" And he adds that it belongs to that question to have repercussion on the questioner and that thus this question "has its ground in a leap through which man thrusts away all the previous security, whether real or imagined, of his life." He adds: "the leap in this questioning opens up its own source—with this leap the question arrives at its own ground. We call such a leap, which opens up its own source, the original source or origin <*Ur-sprung*>, the finding of one's own ground" (Heidegger 1953, 4-5; 1959, 5-6). The origin in Heidegger's sense is at this time a sudden leap through which the Dasein of a people is supposed to confront what is most fundamental in its being.

2. The First Elaboration of the
Questioning on the Origin of the Work of Art

This first elaboration probably dating from 1931-1932 was only published in 1989 (Heidegger 1989, 5-22), edited by Hermann Heidegger, the philosopher's son.[1] It is accompanied by an introductory note in

---

1 The citations of this work have been translated by John Noel Turner and

which the editor reminds readers that, according to the *Postscript* which accompanied the publication of the last version of the questioning on the origin of the work art in *Holzwege* in 1949, his father's considerations on the subject did not claim to "resolve" the enigma of art, but only to make it "visible." There is a certain part of retrospective illusion in this note. If the first elaboration indeed contains signs of an attention to the enigma, these are dominated by a completely different thematic: the thematic of the call addressed to the German Dasein to assume resolutely the project of Being properly itself. It is in this sense that Heidegger writes at the very beginning of this first elaboration that for him "*one thing* only" matters: "Namely, in spite of all appreciation of that which has long been thought and said of an essential determination of art, to prepare a changed fundamental position of our Dasein toward art" (Heidegger 1989, 5). The possessive adjective used by Heidegger is significant of the broadening of his problematic to the Dasein of a people. It is by virtue of this broadening that the questioning on the origin of the work of art will be able to exclude from its field any borrowing to accepted views and thus to concentrate on the conditions of a German return of Greece.

According to Heidegger these accepted views regarding art suffer from a real ontological deficiency to the extent that they reduce the work of art either to being only the result of a lived experience (*Erlebnis*) of the artist awakening in the spectator this other *Erlebnis* of aesthetic enjoyment, or to being only objects around which historians, art critics, museum curators and amateurs busy themselves.

In both cases, one does not recognize that the "authentic" work—and only "great art" has this quality—is an epoch-making event and is endowed with the totally inaugural power of historization which is accompanied by a rupture with accepted views. In this regard it is striking to note that the continuity with the problematic of *Being and Time* imposes itself right away at the beginning of the questioning, to the extent that the separation between everydayness and authenticity is what rules the rejection of current views. At close inspection it turns out indeed that the goal is to give back its rights to the Being, in the verbal sense, of the work, to its working character. If, in order to do that, one has to free oneself from the habitual reducing of the being-work to the level either of the being-product or of the being-object, it is not for subtracting the work from any relationship but to take it away

been provided by the author, Jacques Taminiaux.

from a certain type of manifestation which concerns publicness. What characterized the inauthentic mode of existing in everydayness in *Being and Time* was precisely the submission to publicness, to the realm of the "they," to all-purpose clichés; and it was by opposition to all this that the indeclinable individuation of the Being proper to Dasein was described. Following this contrast and transposing it Heidegger can now write: "To the 'public,' where there is one, it has only the relation that it destroys the public. And in this destructive force the greatness of an artwork measures itself" (Heidegger 1989, 8).

2.1 The work of art as work

It remains to be seen whether this continuity is confirmed when we examine the two features characterizing the being-work of the work: the setting-up (*Aufstellung*) of a world and the setting forth (*Herstellung*) of an earth.

With regard to the setting-up of a world, the continuity is confirmed in that the world established by the work is presented as something "uncanny [*Unheimische*]" which is not only "more real [*seiender*, "beinger"] than any of the tangible present at hand things in which we believe ourselves in everyday life to be at home" but which also has a function of "rejection of the usual presence at hand" (Heidegger 1989, 9). It is thus a reformulation of the opposition emphasized by *Being and Time* between the disquieting character of the world in the proper and authentic sense and the securing character of everyday world. It is thus in fundamental ontology that the ontogenesis of the questioning on the work of art lies.

However, since for some years fundamental ontology has moved beyond the limits of individual Dasein to bear on the Dasein of a people, these echoes of existential analytic are intermingled with the echoes of some German precursors for whom Ancient Greece had the rank of a paradigm.

Like Hegel and his friends, Schelling and Hölderlin, like Schiller before them, Heidegger greets the example of "great art" among the Greeks. And like these precursors, Heidegger argues in a metaphysical perspective. Like them lastly, he appeals to types and not to designatable works, for one seeks in vain, when he grants to "the building of a certain temple of Zeus, or the putting up and erecting of a certain statue of Apollo" (Heidegger, 1989, 8-9) the function of establishing a world, which designatable work he had in mind. More precisely, in continuity with the chapter of the *Phenomenology of Spirit* on the "Religion of art" which for Hegel was the religion of the Greeks, Heidegger grants a theophanic function to the Greek works which are supposed to establish a world: "Such setting up as *establishing* is consecration and praising. To consecrate means to 'bless' in the sense that in the workly offering the holy as holy opens up and the God gets wrested into the open of his presence." (1989, 9)

By virtue of this theophanic setting-up, the world gains a verbal and active status: it "worlds" in the manner of a "guiding escort" which "never comes upon us as object. Rather, indicating, it holds our doings enraptured in a structure of reference out of which the beckoning grace and striking fate of the Gods arrives and—remains absent" (Heidegger 1989, 9). The first feature of the being-work of the work, through this contrast between worlding and innerworldly, between the non-familiarity of the former and the familiar character of the latter, concretizes at the level of a "we" the opposition *Being and Time* stressed between everydayness and the disquieting character of one's own Being.

How about the second feature, the *Herstellung of an earth? Herstellung* in German sometimes means production, sometimes setting forth (or even restoration). Heidegger makes use of these two meanings but he intends to emphasize the second.

Heidegger acknowledges that "every work, insofar as it is, is set forth *out of* stone, wood, ore, color, tone, and language" and that "in production utilization this is called the *matter*. It is brought into a form." He then claims that this conceptual doublet matter-form inherited from Plato and Aristotle involves an "interpretation of the Being of beings [which] is nevertheless not only not transparent, [but] not even fashioned out of the experience of the artwork as *artwork* at all" (Heidegger 1989, 10-11). It is here that Heidegger brings to the fore the second meaning of the word *Herstellung*.

He writes:

> Just as the work towers up in its world it also sinks itself back in the massiveness and weight of the stone, in the hardness and splendor of the ore, in the firmness and pliability of the wood, in the light and dark of the color, in the sounding out of the tone, and in the naming power of the word. Is all this only and chiefly matter, which just gets picked up from somewhere, used, and consumed in the making—and then through the forming no longer appears as mere matter? Does

not all that first come to light in the work? Are weight, splendor,
light, sounding—matter that gets 'dealt with'?"

To produce an earth is to restitute, to give this manifestation back
to itself, to manifest its "unparalleled fullness [unüberbietbaren Fülle]"
as "a ground which, because essentially and always self sealing off, is an
abyss" (Heidegger 1989,11).

Such are the two features constitutive of the being-work of the work.
Since the world is "an unveiling escort" while the earth is a "self-sealing
off," their relation could only be conflictual: "World is against earth and
earth against world. They are in contest [Streit]" (Heidegger 1989,12).

This conflict is at the heart of the work. The work is what animates
the conflict by establishing a correspondence between "the self-squan-
dering of the sealing itself off of the earth" and the parallel rigor of a
"feature" which, through "the countour, sketch, and outline," in short
through a "form," which is no longer the mastery of a material, succeeds
in drawing into the open the abysmal character of the earth (Heidegger
1989, 12). This is by virtue of which the work "grounds" and "opens" a
"leeway" (Spielraum) in which "the earth, world-like is sealed off and the
world, earth-like, is open." This leeway, Heidegger adds, appealing once
more to the paradigmatic example of the Greek temple, is the "openness
of the There, in which things and humans come to stand, in order to
stand it [bestehen]" (12).

On this point one could be tempted to agree with Heidegger's son that
the description I just summarized, through its insistence on the overlap-
ping over each other of opening and closing, invites to pay attention to
an enigma. But the invitation is short lived as soon as it appears, always
on the example of the Greek temple, that the There open by the work
is defined as that "in which a people comes to its own—i.e., comes into
the ordaining [fügende] power [Macht] of its God" (Heidegger 1989,
12). The chiasma of opening and closing thus calls for less a meditation
than a conquest of oneself by the broadened Dasein of a people.

It is thus the thematic of resolute selfhood which prevails over the
thematic of the enigma as is shown by the function assigned in parallel
to the word of the great poet: thanks to him "a people finds its great
concepts of being as a whole predetermined for it" (Heidegger 1989,
13). This is confirmed shortly after by the introduction of a motif which
will play a determining role in the following of this first version of the
questioning on the origin of art: the motif of decision (Entscheidung).

The decision in question is imposed by the dominance throughout the history of Christian West of a conception of art inherited from Plato and which granted to works the function of representing something, not in the sense of a servile imitation of what is given ready to hand, but in the sense of a symbolization.

The reference to the Greek temple and to the theophany inaugurated jointly by the *Aufstellung* of a world and the *Herstellung* of an earth cannot be dissociated in Heidegger from a polemic against *Darstellung*, representation. Of course it is an ontological polemic. Not content to hold the work of art as a material dressed by virtue of a form, and thus to duplicate the work in *hyle* and *morphe* as any tool, the conception Heidegger criticizes suffers from intensifying the drawback of the duplication by granting to the form of the artistic product the additional role of referring as an allegorical imitation, to a reality situated elsewhere. It follows that the work is only the unreal appearance of a genuine being of which it is only a weakened echo, a derived copy. Whatever may have been the modalities of the *Darstellung* throughout the history of the West, whether the function of symbolizing the invisible, the intelligible, the supra-sensible, the supernatural granted to the work or conversely the function of symbolizing the visible, in all cases the work is held as secondary compared to a genuine being which is considered primordial.

Against that Heidegger rebels:

> But the artwork does not represent anything—and this for the sole and simple reason that it has nothing that it should represent. For while the work in the contesting of the contest of world and earth ever opens this contesting in its way, the work wins for the first time the open, the clearing in whose light what is as such encounters us as on the first day or—if become everyday-like—transformed" (Heidegger 1989, 13).

By contrast to the unreality and the secondary character granted to works of art by the *Darstellung* so dear to the West since the time it claimed to vindicate the legacy of Plato, the Greek temple is there to prove the contrary:

> The temple, which towers up on a promontory or in a rocky valley, the statue, which stands there in the holy district—these works amid everything else—the sea and land, the springs and trees, eagles and snakes—are not simply at best present at hand also. Rather,

they keep the midst engaged in the lit up leeway of the appearing of things. They are realer than any thing because each thing can only first show itself as a being in that open that is won by the work (Heidegger 1989, 15).

It thus follows that the work, far from being subjected to an external norm, "itself is standard of being and unbeing [*Unseienden*]" (Heidegger 1989, 15).

In *Humanisme de l'autre homme*, Emmanuel Levinas notes that, in Heidegger's conception of the history of being, biblical verses do not seem to be entitled to be quoted and he thus raises the following question: "Have the Holy Scriptures, read and commented in the West, inclined the Greek writing of philosophers or are they united to it only teratologically?" (Levinas 1972, 96). Upon a closer reading of the text I analyze here, the answer is that Heidegger presents the Western heritage of Platonism as a teratology, i.e., as a monstrosity. According to the proclaimed ambition of this text which is "to prepare a changed fundamental position of [the German] Dasein towards art" (Heidegger 1989, 5), the transformation in question imposes to totally disregard the long dominance of the *Darstellung* which is inherent to this heritage where Platonic inspiration and commentary of Holy Scriptures intermingle. What Levinas called "transcendence" is thus totally disregarded.

The careful reader, surprised by the vehemence of this recusation of *Darstellung*, can with good reason wonder whether Heidegger's argumentation does not come close to contradiction. If the Greek work around which the argumentation gravitates is "the standards of being and non-being," how can it escape the duplication real-unreal which is blamed on *Darstellung*? More generally, if such a work does not draw from "common reality," but produces "shock and refutation" (Heidegger 1989, 15), is the duplication real-unreal, against which the polemic is directed, abolished or simply displaced and transposed in another duplication: the anti-thesis of the common and the authentic? Be it as it may, since this polemic is supposed to contribute to the transformation of the German Dasein's attitude toward art, how can it escape the realm of imitation which it denounces in all respects, since it takes as its model an Ancient work which should inspire the German return of the Greek beginning?

2.2 Art as the Origin of the Work

Whatever these difficulties may be, the vehemence of the polemic, its appeal to a "decision" suggests that the voluntarist thematic of resolution wins over the attention to the enigma. This is confirmed by the second part of Heidegger's analysis. It begins with a question: "Why is strife the essence of art?" To which it can be answered: "The work-being of the work has the fundamental trait of contesting because and insofar as the work is a work of 'art' [*der* Kunst]." This only pushes the question further: what is thus "art"? (Heidegger 1989, 18) For fear of reducing art to a simple multi-purpose label, one has to start from the essential features of the being-work of the work and move back toward art as what founds them and is at their origin.

Reminding us that the work opens the There, the *Da*, "the midst of the open in whose clearing which is as such stands in and shows itself," and that "this open contains the awakening of a world together with the sealing itself off of the earth," Heidegger adds: "while this intimacy of the open conflict of the self-concealing and the self-unconcealing occurs, that which up to now was reckoned the real becomes manifest as unbeing. It comes to light—that means into the open—that up to now hiding and pretense and distortion of being prevailed. What thus occurs in the contesting—the opening up of the openness of the conflict of the unconcealed and concealed, the emerging from hiding and pretense—this by itself decreed occurring is the occurring of that which we call *truth*. For the essence of truth does not consists in the agreement of a sentence with a thing. Rather, truth is this fundamental occurring of the opening up of the openness of what is as such. That is why the concealed and the self-concealing (the secret) essentially belong to truth just as much as do the hiding and pretense and distortion—un-truth" (Heidegger 1989, 16). If this event of *aletheia* is what is fundamental in the strife of the conflict world-earth, the answer to the question "what is art?" readily follows: "*The setting to work of truth is the essence of art*" (1989, 16). As presented, the bursting open of *aletheia* which characterizes the essence of art according to Heidegger has enigmatic features: what is more enigmatic than a truth which makes undecidable the discrimination between secret and sham? One could believe that the attention to enigma bounces back. In reality, however, it is as if the insistence on the undecidable only intensified the decisionist appeal to the resolution of being oneself by cutting through at the heart of the entanglement between concealment and unconcealment. What follows in this analysis of art as origin of the work does not gravitate around the meditation on an enigma but on a historical project. The analytic of Dasein defined this historical project as a thrown project, the authenticity of which pertained to the resolute assumption of its ekstatic temporality with regard to the everyday fixation on the present. Following this analytic now broadened to the Dasein of a people, Heidegger tries to make it clear "why there must be work in order for truth to occur" (Heidegger 1989, 17).

Some quotations will suffice to manifest this furthering. Heidegger writes:

> If truth first comes to work *with* the work and *in* the work and is not present at hand anywhere beforehand, then it must *become*. From where does the opening up of the openness of what is come? From the nothing, say? Indeed, if by not-being [*Nichtseienden*] that presence at hand is meant which, just like the allegedly true being, was refuted and shocked by the work. The truth is never read off from this presence at hand. Much more does the openness of what is occur while it is projected, *poetized*. All art, in essence, is poetry—i.e., the blazing up of that open in which everything is otherwise than usual. By virtue of the poetizing projection the usual and the up-to-now turn to unbeing (Heidegger 1989, 17) .

It is impossible not to recognize in these formulations, in their insistence to invert signs—ordinary being becoming non-being—and to emphasize the inherent rupture from historization, the echo and the transposition into the work of art of the problematic which was central to the analytic of Dasein: the unveiling project breaking up with the inauthentic in order to gain access to the sight of the most proper capacity to be.

There are other quotes. Since the word *Dichtung* designates in German most of the time the art of language which is poetry, Heidegger is careful to note that he understands this word etymologically as an activity of composition, what the Greeks called *poiesis*, thus a poietic project broader than the one of poetry in the narrow sense of a linguistic art. "Nevertheless the language work, poetry in the narrower sense, has an *exemplary* position in the whole of art" (Heidegger 1989, 17). This is the occasion for Heidegger, in order to grasp more closely the meaning of his definition of the essence of art as *Dichtung*, on the one hand to reject the current views of specialists who judge the quality of works with regard to their power of "expression" and on the other to propose against this notion of expression his own conception of the essence of language. Heidegger writes:

> But this boundlessly correct and yet essenceless characterization of art as expression does not accord at all with language. It is true that language serves for communication, conversation, and agreement. But it is neither only nor primarily a vocal and written expression of that which is to be imparted, whether of the true or the untrue—i.e., whether of manifest or disguised being *as* manifest or disguised. Language does not just impart the manifest and pass it along. Rather, before this and properly it is the essence of language to raise the being as a being in to the open for the first time ... This naming and saying is a projecting in which the being is *announced* as what is open (1989, 18).

It is impossible not to recognize that this formulation furthers the analytic of Dasein which, when treating *logos* ("discourse") as an existential, granted it the primordial function of an ontological revelation and not of a communication with others. Now as before, to speak is not primarily to speak *to* somebody but to speak *of* being in its being and eventually to talk to oneself of one's authentic capacity to be. Emmanuel Levinas has dedicated himself to reverse this marginalization of communication—the ground of ethics but also of politics—in *Totality and Infinity*: he sees the face to face with the other as the primordial site of discourse, tearing discourse away from the apophantic and thematic project of discourse and rehabilitating expression as the "manifestation *kath'auto* of the face of the other" (Levinas 1961, 37).

However, since Dasein is no longer of an individual but of a people, it is now incumbent on this people to transpose the existential problematic of discourse. This is the reason why Heidegger specifies in these terms the nature of the ontological projection which defines according to him the essence of language: "The projecting saying is poetry, the saga of world and earth and therewith the leeway of the nearness and distance of the Gods. The primal language (*Ursprache*) is such saga (*Sage*) as the primal poetry of a people in which its world rises up and its earth *as* its own begins to seal itself off." Thus broadened to a people, the existential problematic of discourse has now its site in the language of a people and the ontological projection this language enjoys. Just as the acute point of discourse in *Being and Time* was the call individual

Dasein addressed to its resolution to be itself, the language of a people is accomplished in the call it addresses to the people to be resolutely and exclusively itself. Heidegger writes:

> Truth as openness is always openness of the There in which all being and unbeing stands, out of which every being as the sealing itself off takes itself back. And so the 'There' itself remains rooted in this abyss. Nevertherless, this 'There'—how is it? Who takes it upon himself to be this 'There'? Answer: man—not as individual, also not as community. These two ways of human-being are only possible at all if man previously takes on the There—i.e., stands in the midst of being *as* being and unbeing—i.e., stands with Being as such. This way of being the There we call history. When man is the There—i.e., is historical—he becomes a people. (Heidegger 1989, 19)

It is useless to seek in these considerations on language, on the legend of the world and the earth, on the people, on history, any opening to what linguistics, philology, mythology, sociology, historiography could teach us on these themes. In the wake of fundamental ontology, they have become the object of such an ontological epuration that they are radically subtracted to these disciplines just as the work of art was beforehand subtracted to the specialists of art and just as the analytic of Dasein wanted to escape any psychology or anthropology. In these conditions, the refusal of any positivity is no less than the refusal of any transcendence. In both cases, what justifies such a refusal is a possibility to be which is equal to none and rebellious to any generality, improper and inauthentic by definition.

Heidegger writes about the There which a people attempts to be: "This There itself is never something general—rather, ever a this and a singular [*ein einziges*]" (Heidegger 1989, 20). Just as before Dasein at each time mine was individuated through its confrontation with its proper death, the Dasein of a singular people to which Heidegger speaks has no other historicity than the one of a thrown project opting for being despite the non-being which threatens it.

It is at any rate on the axis of the resolution to be one's own properly and exclusively that this first elaboration of the question of the origin of the work of art concludes. Heidegger writes: "Knowing about the essence is just knowing as decision. In the question about art, the decision runs thus: Is art essential to us? Is it an origin and with that an endowing *start* to our history? A start or only still a *supplement* that gets brought along as 'expression' of the present at hand and pursued further for ornamentation and amusement, for relaxation and excitement? Are we in the nearness of the essence of art as origin or are we not? And if we are not in the nearness of the origin, do we know this or do we not know it and just stagger on in art management? If we do not know it, then the first thing is to raise it up to knowledge. For clarity as to who we are and who we are not is already the decisive leap into the nearness of the origin. Such nearness alone guarantees a truly grounded historical Dasein as genuine autochthony on this earth" (Heidegger 1989, 22).

It is impossible to understand the alternative thus formulated both in terms of knowledge and in terms of will as something other than the reminder of the very program of the analytic of Dasein: to be clear about who Dasein is and what it wants to be by contrast to what it is not. Heidegger wrote at the beginning: what we are seeking, the origin, we must already have it, and what we have we must first seek. In reality, upon closer reading of this text, one realizes that what matters, by virtue of this circle, is not to dispossess ourselves in an enigmatic and mysterious origin, but to find ourselves: brought to its origin, the work, even if it illuminates all things differently than ordinarily, has nothing surprising: however inaugural it is claimed to be, the work does not bring about strange surprises, for what is otherwise than ordinary is in fact nothing strange. The only surprise involved is to be understood in the literal sense of an overtaking, of a supplementary taking hold that the Dasein of a people is called to exercise over itself. Seeking the origin is simply taking again hold of oneself.

Translated from the French by Dominique Poncelet

Works Cited

Heidegger, Martin. 1953. *Einführung in die Metaphysik*. Tübingen: M. Nie-meyer.

———. 1959. *An Introduction to Metaphysics*, trans. Ralph Manheim. New Haven, Conn.: Yale University Press.

———. 1962. *Being and Time*, trans. J. Macquarrie and E. Robinson. New York: Harper & Row.

———. 1989. "Vom Ursprung des Kunstwerks: Erste Ausarbeitung." *Heidegger Studies* 5: 5-22.

————. 1992. *Platon: Sophistes. Gesamtausgabe* 19. Ed. I. Schüssler. Frankfurt am Main: Klostermann.

————. 1997a. *Plato's Sophist*, trans. Richard Rojcewicz and André Schuwer. Bloomington: Indiana University Press.

————. 1997b. *Vom Wesen der Wahrheit. Gesamtausgabe* 34. Ed. H. Mörchen. Frankfurt am Main: Klostermann.

————. 1999. *Hölderlins Hymne "Germanien" und "Der Rhein." Gesamtausgabe* 39. Ed. S. Ziegler. Frankfurt am Main: Klostermann.

————. 2000. *Reden und andere Zeugnisse eines Lebensweges, 1910-1976. Gesamtausgabe* 16. Frankfurt am Main: Klostermann.

————. 2002. *Grundbegriffe der aristotelischen Philosophie. Gesamtausgabe* 18. Ed. M. Michalski. Frankfurt am Main: Klostermann.

Kisiel, Theodore. 1995. *The Genesis of Heidegger's Being and Time.* Berkeley: California University Press.

Levinas, Emmanuel. 1961. *Totalité et infini: essai sur l'extériorité.* The Hague: M. Nijhoff.

Levinas, Emmanuel. 1972. *Humanisme de l'autre homme.* Montpellier: Fata Morgana.

Taminiaux, Jacques. 1989. *Lectures de l'ontologie fontamentale: essais sur Heidegger.* Grenoble: J. Millon.

2

OF SARTRE, KLEE, SURREALISM & PHILOSOPHY
TOWARDS A 'NON-PROSAIC'
CONCEPTION OF CONSCIOUSNESS

STEPHEN WATSON

"I recognize in no uncertain terms that surrealism is the only
poetic movement of the first half of the twentieth century."
Sartre (1978, 190-1)

Phenomenology is "the only philosophy which lives."
Bataille (1988, 8)

"Perhaps in our uncertain space we are closer to those who excavate:
to Nietzsche (instead of Husserl) to Klee (instead of Picasso).
Breton belongs to that family."
Foucault (1997, 171)

"The greatness and error of Klee lie in his attempt to
make painting both sign and object."
Sartre (1978, 29n)

The relationship between philosophy and surrealism remains
unwieldy. At stake, to use Blanchot's words is a "strange plurality" (1992, 408). The significance of this plurality, moreover, has been difficult to evaluate. Seen from either perspective each
is the site of a certain interruption. As Blanchot has noted, discussions
of the issue tend typically to restrict such evaluations to an explication
of sources, Breton's readings of Hegel, for example, or his relation to
Bergson. The resulting analyses not only rarely rise to the level of ad-
judication in themselves but also rarely engage the status of surrealism
as a theoretical 'source' for other matters, as far ranging as accounts of
the primitive in anthropology, or the unconscious in psychoanalysis,

or even the account of the sacred in theology. We are at risk of losing,
thereby, the debates and dialectics through which surrealism might be
more than simply a historical fact. Granted the complexity of these
relations, it is understandable how such debates (not only between
artists, but artists and critics, the 'silence' of artistic practices and the
'noise' of theoretical discourse) go largely unexplored. And, like other
such lacunae, the historical effects of surrealism would thus remain
largely 'unconscious' in our accounts.

The relation between Picasso and Klee, for example, has similarly
been described as both classical to, and inherently dialectical within, the
history of aesthetic modernism; it involves a clash between a vigorously
inventive systematic, engaged practice and its 'cooler' more labyrinthian
explorative demurrals. Granted the diversity of these painters' works
and the immensity of their impact, any final appraisal concerning such
a dialectic inevitably itself remains conditional. Adding to such internal
dialectics of artistic posture and commitment, the complications of
'philosophy' only further underdetermines the event—an event that
involves not only the 'differends' of theory, but those of criticism and
the dialectics of both theory and praxis. To say all this is doubtless to
say something about the uncomfortable relations not only between
philosophy and art (or at least the painterly), but philosophy and poetry
(or at least the literary). Ultimately, however, it forces us to confront
the difficult space that separates the 'hieroglyphics' of the textual and
the 'propositional.' In all of these cases, like much of the impact of
avante-garde, the practices at stake seemed inevitably to question the
contingency of the distinctions themselves.

In the case of philosophy and writing, these issues (as well as the
troubling status of surrealism) were certainly thematic by the time of
Sartre's _What is Literature?_ (where, not incidentally, the dialectic between
Picasso and Klee is likewise at work). Moreover, as will become evident,
Sartre's protocols form something of a legacy for the interpretation of
these matters. Strikingly however, in an opening chapter ("What is
Writing?") Picasso's "Guernica," often cited as an exemplar of political
engagement, becomes for Sartre a certain exemplar of the painter's muteness: "does any one think that it won over a single heart of the Spanish
cause?" (Sartre 1978, 5). Having invoked Merleau-Ponty's claim that no
quale is "so bare that it is not permeated with signification," Sartre states
that in the Guernica "something is said that can never quite be heard and
that would take an infinity of words to express." This infinity however

speaks to a crucial problem within the Sartrean text. For Sartre, this "infinity" spoke less to a wealth to be mined (as it had already in Kant) than a limitation concerning the work of art's conceptual determinability—and not only relevance but also reference.

Kant himself claimed that we are compelled within this 'infinity' to ascribe reality to an aesthetic predicate "as if it were a property of things" (Kant 1987, 56). The problem that Sartre's text will raise is prefigured in his citation of Merleau-Ponty, where this 'adventure of the aesthetic dialectic' had already begun. The question for Merleau-Ponty had emerged as to the originality (and difference) between the said and the unsaid, the relation between the sensible and the intelligible. In the problem of the painterly concept, however, Merleau-Ponty had encountered not simply the problem of finite sensoriality, i.e., not simply the metaphysical relation between the sensible and the intelligible but, in their difference, the limitations of that strict distinction—and in the issue of their significative difference, precisely different domains of intelligibility itself. In this silence that speaks otherwise than the said, Merleau-Ponty argued—and would increasingly in the wake of Sartre's citation—there lurks a polymorphism in what Kant called the schematism, the event in which Kant argued transcendental imagination linked intuition and concepts (Merleau-Ponty 1962, 326 f.) As Blanchot saw, there lay lurking equally in this difference a certain alterity before the demands of strict theoretical determinability. Schelling, who had linked this difference to art and the unconscious, wrote that a certain surpassing or surprise, literally an 'overtaking' (*Über-raschung*) occurs in the work of art that challenged the Kantian honorifics attending cognitively determinate discourse (*Erkenntnis*: Schelling 1978, 221 f.). Indeed Merleau-Ponty was willing to say that in this moment words surprise me and "teach me my thoughts," calling into question the simple link between reflection and the intention to communicate (*vouloir dire*). In linking himself to Merleau-Ponty's more expressive archive in 1948, Sartre never saw the objections that would sink his simple opposition between the silent and the said.

Nevertheless, the invocation of such a 'polymorphism' seemed non-phenomenological in the classical, Husserlian sense, where paintings are simply iteratively available as pre-linguistic phenomenological *Sinn*—not 'differently' but restrictly: the painterly *Sinn* remains, unlike the mathematical, bound to time and place, and even materiality. Sartre's account of the imaginary follows Husserlian premises: the imaginary is an immanent object strictly distinct from the real. Correspondingly, the semantics of "What is Literature?" strictly distinguishes between meaning and use in precisely this regard: designation or real reference and imaginary reference are two strictly distinct significative "layers". While from the outset Merleau-Ponty had rendered this distinction problematic, Sartre cites Merleau-Ponty only to note that the painterly (like the sensible) is significative—though for Sartre in strictly distinct (but analogous) manners (Sartre 1978, 4-5). As his 1940 work on the *Imagination* had declared, the image is an analgon but precisely an analgon of the real upon which it remains always semantically and ontologically parasitic.

In *What is Literature?*, Sartre again insists on the difference, the hierarchy and its valorization. The writer's vocation is that of responsibility, as it were the existential speech-act of engagement. The painter and the poet undertake the exploration of their media, which becomes like the image, merely an object in itself. Here the writer's responsibility is absolute and absolutely distinct from the irresponsibility of painting. The writer's silence is not different, a difference among *modi significandi*, but rather an (irresponsible) refusal to speak (Sartre 1978, 19). Hence Sartre claims, one has the "right" to ask "Why have you spoken of this rather than that" (Sartre 1978, 19). Except in certain precisely 'exceptional cases'; while for the painter the color is a thing, Klee has transgressed the protocols or limits of the painterly imaginary: "The greatness and error of Klee lies in his attempt to make a painting both sign and object" (Sartre 1978, 29 n.) The writer does not (analogously) explore words, does not allow language to resonate, rather the prose writer "makes use of words" (Sartre 1978, 13). And this 'prosaic' use removes the writer from the poetics and the imaginary of the avante-garde leaving the writer's discourse, meaning and use—or responsibilities—untouched:

> The crisis of language which broke out at the beginning of this century is a poetic crisis. Whatever the social and historical factors, it manifested itself by attacks of depersonalization of the writer in the face of words. He no longer knew how to use them, and, in Bergson's famous formula, he only half recognized them. He approached them with a completely fruitful feeling of strangeness. They were no longer his; they were no longer he; but in those strange mirrors, the sky, the earth, and his own life were reflected. And, finally, they became things themselves, or rather the black heart of things. And when the poet joins several of these microcosms together the case is

like that of painters when they assemble their colors on the canvas. One might think that he is composing a sentence, but this is only what it appears to be. He is creating an object. The words-things are grouped by magical associations of fitness and incongruity, like colors and sounds. They attract, repel, and "burn" one another, and their association composes the veritable poetic unity which is the phrase-object (Sartre 1978, 10).

The existentialist's speech act, instead, *uses* language to communicate; "he designates, demonstrates, orders, refuses, interrogates, begs, insults, persuades, insinuates" (Sartre 1978, 13). While all this sounds like rhetorical figure, the more basic theoretical claim is that, "words are first of all not objects but designations for objects; it is not first of all a matter of knowing whether they please or displease in themselves, but whether they correctly indicate a certain thing or a certain notion" (Sartre 1978, 14). The writer's praxis is thus "action by disclosure."

The dichotomy here between poetry and prose could not be made stronger. When Michel Foucault would later analyze the account of language as an economy of analogy, or a hermeneutics of resemblance he would link it to pre-representational significative practices that emerged in the wake of the middle ages (Foucault 1970, 17 ff.). Like Foucault, Sartre would not rest easily with such a 'hermeneutics.' However, the problem with such an account of signification for him was less theoretical than practical, less a matter of linguistics than politics. The problem, for Sartre, was "What is the structure of our society that provokes the appearance of this emphasis on hermeneutics?" (Sartre 1992, 435). Sartre had linked hermeneutics to the medieval clerk's linguistic "techniques," which "were not practiced for their own sake like spiritual exercises" (Sartre 1978, 78). The writer remained fully accommodated to the ruling class and at the service of its ideology. Only when these techniques became capable of distinguishing themselves from the object could they become explicitly an object in themselves, ideological (Sartre 1978, 77). This legacy lives on our own practices. The poet, on Sartre's account, risks, in objectifying language, becoming simply ideological, while the existentialist, in contesting such alienated objectifications, resumes the medieval clerk's non-spiritualized technique—albeit now fully rationalized in self-conscious responsibility.

His existentialist criticism of Husserl notwithstanding, Sartre's account of signification is staunchly transcendental: transparently devoid of the contingencies of convention, history, stylistics. It is almost as if the radicality of modernist poetics had forced a certain transcendental regression. If the "speaker is in a situation"—indeed "within language like we are in our body" (Sartre 1978, 7; 14)—this is not a limitation but a transcendental epistemic condition. It is still true that "words are transparent and the gaze looks through them" (Sartre 1978, 19). While the poet "more often has the scheme of the sentence in his mind, and the word follows" (Sartre 1978, 10), prose has been detached from the question of the schematism or the "verbal scheme" and linked directly to signification. "There is nothing to be said about form in advance, and we have said nothing. Everyone invents his own, and one judges it afterward" (Sartre 1978, 20). Rather than "utilizing" words, the poetic attitude is an autonomous function: the poet's words are magical, a self constituted microcosm. "Thus in each word he realizes, solely by the effect of the poetic attitude, the metaphors which Picasso dreamed of when he wanted to do a matchbox which was completely a bat without ceasing to be a matchbox" (Sartre 1978, 8-9).

Now it is clearly the surrealists that were the focus of Sartre's ire. He found the same "error" that he had found in Klee. Again the prose of the everyday becomes transformed into poetic object. This poetic transformation was generated, he claimed, in the wake of "Baudelairian dissatisfaction," arising out of the "obscure spot of the most bourgeois soul where all dreams meet and melt in a desperate desire for the impossible" (Sartre 1978,154; 167). Thus, the surrealist's account of automatic writing was, for Sartre, to use Hegel's terms, "the inverted world" to l'homme engagé. [1] Indeed, such automatic writing was, above all, 'destruction of subjectivity':

> When we try our hand at it, we are spasmodically cut through by clots that tear us apart; we are ignorant of their origin; we do not know them before they have taken their place in the world of objects, and we must perceive them with foreign eyes. Thus, it is not a matter, as has too often been said, of substituting their unconscious subjectivity for consciousness, but rather of showing the object as a fitful glimmering at the heart of an objective universe (Sartre 1978, 170).

Like Klee, the surrealists had confused object and sign, inverted the voluntary for the involuntary in "the ruins of subjectivity," inverted the subjective and the objective, a mixture of virtue and vice, "greatness and error." But this was not all surrealism did: for "the surrealists' next step

---

1   See Hegel 1977, 90 ff.

was to destroy objectivity in turn" (1978, 170). And it is just this that constitutes the ambivalence of their own "greatness and error":

> Whence, the ambivalence of the surrealist works: each of them can pass for the barbaric and magnificent invention of a form, of an unknown being, of an extraordinary phrase, and, as such can become a voluntary contribution to culture; and as each of them is a project for annihilating all the rest by annihilating itself along with it, Nothingness glitters on its surface, a Nothingness which is only the endless fluttering of contradictions (Sartre 1978, 172).

This Nothingness is obviously close to Sartre's heart—or in any case the "heart of Being" on his account, wherein Sartre had discovered the very essence of consciousness or the "for-itself." Yet surrealistic nothingness, far from inhabiting the heart of being, occurs only "at its surface." For Sartre, this is its failure; if the surrealists had caught the radical spontaneity of the creative act, or the upsurge of the for-itself, it had not been connected to Being (or to its transformation) but rather to its impossibility. The "*esprit*" of surrealism, Sartre goes on to state, "...is neither Hegelian negativity, nor hypothesized Negation, nor even Nothingness, though it bears a likeness to it; it would be more correct to call it the Impossible, or, if you like, the imaginary point where dream and waking, the real and the fictitious, the objective and the subjective, merge" (Sartre 1978, 172).

While it may be suggested that such a unification is what Idealism always sought, again, it is its "inverted world" that rules here: a flux of difference expelled from the world of eidetics. Rather than "dominating and governing its internal constructions" in synthesis, surrealism "wants to maintain itself in the enervating tension which is produced by an unrealizable intuition" (Sartre 1978,172-3).

This stress upon the irrealizable and the impossible fulfillment of this experience was perhaps especially made by Georges Bataille, whom Sartre quotes at a number of crucial points in this text. Such "limit experiences" were precisely invoked as the alterity to the limitations of communicability or even community itself by which we are always 'insufficiently' in the world. In searching for pure experience we are inevitably led to give up the desire to be everything through knowledge, therefore to communicate. A "new knowledge" emerges in its transgression and once again communication is given to me (Bataille 1988, 53-4). But such an "excessive" singularity encounters this new knowledge only in acknowledging its impossibility—that is, its failure as knowledge. If Bataille agrees that phenomenology is "the only philosophy that lives" (as did Sartre that surrealism is "the only poetic movement of the first half of the twentieth century") the problem is that experience is not limitable to such a goal. "The limit which is knowledge as a goal must be crossed" (Bataille 1988, 8). For Sartre, however, the hopes of the poetic transgression itself remain too imaginary, too detached from the real.

Interestingly, Sartre's transcendental regressions take hold here. At most, on Sartre's reading, surrealism remains simply the enactment of the *epoche*. Instead of Husserl's scientific *epoche*, however, the surrealists' *epoche* is like the third century skeptics Carneades and Philo, who, after enacting the *epoche* and "sure of not compromising themselves by an imprudent adherence, lived like everybody else"(Sartre 1978, 173). Sartre directs this (still Hegelian) critique of skepticism at the surrealists themselves: "In the same way, the surrealist, once the world is destroyed and miraculously preserved by its destruction, can shamelessly give full play to their immense love of the world" (Sartre 1978, 173).[2] The tension which arises out of destruction never then gives way to positive 'revolution.' Indeed, if Sartre does claim that "surrealism is the only poetic movement of the first half of the twentieth century," he adds that "what it liberates is neither desire nor the human totality, but pure imagination. Now, the fact is that the purely imaginary and praxis are not easily reconciled" (Sartre 1978, 191).

Bataille himself responded that "it is true that the operation is not without difficulties, which surrealism has revealed but not resolved" (Bataille 1994, 66). His point remained that there is a (pseudo-) logic of domination that forestalls Sartre's own account. Here he was direct. In his 1943 article on Bataille, "Un Nouvelle Mystique," Sartre had already claimed that Bataille's work violates the conditions of meaningful discourse. Sartre aligned the latter's account of nothingness and the dark side of knowledge with Schelling's—and again Hegel's critique of Schelling's indeterminacy, that at night all cows are black (Sartre 1947, 184).

> It appears that to give oneself to the night is rapturous. I wouldn't doubt it. It is a certain way of dissolving oneself into nothing. But

2 On Hegel's Critique of Skepticism, as "a consciousness which is empirical, which takes its guidance from what has no reality for it, see Hegel 1977, 125.

> Mr. Bataille...satisfies his wish 'to be nothing' in a roundabout way. With the phrases 'nothing,' 'night' and 'a non-knowing laid bare' he has simply presented us with a fine little pantheistic ecstasy. I call to mind what Poincare said of Riemanian geometry; replace the definition of the Riemanian plane with that of the Euclidean sphere, and you have Euclidean geometry. Indeed. And in a similar fashion. Spinoza's system is pantheist of the right-handed type, while that of Mr. Bataille is the left-handed variety (Sartre 1947, 185).

To which Bataille adamantly replied: "At this point, however, I am the one who should elucidate Sartre, instead of the other way around. He should have me say that it 'would be a left handed pantheism,' if this infinite turbulence of mine had already ruled out even a possibility of stopping" (1992, 182).

Unlike either Schelling or Hegel, Bataille's 'experience' neither rises to the level of a proposition nor resides in a system, both of which are arguably still implicitly demanded in the existentialist phenomenological performative. Like the Hegelian account to which it appeals, Bataille claims, it "assumes a coincidence of subjective and objective aspects and at the same time a fusion of subject and object" (Bataille 1992, 186). If modern phenomenology is "replying to changing thought" it "is only one moment among others; a sandcastle, a mirage of sorts" (ibid.). Some would see in de Beauvoir's critique of "masculine logic" in *The Second Sex*, a similar account of logic of domination in Sartre—or what Merleau-Ponty referred to as Sartre's "cursed lucidity."[3] Rightly or wrongly, however, Bataille had already made the critique in 1945:

> "The profound difference between surrealism and the existentialism of Jean-Paul Sartre hangs on this character of the existence of liberty. If I do not seek to dominate it, liberty will exist: it is poetry: words no longer striving to serve some useful purpose, set themselves free and so unleash the image of free existence, which is never bestowed except in the instant" (1994, 66).

This logic of the instant is Kierkegaardian, a *kairos* appealed to not only by him but others in his wake, e.g., Heidegger, Benjamin, or Gadamer—and Sartre himself in the account of existential decision. As close as it may be to Sartre, here he could find in the poetic invocation of the instant only the game of loser wins. Acknowledging the failure of communication, "poetic language rises out of the ruins of prose." The

---

3   See de Beauvoir 1968, 612 and Merleau-Ponty 1964, 24.

word, in ceasing to become an effective means, is metamorphized and each word recovers its individuality and salvation (Sartre 1978, 30). Bataille claimed—against Sartre—that what is decisive is the spontaneity of automatic writing: surrealism "is founded on automatic writing. In so doing it extricates the human mind from any other end than poetry" (Bataille 1994, 57-8). It opens up the domain of "inner experience" that Sartre's logic of domination foreclosed—and precludes the disclosure of a realm that Sartre's "responsible praxis" had lost in being guided by the goal of knowledge.

Thus we are beset with antinomies concerning the expressions of the imaginary: if not dominated or responsibly engaged, then art is not related to the 'real;' but if so related to the 'real,' it is still dominated by utilitarian convention, pre-accommodated, "committed to useful activity" (Bataille 1994, 46). Imagination and reason, *praxis* and the imaginary are all but irreconcilable. Sartre criticized these surrealists' utopianism, "not easily reconciled" (Sartre 1978, 191). If imagination and reason are "not easily reconciled," however, does it follow that they are simply opposed, that there is no such thing as historical imagination and hermeneutic invention? Does poetic engagement exist beyond the antinomies of meaning and use, signification and object, immanence and transcendence, 'responsibility' and 'license?' But what would it be like?[4]

Not without irony, this internal tension is never dissolved from Sartre's account. It is perhaps the problem of irony in the Sartrean text, even while it reinvokes the Hegelian critique of irony to overcome the destruction of tradition, the classical (Sartre 1978, 85).[5] Granted this

---

4 This is not to deny that such oppositions can be justified but to claim that such articulemes are "schema specific." That is, they are always articulated against a background that, in turn, delineates 'possibility' and 'impossibility' and remains (indeterminately) open to transformation. As 'antinomies,' to speak Kantian, they are less 'mathematical' than 'dynamic.' We may say of Sartre's hope to strictly distinguish signification and object, (e.g. between experience and proposition, signification and object, the lived and its systematic 'correlate') maintaining its inner historicity, what Merleau-Ponty said of Kant, that what he had learned in the Transcendental Dialectic he seems to have forgotten in the Analytic (1962, 304).

5 On Hegel's criticism of the beautiful soul, see Hegel 1977, 406f. On the critique of irony as a "longing which will not let itself go in actual action and production," see Hegel 1975, 160. Sartre's account of irony remains underdeveloped, though always presupposed. It plays an explicit part in his classical

logic of opposition between the silent and the said, the writerly and the painterly, there are perhaps few options. Again, Merleau-Ponty's account of the historical imaginary had sought to overcome such distinctions while, as Blanchot saw, still acknowledging a certain alterity in its midst (Blanchot 1980, 1-3). With Sartre we are confronted with a logic, if not of strict representation, then of strict phenomenological presentation, complete with its principle of presence and its logic of significative fulfillment: what is significative will be referentially significative when, and only when, it is adequate(d) to the real. It is in this sense that Sartre's analysis remains consistent with Husserl's famous tour of the Dresden Gallery in *Ideas* I, where "depictive objectification" and "sign objectification" distinctly inter-refer without ambiguity:

> A name reminds us, namingly, of the Dresden Gallery, and our last visit there: we walk through the halls and stand before a picture by Teniers which represents a picture Gallery. If let us say all the pictures in the latter would represent again pictures which, for their part, represent legible inscriptions, and so forth, then we can estimate which inclusion of objectifications and which mediacies are actually produced with respect to objectivities which can be seized upon (Husserl 1982, 246-7).[6]

In such analyses all historicity and all convention have seemingly become superfluous, identically parsed in the sheer givenness in which the pictorial and the significative have been distinctly isolated before the cognitive regard. But this seems just what Sartre's honest historical engagement and its concrete situation seemed to want to deny; for Sartre, the writer is both situated and historically engaged and responsible.

Granted this complication, one option is to deny that painting has anything at all to do with such reference, signification or reality. This emancipation from the frame of "discursivity," on Michel Foucault's terms, is precisely what is internal to the transgressions that compose the history of painterly modernism from Manet to Warhol. Here he declared we are more like Klee than Picasso.

Paul Klee's links with surrealism were immediate and substantial. And those perhaps most influenced by surrealism have not missed its importance. This was especially true not only of the painters that Klee

---

account of bad faith (1996, 87) but arguably underlies the dynamics of the for itself generally, as "being what it is not and not being what it is."

6 See the classical analysis of Jacques Derrida (1973, 104).

directly influenced but the 'renaissance' that occurred in French letters in the 1950's-60's, reconnecting it to the issues accompanying the aleatory, chance, unconscious, phantasy and their limits. While Merleau-Ponty had already privileged Klee in his analysis of painting, beginning with Michel Foucault's reading of Magritte, perhaps a different, more sur-realist Klee came to the forefront. Indeed instead of the neoclassical or neomarxist readings of Klee, for example, both of which were grounded in the naturalist symbolism of Goethe, Foucault had declared "Breton is our Goethe" (Foucault 1997, 172).[7]

Still, Foucault, like Breton before him, believed that Klee challenges but does not fully repudiate classical painting. Breton had character-ized Klee's work as "partial automatism"; Foucault similarly claims of Klee that his emancipation from "external" representation is only partial (Breton 1972, 64). While Klee steps beyond classical painting's representationism (and hence its 'silent' constitution within a discursive space) he does so, for Foucault in the invocation of a "new space," one that is "simultaneously page and canvas, plane and volume, map and chronicle" (Foucault 1983, 41; 33). Foucault had said elsewhere that the question of space is integral today "no doubt much more than time." Unlike time, "which was 'desacralized' in the nineteenth century," it seemed to Foucault that "contemporary space is not yet entirely desacralized" (Foucault 1997,177). At the same time, he suggested that if this desac-rilazation is not complete, it is also true that "our life is still dominated by a certain number of oppositions that cannot be tampered with, that institutions have not ventured to change," e.g., that between public and private space, or the space of leisure and the space of work (Foucault 1997, 177). Doubtless this remains true, for Foucault, of the opposi-tion between discursivity and the silence or the 'beyond' that escapes it. Our "uncertainty" here, consequently, brings us closer to those who excavate, to Klee, to Nietzsche and Breton—and yet in Klee's case not without certain restrictions

If Klee emphasizes precisely the uncertainty of pictorial 'space' he does so with invocation of a "new one," Foucault claims, and this doubtless also is not yet fully released from the space of representation and its 'sacred' opposition. Somewhat in opposition to Klee, consequently, Magritte is

---

7   Recent Klee interpretation has been divided between a neoromantic in-terpretation (e.g., Glaesemer) and, following Walter Benjamin, a neo-marxist interpretation (e.g., Werckmeister). See for example Glaesemer 1986. Also compare Werckmeister 1982.

privileged by Foucault, albeit by a certain complementarity (1983, 35). Instead of Klee's 'hieroglyphic' "weaving of signs and images" resulting in a "new space," Magritte "allows the old space of representation to rule, but only at the surface, no more than a polished stone, bearing words and shapes: beneath, nothing. It is a gravestone" (1983, 41). Indeed, this 'nothing' itself seems almost as impossible as Sartre had claimed of the surrealists' "surface" and space.

Analyzing Magritte's "'This Is Not a Pipe,'" where text and image play off one another, Foucault claims that, in Magritte's apparently representational and discursive space, "negations multiply themselves" and "the common space (*lieu commun*) has disappeared" (1983, 30-1). External resemblance has not simply been rendered uncertain but has vanished and similitude in particular, (the similitude between discourse and image), is rendered unstable in a series of multiplicities "referring" to nothing other than themselves. Foucault concluded: "A day will come, when, by means of a similitude relayed indefinitely along the length of a series, the image itself, along with the name it bears, will lose its identity. Campbell, Campbell, Campbell, Campbell" (1983, 54). 'Campbell' would thus no longer, to speak Husserlian, infinitely iterate a timeless *Sinn*, but would inexhaustibly differ from such identical 'sameness.' Here painterly modernism becomes a *progressus ad* Warhol and as such, exhibits a step beyond the interwoven space of Klee, ironically fulfilling the Sartrean account of the objectification of pure poetry, its opposition to discursivity complete. Moreover, what is true of painting is true of literature. Foucault's own analysis of Bataille (or Hölderlin or Roussel) reveals a language to infinity, which, in opposition to "a purified metalanguage," finds itself "in the thickness of words enclosed by their darkness by their blind truth" (Foucault 1977, 41). Here, too, Sartre's oppositions between form and matter were not far removed. Ironically, in their opposition, they had divided up the grand synthesis of classical phenomenology between pure logical form and the immanent acts of consciousness. They concur in demoting the significative nexus of art from objective reference. If Duchamp, Sartre claimed, sculpts false pieces of sugar, actually cut in marble, he produces imaginary objects so constructed that their objectivity does away with itself. And, so did literature:

> Literature also did its best to make language go through the same kind of thing and to destroy it by telescoping words. Thus the sugar

refers to the marble and the marble to the sugar; the limp watch con-
tests itself by its limpness; the objective destroys itself and suddenly
refers to the subjective, since one disqualifies reality and is pleased
to "consider the very images of the external world as unstable and
transitory" and to "put them into the service of the reality of our mind."
But the subjective then breaks down in turn and allows a mysterious
objectivity to appear behind it (Sartre 1978, 171).

But all this, again, for Sartre, is futile or even puerile before the duty of
existentialist prose: "All this without even starting a single real destruction" (Sartre 1978, 171).

We should nonetheless read Foucault as trumping Sartre's description
on two grounds. Provisionally accepting the strict Sartrean opposition
between image and sign, Foucault invokes Magritte's "Ceci n'est pas une
pipe" to internally call into question the idea of a 'text' simply regulated
by discourse. Secondly, as Sartre had sought to render the poetic into an
autonomous (or analogous) fictional realm of objects, Foucault called
into question the very idea of such autonomous prose as regulated and
directed by an independent subjectivity. In both cases, Sartre's thesis
about art had been denied. The work of art, Sartre declared, "has no
other substance than the reader's subjectivity" (Sartre 1978, 39). Indeed, while realized in a medium, in painting or "through language (it)
is never given in language," and has value only as an appeal to engaged
responsibility (Sartre 1978, 38). Foucault denied this reduction and the
ahistorical purity of the gaze that would constitute it. "The breakdown
of philosophical subjectivity and its dispersion in a language that dispos-
sesses it while multiplying it within the space created by its absence is
probably one of the fundamental structures of contemporary thought"
(Foucault 1977, 42).

Sartre, himself, acknowledged that language is a limit upon our situation, but he continuously drew not upon the epistemic or semantic
account but his 'ethical' conclusion: "Since he has once engaged himself
in the universe of language, he can never pretend that he can not speak.
Once you enter the universe of significations, there is nothing you can
do to get out of it" (Sartre 1978, 18). What Sartre held was that this
silence "is defined in relation to words" and that "words are transparent;"
he hoped to acknowledge, thereby, both the historicity of language and
the phenomenological purity of prosaic enunciation. As he had replied
to the 'thomist' in "Existentialism is a Humanism," granted, the signs
are there, but they must be interpreted and this implied a reduction of

meaning to 'use'—or in Sartre's terms 'creation': "in any case, I myself choose the meaning they have" (1957, 28). Foucault (and those more closely related to surrrealism) rightly saw the "impossibility" of this position and the impossibility of its strictly transcendental foundation. Indeed the very idea of 'prose' and analogical image (uniting discourse and image in resemblance and similitude) struck Foucault as no less "magical" itself, based historically on the 'magical' or the analogical hermetics of resemblance that Foucault had traced in the hermeneutics of the renaissance—and arguably still dominated by medieval analogical accounts. Indeed, while Sartre had limited myth (and the classical) to a strictly regulated society which "confounds the present with the eternal and historicity with traditionalism" (Sartre 1978, 85), the idea of a pure creative subjectivity devoid of myth surely itself risks turning mythic for the same reason. Indeed, as Bataille had rightly seen, "the absence of myth is also a myth"—even if it is our myth (1994, 48). Sartre affirmed the opposition of text and image. Foucault's response went further; he traced their dissolution through Magritte. Henceforth—and beginning with Flaubert and Manet—art and literature would, Foucault claimed, be erected "within the archive." This would occur not out of classical lamentation for the origin but rather in order to explore the space that had been opened up: "the aspect in painting or writing that remains essentially open" (Foucault 1977, 9). The result would, consequently, be less concerned with the figuration of another transcendent or external space but only with "the square and massive surface of painting" and "the indefinite murmur of words" (Foucault 1977, 93). But this was surely not the only option.

While Foucault attempted to articulate the 'silence' intrinsic to painting by distinguishing it from the space of representation, Jean-Francois Lyotard, for example, attempted to articulate the silent significance that exceeds "the said." More explicitly Freudian, Lyotard articulates an account of the figure-matrix through which the silence of original phantasy is expressed outside and excessive to discursivity. Even though he retains an account of painting as original expressivity, for Lyotard, the artist does not simply communicate originary phantasies. Iteration here would demand precisely an identity of such phantasies in the spectator. Rather the figure-matrix schematizes such phantasies in the work of art. In a sense, the figure-matrix makes possible iterability between 'subjects', as does the Husserlian noema—but precisely as more originary than it. Incapable of reduction, the figure is not restricted (nor regulated) by discourse, image, or form (or conscious regard) since it expressively resides in the three spaces together and makes possible both identity and opposition among them (Lyotard 1971, 278).

Accordingly, while Foucault sees Klee to be constructing representationally, i.e., discursively, a "new space," Lyotard invokes Klee's work as an example of a more primary figure-matrix process. He argues that Klee increasingly explores thereby a more primordial expressivity, antecedent to representation. Lyotard claims the transformation in Klee's work occurs as he increasingly acquires a more critical relation to the figure-matrix. Early on, Klee attempted to more directly communicate phantasy, while the later works' 'glyphic' forms articulate neither sheer lines nor drawings—as Sartre, too, remarked. In these works discourse and figure are explicitly, albeit indeterminately and expressively, together within the visual field. As art historians have noted, moreover, this heterogeneity further explains the prominence of mythic themes. This is especially true in the late works, where the figure-matrix allows for the expression of meaning to transcend both discursive and representational (including facist) myth.[8]

This re-raises the question of the importance of myth, and in particular its political implications. While we are not concerned with the political, throughout Klee's career the latter surely accompanies the issues of 'primitivism' in his art (the ethnographic, the art of the insane, or the art of children). Moreover it accompanies the issues that cluster around spontaneity (or automatism) that accompanied the problem of surrealism from the outset, and have overdetermined discussions here. If Sartre had condemned such views to the irrational, Foucault spent much of his career arguing against such condemnations. And the charge of primitivism or irrationalism accompanied Klee's work as well, as we have seen. Historians have noted that such charges miss his point, however, as the following evidences from his 1912 review of the joint exhibition of the Neue Kunstlervereinigung and the Blaue Reiter, Klee states:

> For there are still primal beginnings in art, which one is more likely to find in ethnographic museums or at home in the nursery (don't laugh dear reader); children can do it too, and that is in no sense devastating for the latest efforts; on the contrary, there is positive wisdom in this state of affairs. The more helpless these children are,

---

8 See Werckmeister 1985, Introduction.

the more instructive is the art they offer us; for there is already a corruption here: when children begin to absorb developed works of art or even imitate them. Parallel phenomena are the drawings of the mentally ill, and so madness is not an apt word of abuse either. All that, in truth, must be taken far more seriously if present-day art is to be reformed. So far back will we have to go if we are not simply to imitate antiquity.[9]

As Klee's historian, Marcel Fransiscono, rightly sees, this step beyond 'antiquity' involves neither primitivism, nor regression nor even the affirmation of insight into a spontaneous "unconscious enormous power" (Franciscono 1991, 167). Instead Klee saw such interest or investigations to be part of the exploration and 'reformation' (and rational potential) of contemporary art. Blanchot will make defenses (on behalf of Webern and Klee) concerning similar charges by Adorno (Blanchot 1992, 345 ff.)—though he also would distance himself from the "temptation to which surrealism risks succumbing when it lends itself to a search for the immediate" (1992, 410).

How are we to escape the apparent antinomies regarding the imagination that result, that affirmation of such 'spontaneity' is either beyond the reach of reason or wholly contained within it? As Sartre had put it, since the image is a function of spontaneity, there is nothing in the image that I have not put in it. Phenomenological imagination, for Sartre, is strictly contained by the reflective regard and, therefore, "there is nothing new to be found in the imagination because I have made it" (Sartre 1968, 10). That is, phenomenologically, subject and object are not only intentionally parallels, but coefficients: as Fichte had put it, Ich = Ich.[10] Hence, the result: "nothing can be learned from an image that is not already known" (Sartre 1968, 11).

Arguably, even phenomenologically construed, this fails however. If I am intentionally related to imaginative acts, "I" am not their simple coefficient. This is precisely how it can be that I might be taken by "surprise" in such imagining, as Schelling saw. Klee invokes the term, too, for the account of figurative invention. Moreover the reference to Schelling further explains Klee's cosmological 'mytheme', that nature as 'Will' works itself through me. Such an account was in the background

---

9 Cited in Franciscono 1991, 167.

10 See Casey 2002, 93n. For the Fichtean 'protocol' see the 1794 *Wissenschafts-lehre* (i.e., "the first absolutely unconditioned principle": 1982, 93 f.)

of surrealism, as Bataille noted in his piece on Sartre, in aligning surrealism and Romanticism, the former radicalizing romanticism by bringing everything into question (Bataille 1994, 57). Still, for Klee (and this is why, perhaps, his is only a "partial automatism" for Breton), it is not the case that I am simply 'over-taken' by such imaginative events, delivered over or forced to ascent to their naive immanence; this would involve the return of primitivism that he has denied. As Husserl had seen in replying to Hume, the explicative series in passive synthesis does not succumb to causal association but to adumbrative explication. No more does the series of 'imaginings': both are examples of transcendences—albeit still 'motivated,' a step into the unknown.[11] The "interruption" of reason is not reason's inversion—any more than it is its completion.[12] Instead, against the reduction of phenomenological immanence, such interruptions or transcendences trace an irreducible excess. Accordingly, subjectivity here, to use Merleau-Ponty's terms "is not motionless identity: as with time, it is of its essence, in order to be genuine subjectivity, to open itself to an Other and to go forth from itself" (1962, 426).

This opening arrests, to use Blanchot's terms, the attempt to conceive intentionality "in order to guarantee judgment" (1992, 251). Indeed, Merleau-Ponty, whose account of sense and significance provided a protocol for Sartre, found therein "typical relationships" transcending the distinctions between nature and convention, sense impression and categorical act, a body-synthesis he identifies with Kant's transcendental imagination (1962, 168; 192). Indeed at stake is an event in which the question of transcendence is never exhausted; it is always an 'incarnate' event irreducible to an act, a "gift" which the mind "makes use of beyond all hope" (1962, 127).

As Sartre argued in the *Transcendence of the Ego*, it may seem the case that the "I think" must accompany all our representations. But the question is, does it? (1971, 32 f.) While Sartre distinguished these he retained the "I think's" immanence for the contents of consciousness. Too often Sartre confused phenomenological immanence and transcendence: where transcendence is not the simple sign of inadequateness (or illusion) but an excess never finally reduced or cognitively adequated—and yet still relied upon. Sartre's subreptions regarding transcendence were certainly at work in his dealings with the imaginary, certainly present in

---

11 See Husserl 1973, Appendix II.

12 See Watson 1992, Ch. II.

his account of the imaginary, too often reduced by him simply to what I 'create' and am consequently reflectively responsible for. The difference between image and reality is not absolute but equally historical, a matter always of "intentional implication;" perception is co-determined by the possibility of phantasial modification and vice versa. Without reducing the distinction to "degrees of evidence," it should be admitted that the centaur too has its transcendencies, indeterminacies, problematic status and horizonal (i.e., historical) coherence. If the real and the imaginary remain phenomenologically distinct, where does the imaginary begin and where does it end if it is devoid of the ego's domination? The result looks, beyond the attempt to guarantee judgment, like a very different domain, one perhaps Blanchot has aptly caught in a lengthy passage with significant consequences for the issue that dogs Sartre:

> By showing there is a rigorous correlation between the determinations of the object and the steps of the "consciousness" that intends them or takes up their evidency, phenomenology made thought familiar with the idea of a relation that is empirical and transcendental. Or, to state this more clearly: it is intentionality that maintains the empirical and the transcendental within a structured relation—an alliance that is essentially modern, that is to say, explosive. As a result, the empirical is never in and of itself the empirical: no experience can claim of itself to be in itself knowledge or truth. And also as a result of this, the "transcendental" will find itself nowhere localized: neither in a consciousness that is always already outside itself, nor in the so called natural reality of things (which must always be suspended or reduced). Rather it will reside in the emergence of networks of relations that neither unite nor identify but maintain what is in relation at a distance, and make of this distance, recaptured as a form of alterity, a new power of determination (1992, 251).

This network of relations, Blanchot realized, has much then in common with his account of "the game, the aleatory, the encounter" and the "new space" of surrealism (1992, 421). In this guise, it impacts Blanchot's own account of Klee, for whom, like for Foucault, Klee "dreams of a space where the omission of every center would at the same time do away with any trace of the vague or the indecisive" (1992, 350). Moreover, far from being simply contradictory or nihilistic, or even simply impossible, *tout court*, there is a sense in which, freed from 'knowledge' or the constraints of *strenge Wissenschaft*, all this remains 'phenomenologically' a matter of the everyday, precisely insofar as the (aleatory) everyday escapes strict phenomenological adequation (1992, 241-4). Such a phenomenology, consequently, would require a step beyond its classical formulations.

Writing in 1948, Levinas said of the captivation or incantation of poetry and music: "It is a mode of being to which applies neither the form of consciousness, since the I is stripped of its prerogative to assume its power, nor the form of unconsciousness, since the whole situation and all its articulation are in a dark light present. Such is a waking dream" (1987, 4).

The image is a shadow of reality, not its representation, literally beyond the world of judgment. And he adds:

> Here we have really an exteriority of the inward. It is surprising that phenomenological analysis never tried to apply this fundamental paradox of rhythm and dreams, which describes a sphere situated outside of the conscious and the unconscious, a sphere whose role in all ecstatic rites has been shown by ethnography; it is surprising that we have stayed with metaphors of "ideomotor" phenomena and with the study of the prolongation of sensing actions (1987, 4).

This opening beyond the "ideomotor" is precisely where Levinas himself would surpass classical phenomenology, transforming its other into the sacred understood as the ethical. He did so ultimately by articulating an event that opened beyond the image in announcing both the exteriority and the imperative of the ethical—the obligating appearance of the 'face of the other.' The protocols for this passage through ethnography (and beyond) had been prepared for by phenomenologists of religion such as van der Leeuw or Buber or Rosenzweig.[13] This "relationality" of the "beyond" (or to demystify perhaps, according to Wittgenstein, the "family resemblance" or Blanchot the "strange plurality") is what connects (and interrelates) the other, the primitive, and the sacred at the limit of phenomenology. This doubtless turns its Husserlian theater of immanence into something more resembling the dramatics and reversals of the Hegelian series of figures (*Gestalten*). As such it is the opening

13 Of these thinkers perhaps van der Leeuw remains the least now known in this context but his work in the phenomenology of religion (especially in what Levinas calls its ethnographic or comparative), surely makes it critical at this point. See Van Der Leeuw 1986. For further discussion of these issues and, in particular, the question of surrealism, see Rabinovitch 2002. Also see Clifford 1988, "Ethnographic Surrealism." "The surrealist moment in ethnography is that moment in which the possibility of comparison exists in unmediated tension or with sheer incongruity" (146).

of a 'hermeneutics' (or even an account of the 'sacred') that was beyond the discursive regulations to which both had been previously bound.[14] Its topos 'strangely' would unite thinkers as diverse as Levinas, Bataille, Blanchot, Kristeva, Callois, and Breton. Emphatically, Foucault had made a similar point in his own evaluation of surrealism:

> There is no doubt that the whole network connecting the works of Breton, Georges Bataille, Leiris, and Blanchot, and extending through the domains of ethnology, art history, the history of religions, linguistics, and psychoanalysis, are effacing the rubrics in which our culture had classified itself, and revealing unforeseeable kinships, proximities, and relations. It is very probable that we owe this new scattering and this new unity of our culture to the person and the work of André Breton. He was both the spreader and the gatherer of all this agitation in modern experience (Foucault 1997, 174).

This is admittedly overstated; Foucault acknowledged that much of what we find in Breton is to be found like in others, complicated in relation to the archive, "prefigured in Goethe, in Nietzsche, Mallarmé or others." It is critical that Foucault also claims that "what we really owe him is the discovery of a space that is not that of philosophy nor of literature, nor of art, but that of experience" (Foucault 1997, 174). This is precisely the realm which Sartre's phenomenology had sought to free in his attacks on surrealism (174). But for Foucault this space of new relations belies the distinctions between philosophy and poetry. To use a term of Derrida's, who through the notion of *archi-écriture* was still trying to "attain by deconstruction its ultimate foundation," the concept of experience is "unwieldy," indeed "embarassing (*embarrassant*)" (Derrida 1976, 60). Experience remains divided between intuition and concept, event and history, "archesynthesis" and what inevitably escapes. Doubtless in all these cases, experience, history—and even perhaps 'phenomenology' itself, unwittingly—both thinkers, unlike Sartre, were replanking the raft as they went.

Both as experience and concept, however, this space of new 'relations' is also the very space opened by imagination, as Blanchot saw. What Sartre may have forgotten in all this (and in his own attack on surrealism on the question of writing and the imagination) was the dependence of phenomenological reflection itself upon fantasizing. The 'free varia-

---

14 See "Hermeneutics and the Retrieval of the Sacred," Ch. III in Watson 1992.

tion' that discloses (and conceals) pure possibility (and necessity) also explicates the phenomenological return to origins through the 'texts' of 'time' and 'image,' reflection and dream, consciousness and its own 'fictions' as Husserl put it in *Ideas I*. He famously wrote: "free phantasies acquire a position of primacy over perceptions and do so even in the phenomenology of perception itself..." (Husserl 1982, 158-9). In the extended passage quoted above, Klee articulates the differentiation of such possibilities in the attempt to escape the limitations of factical antiquity, articulating what he will call elsewhere "the prehistory of the visible"(Klee, 1978a, 60) The question of the return to origins (*Rückfrage*) cannot simply be reduced to the conscious gaze but is equally dependent upon what escaped it in the 'text' of the imaginary and what, perhaps reflectively construed then, remains 'unconscious,' conditional and 'excessive' to the regard of significative intention. But both Husserl and Sartre problematically sought to contain such 'transcendence' by reflective or 'transcendental immanence,' conflicting the transcendence of dialectical possibility with analytic necessities.

Having encountered this "strange plurality" one can see the ease, the complicities and the complications at stake when post-Sartrean phenomenologists like Edward Casey must take up the matter. An author of the classical study on phenomenological imagining in English, even Casey found here a convergence between Husserlian *phantasieren*, which reveals essential possibility through imaginative variation, and something like the Jungian unconscious.[15] In this convergence, Jung's so called 'archetypes' would need to be understood more 'eidetically' or at least as 'eidetic variations' rather than as set of primitive natural facts (as he too often interpreted them). As Jung himself had likewise declared, in this regard they are an a priori condition of possibility.[16] Like the problem of the Kantian "schematism," Jung thought, such archetypes revealed an "art hidden in the depths of the human soul, a treasure in the realm of shadowy thought" that is exhausted by none of its exemplifications (Jung 1990, 84). Similarly, Jung's archetypes are 'transitional' analogs always in need of interpretation or refiguration ('symbolic' as he argued—and in their alterity, doubtless allegorical

15 See Casey 2002, 212 ff.

16 See Jung 1990, 66. Cp. Klee's self description: "I place myself at a remote starting point of creation, whence I state *a priori* formulas for men, beasts, plants, stones and the elements, and for all the whirling forces." See Klee 1964, 345.

in Benjamin's sense).[17] It is not surprising that Adorno suggested to Benjamin that he would need to confront (and criticize) Jung's account of the collective unconscious, especially singling out Jung's reading of aesthetics.[18] This task surely played a role in what Benjamin called "the epistemological foundations" of the *Arcade's Project*.[19]

As Jung's account blinkingly acknowledges, such possibilities require that we need to add the limitations (and excess) of the Kantian schematism to the phenomenologists' reflective variability. Thereby we encounter again the problem of transcendence, the problem of finitude or historicity. Taken together they imply that phenomenology must be understood to involve less an apriori possibility or pure factum but rather, as Heidegger put it in his study of the schematism, an event that is always already "exploratory."[20] Hence Heidegger's penchant for translating the Platonic *eidos* phenomenologically, always as its adumbrative *Aspekt*. Correlatively, at stake is not simply a description of self-contained mental facts (this is Husserl's lingering cartesianism). Rather such a 'phenomenology' involves the exploration of a transcendent or adumbrative event that exceeds us and which encounters its own limits—perhaps to use Benjamin's term, even "the death of intention," strictly construed. And Klee's exploratory defense of the primitive in his extension beyond the classical tradition doubtless should be understood in this light. The encounter with the primitive is by no means an encounter with an immanent essence more true than the classical but an alterity that articulates in the encounter itself more than the past might contain—and where, granted both the coherence (or textuality) of the past and the alterity of the present, 'image' and 'text' become interspersed as an adumbrative complex in

---

17 See Jung 1971, 111. This text makes Jung's account's links with post-Kantian aesthetics of symbol and allegory clear—an archive I have traced more fully with respect to Gadamer and Benjamin elsewhere. See Watson 2004.

18 See Adorno and Benjamin 1998, 61. Adorno notes the "not insignificant essay on Joyce" that appears, along with Jung's writings on Picasso in Jung 1966.

19 Adorno and Benjamin 1998, 61; 201.

20 See Heidegger 1990, 127. Compare Merleau-Ponty's similar invocation of "an operative imaginary," in his later critique of Sartre, which is "part of our institution, and which is indispensable for the definition of Being itself" (1968, 85).

the play of possibility, one always in need to interpretation (Benjamin 1999, 463).[21]

This only emphasizes the ambiguity involved: such adumbrations are theoretically underdetermined. This account for the fact that, while Husserl appeals to James' stream of consciousness for the adumbrations of the perceived world, Jung appeals to James for his account of the symbolic. This is the so-called "free association" in the unconscious and the active imagination: "much of our thinking consists of trains of images suggested one by another."[22] Moreover even James himself had interests in such matters as the unconscious and "automatic writing."[23] Jung however denies rational access to this realm as well, almost on 'Sartrean' grounds: "the rational functions are, by their very nature, incapable of creating symbols, since they produce only rationalities whose meaning is determined unilaterally and does not at the same time embrace its opposite"—tantamount, again, to declaring that reason only understands what it has itself put in it, i.e., univocally determined.[24] The 'symbolic' exceeds such parameters, and exceeds the real only by being rediscovered at its heart. Jung's search for the archetypes remains less a return to primitive facts (or as Blanchot puts it, an attempt to retrieve "a respectable spirituality" (1992, 299) than it is perhaps grasped as a matter of the social or historicity. Jung himself had articulated the antinomies of artistic possibility in the work of Picasso and Joyce.[25] It

21 Benjamin invokes "this point of explosion" in the image that is the death of intentio precisely against phenomenology and even Heidegger's "vain" attempt "to rescue history for phenomenology abstractly through 'historicity'"(462). Without mediating between these accounts, I am simply suggesting the plurality that conjoins them. Much more would need to be said. In the "ruins" of phenomenology however, much hangs upon the "adumbration" of images. Benjamin's account of the death of 'intentio,' was written, obviously unaware of the later writings of Husserl, which arguably leads beyond the restrictions of the *Ideen* account.

22 See Jung 1967, 17.

23 See Gertrude Stein's account of experimenting with automatic writing while she worked under James in "The Autobiography of Alice B. Toklas" in Stein 1962, 74.

24 See Jung 1971, 111.

25 See Jung 1966, 109-143. For Jung, both artists articulated the possibilities of a "new cosmic consciousness" albeit under the fragmented conditions of the present and its resulting *drame intérieur*.

remains perhaps similarly at stake in the Picasso/Klee double, divided between the systematic 'invention' or exploratory 'excavation' of expressive form. This is because this double of unity and fragmentation is at work in the symbolic function everywhere. But Sartre could view the resulting expressive images only in terms of consciousness and signification. Doubless it was with this in mind that Blanchot argued that signification, so construed, in a sense detaches itself from iterative or significative *mimesis*: "The image has nothing to do with signification, meaning as implied by the existence of the world, the effort of truth, the law and the brightness of the day. Not only is the image of an object not the meaning of that object and of no help in comprehending it, but it tends to withdraw from its meaning by maintaining it in the immobility of a resemblance that has nothing to resemble" (Blanchot 1981, 85).

Blanchot's followers would not miss this. The network of intentionalities in which "the empirical is never in and of itself empirical" and the "'transcendental' will find itself nowhere localized," will always involve, as Foucault saw, an "empirico-transcendental doublet" (Foucault 1970, 318). Derrida too saw that this intentional network would always emerge "as a warp of language, logic, evidence, fundamental security, upon a woof that is not its own" (Derrida 1976, 67). It is in just this 'crossing' or 'doubling,' belying the simple distinction (indeed the Cartesian 'distinctness') between immanence and transcendence (or active and passive synthesis), that the image becomes, in terms Blanchot (and Benjamin) invoke, always potentially "explosive" with respect to intention.

What Levinas called the 'ethnographic' decentering of the phenomenological image does not involve a naive return to the primitive. Derrida, nonetheless, argued that Levinas' own attempt to simply distinguish the religion of the sacred law from sacred, but still pagan naturalness is forced (Derrida 1998a, 150). In fact, Derrida had argued similarly in relation to Bataille, that such claims to the archaic or the sacred could be accessed only through a double reading that would not simply submit the known to archaicism, but through understanding the latter as equally a proposition, albeit one that opens itself up beyond the predetermined sovereignty of meanings. This looks like the very premises of what he called deconstruction (and it is). It also acknowledges, beyond Bataille's empiricism, a double gesture in the refiguration, the twofold synthesis to the passage from the past to the future "beyond" or "outside," the twofold synthesis of retention and protention.[26] In this respect, beyond the limits of a phenomenology predetermined in sense, another 'phenomenology' emerges, one no longer governed by the 'sovereignty' of a meaningful correlate.

'Phenomenology' thus, for Derrida, could not be understood as a meaningfully isolatable term. Nor could it be simply determined by a semantic context, but would be subject to its own internal (historical) 'drift,' indeed, the very one we have articulated here (cf. Derrida 1978, 273). Here too, as Derrida argued concerning Bataille, "Tradition's names are maintained, but they are struck with the differences between the major and the minor, the archaic and the classic. This is the only way, within discourse, to mark that which separates discourse from its excess" (1978, 272). Yet, such a strategy is equally in accord with what Heidegger saw as the exploratory (and hermeneutic) legacy of transcendental imagination, the 'gathering together' of discourse and its excess, immanence and transcendence, analysis and synthesis, intelligible (i.e., ontic) schema and ontological possibility. In thus elevating the imagination, Heidegger acknowledged he followed post-Kantian thought (explicitly Fichte, Jacobi and Schelling). But this also indicates the false charges about irrationality here. Doubtless Heidegger also followed, thereby, the post-Kantian account of judgement as differentiation (*Unterscheidung*). Here, as Fichte put it, qua mutually interrelated, "every positive judgement can also be considered to be a negative one." But then, as Novalis would interpret Fichte, in this differentiation, all terms—even the ego itself—become 'hieroglyphic.'[27] As we have discovered, Klee's 'hieroglyphic' explorations are equally to be found here. But it is also decisive that Heidegger could still retain the term "phenomenology" for all this.

Such a "phenomenology" would involve, as was the account of time internal to it, the constant reweaving of warp and woof, albeit no longer governed by the 'sovereign' gaze, and no longer governable by the external correlation of form and content. Phenomenology would no longer simply be strictly pre-figured in advance; it would involve a transcendental

---

26 Hence while this "double reading" looks like an extreme or an 'exceptional' account of interpretation, elsewhere I have argued that it underlies the rationality of traditionality more generally. See "Our Reciprocal Rejoinder with the Past: On Heidegger's *Erwiderung*," Introduction to Watson 1997.

27 See the analysis of judgment as differentiation by Manfred Frank (2004, 85 f.)

logic that is neither simply conceptually regressive (or 'reductive') nor predetermined (by a pure form), a schematism whose adumbrative 'texture' remains inevitably exploratory. So interpreted, phenomenology would always already in this regard, be "multi-dimensional," to use Klee's term—indeed even 'aleatory.' And when Derrida cites Klee it is precisely in this regard. For Derrida, Klee's work articulates the aleatory distinction of form and content. In particular, he cites the 1927 "Constructiv-impressiv" where nails ("the points that nail the canvas onto the painting") presumably appear in the painting. Here the image is neither dissolved nor simply opposed to 'discourse' but remains lacking in completeness; its synthesis to speak Husserlian remains (not only uncertain or 'inadeqaute' but) 'transcendent' and indeterminately 'transitional,' the presentation of a "texture" in "an object which has been transfigured" (Derrida, 1987,304).

This perhaps tells us something about Klee's multidimensionality as well. Despite its acknowledgments of abstraction or constructivism, (again unlike Foucault's interpretation of him) Klee's work is neither the construction of a "new space" nor the representation of a propositional space. What after all, would a "new space" mean here? Rather, it explicates the constant raveling and unraveling of the constructive-impressive conjunction (or heterogeneous synthesis) that is involved in *espacement*—as a general phenomenon (or phenomenalization).

As has become now apparent, something similar is at hand in what we have been calling the indeterminacy, 'inadequation' or 'drift' internal to phenomenology. At stake is not simply a step beyond (or behind) reason, nor even simply a kind of *trembulatum* before what Blanchot called the unfigurable universe. It was, in some respect, all of these, confronted with an event in which the intentional *adequatio* has been abandoned—or an event in which 'adequatio' abandons us. It was also the recognition of the problem of the 'dehiscent' or 'textured' plurality articulated adumbratively within the event of intentional implication itself. The problem is that, far from there being too few 'figures' in this event of inadequation, there were also too many; the sacred, the other, could be neither simply allowed in nor simply ruled out. Moreover, devoid of such determinacy there would be no one strictly scientific (or anti-scientific), metaphysical (or non-metaphysical) concept of the other or the sacred—and surely not "the" surreal. And, this would be the lot of more than one of our epistemic practices shorn of scientific pretense. Derrida has similarly noted such an effect in arguing that "there is not one (psychoanalytic concept of) resistance, there is not 'la psychanalyse' whether one understands it here as a system of theoretical norms or as a charter of institutional practices" (1998b, 20). And more to the point, having denied the strictly scientific status of such terms, is his characterization of the result, too often construed as evidence of a theoretical failure or a pseudo-science:

> If this is indeed the way it is, this situation does not necessarily translate a failure. There is also a chance for success, with no need to dramatize things. I don't believe one needs to turn this disjunction, in this case or any other, into bad drama. The inability to gather oneself, to identify with oneself, to unify oneself, all of this is perhaps tragedy itself, but it is also (the) chance and if there is no reason to dramatize, it is not only because that serves no purpose but also because it has not the least pertinence for this alliance of destiny, namely tragedy, and chance as the possible or the aleatory (1998b, 21).

If this logic of "strange plurality" seems still an appeal to the theoretically surreal, (or a sur-rationality, as Bachelard put it), it is what philosophers of science would call the "fertility of theory," gauged by a theory's ability to interact, contest and to advance the rational, even if fallibly or unknowingly.[28] Thus understood, we have been tracing the surrationality of 'phenomenology.' Even so, it might be replied, all this seems far from the sacred, in its purity and exteriority. Yet, sounding very much like Sartre's "we are condemned to be free," Mircea Eliade once said: "Hermeneutics—the science of interpretation—is the Western man's reply—the only intelligent reply—to the demands of contemporary history, to the fact that the West is committed (one might be tempted to say "condemned") to a confrontation with the cultural values of the 'others'" (Eliade 1962, 11).

Surely this occurs out of the "chance" of respecting what we don't know but also in acknowledging (the problem of Enlightenment itself) that we might have something to learn from it (Kant's *sapere aude*).[29] That this 'condemnation' and its chance has been reserved for our classical discourse for disambiguating theological texts ('hermeneutics,' a term no more strictly determinate than 'phenomenology') is perhaps not a matter of chance. To use Blanchot's term, at stake is a discourse of interruptions.

---

28 On Bachelard's term 'surrationality' see "Le surrationalisme," in Bachelard 1972.

29 See "What is Enlightenment?" in Kant 1963, 3.

Such a hermeneutics openly acknowledges its own rational and semantic 'drift,' combining, without resolving, the problem of transcendence and immanence, the same and the other. Both conceptually and historically, it might be said, this hermeneutics has something 'surreal' about it. In its interplay of conceptual and experiential horizons hermeneutics involves the encounter with the unknown, even against our wishes and the 'unconscious' of knowledge and its sovereign gaze.

For Blanchot, this was precisely the site of *écriture automatique*, which formed the legacy of surrealism and "one of literature's principle aspirations:" it provided, that is, both a "weapon against reflection" and a "belief in words" (1995, 86). Accordingly, the legacy of philosophy and *écriture automatique* then becomes somewhat unwieldy, almost inevitably understood in these authors as an encounter with philosophy's beyond, the 'outside,' its limit or its 'hieroglyphic' remainder. As Derrida would inevitably put it, strictly construed, this legacy involves the "becoming absent and the becoming unconscious of the subject"—but without, it should be insisted, succumbing simply to either absence or the unconscious (1976, 69). Even if its phenomenology is to be understood only as a certain 'fictionalization' that subtends the discourse of truth, this occurs without succumbing to irrationality. It is precisely this hieroglyphic structure that forms, Derrida claimed, the structure of interpretation—even Bataille's. "Like every discourse, like Hegel's, Bataille's discourse has the form of a structure of interpretation" (1978, 274). Indeed, as has become apparent, this step beyond (a step beyond that in fact reinvokes both Hegel and Schelling and the question of the 'surprise') is equally albeit "beyond the opposition of the mystic and the rational"—and yet obviously a beyond not without risk. It is also not without relation to Sartre, who had found here only a contradictory *combinatoire* of scientism and mysticism (Derrida 1978, 272; 269). No more than Bataille could remove such a writing from the task of interpretation could Sartre restrict it to the gaze of conscious regard—and neither, as a result, would grasp Heidegger, as Derrida notes (1978, 338). Writing is thus, in becoming other itself, the *espacement* of theory. We are reminded, as Louis Marin once put it that Klee's painting is similarly *peinture-écriture* (Marin 1970, 74-5). Indeed this was his stated intention, the development of a "kind of picture writing"—one in the end, that is neither sign nor object but the hieroglyphic texture

through which both are generated (Klee 1978b, 83).[30] In fact, as Klee
put it himself, its strange plurality remains always "multidimensional,"
an infinite polyvalence of *sens*. But, as we have seen, Klee's work, too, is
by no means unprincipled, if always interpretive. It is just this genesis
beyond 'mysticism' and 'scientism' that makes its 'automotism' always
fragmented and "partial" to use Breton's terms.[31] And, as has become
evident, in the same gesture Klee too had transcended the classical
antinomies of prose and poetry, intuition and concept, 'surrealism' and
'phenomenology'—at least as Sartre had initially construed them.

But even he knew better. The irony is that having posited the adventure of the dialectic between the prosaic and the poetic as he had
defined it, Sartre himself acknowledged a certain internal limitation, if
not impossibility to its expression. Perhaps he had relied on the ironies
of 'impossibility' throughout. The distinction, in any case, he knew was
only pragmatic and 'impure' at best:

> It goes without saying that in all poetry a certain form of prose, that is,
> of success, is present; and vice versa, the driest prose always contains
> a bit of poetry, that is a certain form of defeat; no prose-writer is *quite*
> capable of expressing what he wants to say; he says too much or not
> enough, each phrase is a wager, a risk assumed; the more cautious one
> is, the more attention the word attracts; as Valéry has shown, no one
> can understand a word to its very bottom (Sartre 1978, 31).

As Sartre's best scholars would explain, this dialectic that appears in
the footnotes of *What is Literature?* would inevitably force him to 'de-
ossify' the polarities of prose and poetry.[32] As a result, language itself
would be recognized more and more as a concrete historical materiality

---

30 See the analysis of K. Porter Aichele (2002). Aichele rightly sees that Klee's
heiroglyphics breaks down Enlightenment accounts (e.g., La Fontaine, Less-
ing) that divide poetry and painting, and she traces its antithesis tradition, the
ut pictura poiesis, to Horace's *Ars Poetica*. Before that tradition, it should be
added, Plutarch quotes Simonides as calling "painting silent poetry, and poetry
articulated painting."

31 Similarly we should add, Derrida's own écriture remains 'partial,' a refusal to
substitute the 'mechanism' of automatic writing for the writing of reflection. If
he insisted (still ironically) on the 'act' of writing as the "becoming unconscious
of the subject" or the decisive progress of formalism" he likewise demanded
that both "must discover a field of transcendental experience" (1976, 61).

32 See, for example, Christina Howells 1990.

with which the writer would grapple in order to say what remained unsayable within it. And this unsayble (*indisable*) itself would require us to see the result in terms of a non-knowledge (*le non savoir*) yet to be revealed by means of imaginary transformation. In all this it is clear that Sartre's initial distinctions between prose and poetry, sense and signification—and also 'phenomenology' itself—would need to be transformed. Like the distinction between the imaginary and the real itself, the relation between knowledge and nonknowledge, object and sign had been continuously and lucidly called into question. In retrospect, this was indeed the irony of Sartre's (again footnoted) condemnation of Klee's "greatness and error"—which lies, he claimed, in "Klee's attempt to make a painting both a sign and an object." The irony is that Klee might have become, like Flaubert and Mallarmé concerning the materialities of literature, something of a mentor in grasping the origins and 'drift' of phenomenology itself. Doubtless this accounts for Klee's importance, say, to the later Heidegger, to Merleau-Ponty, or to Lyotard in their attempts to traverse the ossifications of the classical stronghold (*réduit*) of phenomenology.

In all this we can still witness the proximity (and legacy) of Blanchot's own earliest interpretation of surrealism. The latter, he declared, in emphasizing the "transcendence" of language, had revealed a language that, in refusing to be relegated to strict rational construction or cognitive use, might instead be appropriated for the task of freedom itself—a task doubtless, the later Sartre would add, is always a matter of concrete historical necessity (Blanchot 1995, 86-88).[33] But perhaps it would be left to Merleau-Ponty, on whom Sartre relied so much in aesthetic mat-

---

33 As noted previously, by refusing its reduction to rational construction or 'use,' such transcendence is by no means rendered irrational *simpliciter*; rather we articulate a rationality that is, like the schematisms of historical imagination that it relies upon, always schema specific and interpretive. No more than did Klee should we see such affirmations to involve the affirmation of chaos (*sancta ratio chaotica*) (1978a, 70). Indeed, we shall need—as did the later Merleau-Ponty—to understand consciousness as a matter of transcendence, its history as a matter of structured multiplicity, and thereby that there is transcendence, between theories, historical motivations, intentional encroachment (*emptièment*) and transformation—and precisely in these exchanges, development, justification, and right (*droit*) (Merleau-Ponty 1968, 185-187). Such, I have been arguing, is the lot of 'surrealism' and 'phenomenology' itself. Or as Merleau-Ponty put it in relation to Schelling, "He is seeking a Reason that is not prosaic, a poetry that is not irrational" (2003, 50).

ters, to articulate their effect. Turning to Schelling in his final years to
rearticulate this transcendence Merleau-Ponty declared, "this excess of
Being over the consciousness of Being is what Schelling wants to think
in all its rigor. Schelling tries to describe this 'over-Being' (*Übersein*, in
the sense of the word '*surrealism*' (*ce 'Sur-être' Übersein, au sens du mot
'Surréalisme'*)" (2003, 38). Clearly the analogy, for reasons now evident,
would not be merely an external one. But he also saw what was at stake
in this attempt: "Schelling is trying for a non-prosaic conception of
consciousness" (2003, 50).

Bibliography

Adorno, Theodor and Walter Benjamin. 1998. *The Complete Correspondence
    1928-1949*, trans. Nicholas Walker. Cambridge, Mass.: Harvard University
    Press.
Aichele, K. Porter. 2002. *Paul Klee's Pictorial Writing*. Cambridge: Cambridge
    University Press.
Bachelard, Gaston. 1972. *L'engagement rationaliste*. Paris: Presses Universitaires
    de France.
Bataille, Georges. 1988. *Inner Experience*, trans. Leslie Anne Boldt. Albany:
    SUNY Press.
———. 1992. *On Nietzsche*, trans. Bruce Boone. New York: Paregon
    House.
———. 1994. *The Absence of Myth: Writings on Surrealismt*, trans. Michael
    Richardson. New York: Verson.
Benjamin, Walter. 1999. *The Arcades Project*, trans. Howard Eiland, Kevin
    McLaughlin. Cambridge, Mass.: Harvard University Press.
Blanchot, Maurice. 1980. "Le 'Discours Philosophique.'" *L'arc.*
———. 1981. *The Gaze of Orpheus*, trans. Lydia Davis. Barrytown, N.Y.:
    Station Hill Press.
———. 1992. *The Infinite Conversation*, trans. Susan Hanson. Minneapolis:
    University of Minnesota Press.
———. 1995. *The Work of Fire*, trans. Charlotte Mandell. Stanford: Stanford
    University Press.
Breton, André. 1972. *Surrealism and Painting*, trans. Simon Watson Taylor.
    New York: Harper & Row.
Casey, Edward S. 2002. *Imagining: A Phenomenological Study*. Bloomington:
    Indiana University Press.
Clifford, James. 1988. *The Predicament of Culture: 20th Century Ethnography,
    Literature, and Art*. Cambridge, Mass.: Harvard University Press.

de Beauvoir, Simone. 1968. *The Second Sex*, trans. H.M. Parshley. New York: Modern Library.

Derrida, Jacques. 1973. *Speech and Phenomena and other essays of Husserl's Theory of Signs*, trans. David Allison. Evanston, Ill.: Northwestern University Press.

———. 1976. *Of Grammatology*, trans. Gayatri Chakrovorty Spivak. Baltimore: Johns Hopkins University Press.

———. 1978. *Writing and Difference*, trans. Alan Bass. Chicago: University of Chicago Press.

———. 1987. *The Truth in Painting*, trans Geoff Bennington, Ian McLeod. Chicago: Chicago University Press.

———. 1998a. "Faith and Knowledge: the Two Sources of 'Religion' at the Limits of Reason Alone" in *Religion*, Jacques Derrida and Gianni Vattimo (eds.). Stanford: Stanford University Press.

———. 1998b. *Resistances: Of Psychoanalysis*, trans. Peggy Kamuf, Pascale-Anne Brault, Michael Naas. Stanford: Stanford University Press.

Eliade, Mircea. 1962. *The Two and the One*, trans. J.M. Cohen. Chicago: University of Chicago Press.

Fichte, J.G. 1982. *Science of Knowledge*, trans. Peter Heath and John Lachs. Cambridge: Cambridge University Press.

Foucault, Michel. 1970. *The Order of Things: An Archaeology of the Human Sciences*. New York: Pantheon.

———. 1977. *Language, Counter Memory, Practice*, trans. Donald F. Bouchard, Sherry Simon. Ithaca, N.Y.: Cornell University Press.

———. 1983. *This is Not a Pipe*, trans. James Harkness. Berkeley, Cal.: University of California Press.

———. 1997. *Aesthetics, Methodology, and Epistemology*, ed. James D. Faubion, trans. Robert Heard. New York: New Press.

Franciscono, Marcel. 1991. *Paul Klee: His Work and Thought*. Chicago: University of Chicago Press.

Frank, Manfred. 2004. *The Philosophical Foundations of Early German Romanticism*, trans. Elizabeth Millan-Zaibert. Albany: SUNY Press.

Glaesemer, Jürgen. 1986. "Klee and German Romanticism," in *Paul Klee*, Carol Lanchner (ed.). New York: Museum of Modern Art.

Hegel, G.W.F. 1975. *Aesthetics Vol. 1*, trans. T.M. Knox. Oxford: Clarendon Press.

———. 1977. *Phenomenology of Spirit*, trans. A.V. Miller. Oxford: Oxford University Press.

Heidegger, Martin 1990. *Kant and the Problem of Metaphysics*, trans. Richard Taft. Bloomington: Indiana University Press.

Howells, Christina. 1990. "Sartre and the Language of Poetry" in David Wood (ed.) *Philosopher's Poets*. London: Routledge. 140-152.

Husserl, Edmund. 1973. *Experience and Judgment*, trans. James S. Churchill and Karl Ameriks. Evanston, Ill.: Northwestern University Press.

————. 1982. *Ideas Pertaining to a Pure Phenomenology and to a Phenomenological Philosophy, First Book*, trans. F. Kersten. The Hague: Martinus Nijhoff.

Jung, C.G. 1966. *The Spirit in Man, Art, and Literature*, trans. R.F.C. Hull. The Collected Works of C.J. Jung, vol. 15. Princeton: Princeton University Press.

————. 1967. *Symbols of Transformation*, trans. R.F.C. Hull. The Collected Works of C.J. Jung vol. 5. Princeton: Princeton University Press.

————. 1971. *Psychological Types*, trans. R.F.C. Hull. The Collected Works of C.J. Jung, vol. 6. Princeton: Princeton University Press.

————. 1990. *The Archetypes and the Collective Unconscious*, trans. R.F.C. Hull. The Collected Works of C.G. Jung, vol. 9. Princeton: Princeton University Press.

Kant, Immanuel. 1963. *On History*, trans. Lewis White Beck. Indianapolis: Bobbs-Merrill.

————. 1987. *Critique of Judgment*, trans. Werner S. Pluharn. Indianapolis: Hackett.

Klee, Paul. 1964. *Diaries of Paul Klee 1898-1918*, trans. Pierre B. Schneider, R. Y. Zachary, Max Knight. Berkeley: University of California Press.

————. 1978a. *Notebooks Vol. 1: The Thinking Eye*, trans. Ralph Manheim. London: Lund Humphries.

————. 1978b. *Notebooks Vol. 2: The Nature of Nature*, trans. Heinz Norden. London: Lund Humphries.

Levinas, Emmanuel. 1987. "Reality and its Shadow" in *Collected Philosophical Papers*, trans. Alphonso Lingis. The Hague: Martinus Nijhoff.

Lyotard, Jean-Francois. 1971. *Discours, Figure*. Paris: Klincksieck.

Marin, Louis. 1970. "Klee ou le Retour à l'Origine." *Revue d'Esthétique* 23.

Merleau-Ponty, Maurice. 1962. *Phenomenology of Perception*, trans. Colin Smith. New York: Humanities.

————. 1964. *Signs*, trans. Richard L. McClearey. Evanston, Ill.: Northwestern University Press.

————. 1968. *The Visible and the Invisible*, trans. Alphonso Lingis. Evanston, Ill.: Northwestern University Press.

————. 1973. *Adventures of the Dialectic*, trans. Joseph Bien. Evanston, Ill.: Northwestern University Press.

————. 2003. *Nature: Course Notes from the Collège de France*, trans. Robert Vallier. Evanston, Ill.: Northwestern University Press.

Rabinovitch, Celia. 2002. *Surrealism and the Sacred*. Cambridge, Mass.: Westview Press.

Sartre, Jean-Paul. 1947. "Un Nouveau Mystique," *Situations* I. Paris: Gallimard.

―――. 1957. "Existentialism," *Existentialism and Human Emotions*, trans. Bernard Frechtman. New York: Philosophical Library.

―――.1966. *Being and Nothingness*, trans. Hazel Barnes. New York: Washington Square Press.

―――. 1968. *The Psychology of Imagination*, trans. Bernard Frechtman. New York: Washington Square Press.

―――. 1978. *What is Literature?* trans. Bernard Frechtman. Gloucester, Mass.: Peter Smith.

―――. 1992. *Notebooks for an Ethics*, trans. David Pellauer. Chicago: University of Chicago Press.

Schelling, F.W.J. 1978. *System of Transcendental Idealism*, trans. Peter Heath. Charlottesville, Va.: University Press of Virginia.

Stein, Gertrude. 1962. *Selected Writings of Gertrude Stein*. New York: Vintage Books.

Van Der Leeuw, G. 1986. *Religion in Essence and Manifestation*, trans. J.E. Turner. Princeton: Princeton University Press.

Watson, Stephen H. 1992. *Extensions: Essays on Interpretation, Rationality, and the Closure of Modernism*. Albany: SUNY Press.

―――. 1997. *Tradition(s) I: Refiguring Community and Virtue in Classical German Thought*. Bloomington: Indiana University Press.

―――. 2004. "Gadamer, Aesthetic Modernism and the Rehabilitation of Allegory: The Relevance of Paul Klee." *Research in Phenomenology* 34.

Werckmeister, O.K. 1982. "Walter Benjamin, Paul Klee, and the Angel of History" *Oppositions* 25. pp. 102-125.

―――. 1985. *Paul Klee in Exile* 1933-1940. Himeji, Japan: Himeji Museum of Art.

3

HERMENEUTICS
ANOTHER LOOK & OTHER QUESTIONS

RONALD BRUZINA

The approach I wish to take in my essay here is this: While hermeneutics is universally recognized as one of the major currents of intellectual work in the twentieth century, it is not always as clearly recognized how very different one "hermeneutics" can be from another, nor how the paradigm hermeneutical effort may have more in continuity and community with a philosophic current generally deemed its rival than is readily admitted. How this double direction of similarity and difference may pertain to the "hermeneutics" ascribed to Martin Heidegger—on the one hand showing his radical distinctness to other strands of hermeneutics, and on the other his close, even organic methodological linkage with Edmund Husserl's phenomenology—is what I think the full carrying out of the proposal I wish to make here would show. That said, all I can actually do is to sketch out the basics of the reading of texts in Heidegger's corpus that begin this task, and to do so by focusing on *what the issues were* that, being engaged, resulted in each case—for both Husserl's transcendental phenomenology and Heidegger's fundamental ontology—in the inauguration of an entire *program*, a whole philosophic undertaking that has yet to end. The way fundamental ontology eventually was pared down to a more radically focused thinking of being, to the event of being's breaking into human history, is a wider topic that I shall have to leave aside.[1] Here the focus will be on the way one prime element for Heidegger's putting a "hermeneutics" at the center of philosophic interest was his having worked long and hard on issues within phenomenology. What matters most in this is not establishing philosophic *doctrines*—sets of conclusions having thesis-like definitiveness that provide the distinctiveness that enables us to

---

1 This, of course, is the task Heidegger takes up above all in *Beiträge zur Phiolosophie (Vom Ereignis)* (Heidegger 1989).

separate such things as "phenomenology" and "hermeneutics," and at the same time allow application to a wide range of disciplines. What matters most for understanding what either phenomenology and hermeneutics are is what the *issue* is that leads to each program of inquiry, how each program goes about investigating the elements that make up that issue, how the investigation refines and advances the understanding of that issue, and how the program allows self-critique to overcome naïveté and presuppositional elements that may still mark the achievements of its inquiry. What the issue in phenomenology was and is for the Husserl of phenomenology's founding and what the issue was and is for the Heidegger in the hermeneutic restructuring of that phenomenology, and how the inquiry into each issue formed and proceeded through advance and self-correction—it is on this that I wish to focus.

Obviously I cannot cover all this exhaustively in one paper. What I hope to do is at least to lay out certain key points in regard to the whole idea by proceeding in three movements: 1) treating the starting-point issue in Heidegger's hermeneutic; 2) taking account of a retrospective from Heidegger's last years done upon the early work that culminated in *Being and Time*; and 3) noting a fundamental difficulty in the program of "interpreting" Dasein.

1. Heidegger's starting point issue in
Being and Time: the beginning that came later

We have to start with *Being and Time* because it is the statement of the first culmination in Heidegger's own program in its difference from Husserl's, namely, as the inquiry into being as such that is termed *Hermeneutik*, standardly rendered "hermeneutics" with the supposition it means straightforwardly a method of "interpretation." The fact that *Being and Time* doesn't *begin* Heidegger's thinking on this but is the result of a long trajectory of effort makes it essential to understand Heidegger's pronouncements on method in this book in terms of the kind of process from which they themselves result and within which they remain, at least some essentials of which will be laid out here. To begin, let us go straight to the central texts in *Being and Time* on phenomenology as *Hermeneutik*—"hermeneutics"—and first of all, to §7 C where the term is given for the first time in the book.

There are two things to which to pay special attention in this portion of the book. The first is the way the driving issue of *Being and Time* is posed in terms of the problem lying in the situation of bringing something *to show*: How are we to bring something to show that cannot be brought to show except in terms of something else, where the thing to be brought to show is in the peculiar position of being neither the same as nor different from this second something via which to show this first thing itself. This, of course, is the issue of bringing *Sein*—"being"—to show when *Sein* ("being") is precisely not something-that-can-show because, far from standing "behind" *Seiendes*—"something-that-is"—and thus hidden behind it,[2] *Sein* as such is the very *Sinn* and *Grund* of *ein Seiendes*—the very *sense* and *ground* of a something-that-*is*. In point of fact, *Sein* ("being") is not "a something" at all (Heidegger 1963, 35-36; 1996, 31),[3] and therefore cannot be even characterized in terms of differentiating determinateness, in any kind of specific features. *Sein* is neither the same as nor different from *Seiendes*; it is both simply not like *Seiendes* ("something-that-is") and yet "holds" of it (to use a questionable metaphor).

Here is the situation within which phenomenology is to become *Hermeneutik*, to be not an ἀποφανσις, a bringing to show, but rather, Heidegger writes, a ἑρμηνεύειν—which I shall leave untranslated for the moment— "through which [1] the proper sense of *Sein* and [2] the basic structures of Dasein's own *Sein* are *made known* to the *Sein*-understanding belonging to Dasein itself." And the very next sentence is the statement declaring the shift: "Phenomenology of Dasein is *Hermeneutik* in the original signification of the word, by which is designated the business of *Auslegung*" (Heidegger 1963, 37; 1996, 33. Translation modified, italics in the original).

Now, just what this "being *made known*"—*kundgegeben werden*—means as a task, as a procedure of advancing insight and self-critique, cannot be assumed to be grasped adequately here, or anywhere else in Heidegger—or indeed anywhere in Husserl—if we take the familiar words in either German or in any translation as already sufficiently clear for us to understand them in the designation they make in each case. If, for example, we straightforwardly take "interpretation" for either *hermeneuein* or *Auslegung*, we are likely to be misled; for the tendency is to take "interpretation" to mean basically, quite simply, to give a rendering

---

2 One could just as easily say *Sein* is not "inside" *Seiendes*, and hence hidden within it, but Heidegger doesn't mention this here.

3 See also a similar point in Heidegger 1963, 152; 1996, 142.

of an already formulated message of some kind so as to make clear the meaning of that message. But in the present situation what is at issue is precisely the fact that what is to be "made known" is not the meaning of some kind of message-like presentation or declaration; what is to be "made known" is something that has to be *brought* to *"show"* in some sense, and talk about it, or conceptualization of it, is wholly to serve this "showing" (as becomes clearer later in *Being and Time*, rather than in these early sections). Thus, for example, to think that because we have the word *Sein* we have a message-like declaration already on hand, but one that is waiting to be interpreted, would be already to overlook the methodological undertaking Heidegger is beginning to sketch out. That is, one has to begin here to grasp the *manner* in which to bring what is at issue—*Sein*— into clarity when the word for it is anything but a definite "message." What we are told at this point in *Being and Time* is that, if we abide by the "original signification of the term," *hermeneuein* is to be a "making known" in a quite general and noncommittal sense, a "setting out" of something that at that point is *not yet* "made known," *not yet* "set out," a setting out that will in the end "make" it "known" (*kund-geben*, which, while not designating any specific kind of cognition, can connote setting something into view for someone). And the "something" to be thus "made known" by being "set out" is the "proper sense of *Sein*," which this same §7 C has just pointed out is the sort of thing that *cannot show*, even if the second thing at issue, "the basic structures of Dasein's own *Sein*," apparently *is* the sort of thing that can be brought to *show*. Whether this is actually so or not in the case of Dasein, and in what measure and manner it may be, remain to be seen as the study in the book unfolds, and in fact is not really something that can be settled in the present paper.

What we have to do, then, is to let the meaning of *hermeneuein* or *Auslegung* come out more specifically and correctly as it unfolds *in the course* of the inquiry itself that is the program of *Being and Time*, and *as the result* of the way Heidegger proceeds there (including the way from time to time he speaks about how the task at hand is being done). In other words, the point of staying with the "original signification" of the first of these two terms, ἑρμηνεύειν, is to avoid being oriented in terms of possible presuppositional naïveté in what we take "interpretation" to mean. This very effort, now, to allow the investigation to determine the meaning of a term—here "interpretation" in its varieties of expression—which in fact already orients and guides the investigation, defines the procedure of investigation in phenomenology as such as *Husserl* practiced it before Heidegger, and after his relationship with him. Yet despite there being a measure of sameness in this point of method, Heidegger formulates it rather differently than Husserl, and he uses a variety of ways to describe it.

In §2 of *Being and Time* this procedure in investigation is spoken of in terms of the way one formulates a question, with the main point for the present purpose the idea that "questioning needs antecedent guidance from what it seeks" (Heidegger 1963, 5; 1996, 4. Translation modified) even if what is sought is far from clear. In this case, the sense of "being" (*Sein*) is named as what is sought, but just to have the word for it, while indispensable, is not enough. Yet there must be some justification for the word in that what is sought is somehow indicated in the word, even if not clearly grasped in the sense that makes the word meaningful for us. In §31 where the existential structure of "understanding" is explicated, we are introduced to the term *Entwurf*—usually translated "projection"—as the always sketch-like anticipatory openness out to what is meaningfully to come as one continues to be, as one continues to "exist" in Heidegger's technical sense of the word.[4] And in §32 this always still "sketchy""projection" of existential anticipation is spoken of as revisited in the way it *can develop*; and this development of "understanding" is termed *Auslegung*—again, "interpretation," in its usual translation, but rather more nuanced than that. Here the process wherein an "antecedent conception"—*Vorgriff*— of something, already met with in one's engagements, now gets taken up in order to "appropriate" it, to "make it one's own [*zueignen*]" in one's understanding of it, to make it comprehensible. This work of *Auslegung,* not simply acknowledgement of what is understood, but the "working out of possibilities sketchily projected" in one's existential understanding (Heidegger 1963, 148; 1996, 139. Translation modified), can happen in two ways. In the *Auslegung* one can either force a meaning upon the something met with in a way contrary to the kind of being that something has—presumably by too rigid an adherence to the "antecedent conception" one has of it (Heidegger is not specific on this)—or one can "draw from the something-that-is," which is thus to be "*ausgelegt* in the conceptuality belonging to it" (Heidegger 1963, 150; 1996, 141).

---

4 *Entwurf* in German carries both senses: project(ion) and sketch or outline.

It is at this point that Heidegger speaks of the famous "hermeneutic circle," that is, the way in which the anticipatory guiding "sketch-projection" gives inquiry its aim, but acquires its investigationally gained sense "*aus den Sachen selbst*," Heidegger writes, "from the investiganda themselves" (as one might paraphrase it) (Heidegger 1963, 153; 1996, 142).[5] Here it is clear that, far from being a rigid determinacy of meaning, the "sketch-projection" is the way an investigation is given aim and focus, the way in which that which is to be "made known" is provided with a concrete line of meaningfulness in terms of which to be "made known," with the specifics of that meaningfulness coming by force of, i.e., developing from, "*den Sachen selbst*," from the investiganda themselves.

Here is where the parallel has to be made to the methodology in Husserl's investigative procedure. There are two elements I have in mind, one the structural feature that is operative in Husserl's investigations but mentioned by him only rarely, namely, the need to move in a "zig-zag" way,[6] and the other the cognitive principle embodied in the situation of interplay between the "sketch-projection"-element and the "*Sache selbst*"-element, and given in the famous explicit declaration by Husserl of the "Principle of Principles."

On the first element: Husserl's phenomenology is well-known for certain methodological features: epoché, reduction, egoic standpoint, and so on. But there is another feature at play in his investigations as the very dynamic of their movement, and which is directly relevant here, yet is so pervasive that it gets overlooked. It was formulated by Eugen Fink, Husserl's assistant during the last ten years of his life, in draft notes for an introduction to what was originally conceived as an edition of Husserl's Bernau manuscripts but which turned into a massive treatment of time and time-constitution meant to treat the whole problematic of time-analysis. Leaving aside the story of that undertaking, let me simply quote the compact characterizations Fink gives of the way Husserl's phenomenology works:

---

5 Actually Heidegger's first remarks on the circular structure of inquiry in *Being and Time* are in the first Introduction (1963, 7-8; 1996, 6) where the way one already thinks about being in previous ontology is characterized "as not in play availably as a *concept*," i.e., as "that as [or: in terms of which] which it [i.e., *Sein*, being] is being sought" (in my somewhat paraphrastic renderings).

6 See Husserl's characterization of the "zigzag" character of his investigations in volume 2 of his *Logical Investigations*, §6 (Husserl, 1970a); cf. note 7 below.

> With Husserl, his system grows out of the individual analyses. The paradoxical situation, that the concreteness of phenomenological philosophy lies in the manuscripts, which however first make possible the general systematic projections. On the other hand, it is only in the light of these projections that the more comprehensive relevance of the analyses can be seen. These systematic anticipatory perspectives guided things for Husserl. Work done following them sees itself referred to presentations of universal scope.(Fink *n.d.*, 2: B-I 40a)[7]

And, the same thing is said again in a slightly different way, in the same set of notes:

> The peculiarity of Edmund Husserl's way of working is that all systematic projections are not constructions that precede concrete investigations, rather they *develop in the analyses.* But that filled out analyses are made possible also results in the systematic projected design being broken open again, to gain thereby the characteristic of mobility. This is a fundamental characteristic of phenomenology—despite all its rigor [it is an] *open system.* (Fink *n.d.*, 2:B-I 22a)[8]

What is interesting and pivotal here is the characterization of two structural dimensions, that of the conceptions that guide an investigation and serve to unify and articulate its results, and that of the investigational analyses themselves—two interplaying factors that constitute the actual work in their interplay. It is the same pattern of interplaying factors I see in the method Heidegger is elaborating, though in largely different terminology and, a crucial point to develop shortly, with a sharply different focus and aim. And it remains to be seen how these two dimensions need further characterization when methodological self-critique enters the picture.

The second element in Husserl's phenomenology to mention, however, is the famous "Principle of All Principles" enunciated in his *Ideas I* as follows: "that every intuition that gives [its object] on the origin-level

---

7   The last designation gives the manuscript page, retained in the margins of the text as it is to be published. The syntactic incompleteness of the second sentence is not untypical of Fink's notes.

8   Emphasis Fink's, insertion in brackets mine. In more general expression, see also Fink 1995, 7-8. Cf. the near-parallel of the "zigzag" principle in Husserl 1970b, 58 (Husserl 1962, 59), there regarding the relation of origin to sense-tradition but striking in its analogy to the present point.

[*originär*] is a source of *de jure* validity [*eine Rechtsquelle*] for knowledge,
that everything which is offered us in origin-level 'intuition' (so to speak,
in "in the flesh" actuality), is to be accepted as what is given but only
within the limits in which it is there given"(Husserl 1976, 51, §24).[9] The
point of citing this is to show that, even with the wide-ranging change
of terminology on Heidegger's part, the operative principle in his work
is the same as Husserl's in the following way: that what one gets to in
one's program of investigative "seeing"—in whatever way one conceives
that "seeing," that "insight," as long as it is taken on the level and within
the situation of that being which, doing the "seeing," is constitutively, and
in all its powers, in-the-world—is neither a fiction nor a mere mental
projection, but "something-that-is" (*Seiendes*). This is the fundament of
all possibility for both experience and philosophy, not to mention all
science; and the point of a phenomenology, whether a "transcendental"
one in Husserl's manner or an "ontological" one in Heidegger's, is to
show that one cannot argue toward this realization as a conclusion, one's
work must show the necessity of beginning and remaining within it as
the overarching constitutive condition of knowledge-capable human
being as such. The "trick," however, lies in the "showing" and the "seeing,"
and that "showing" and "seeing," I wish to argue, is built into what is the
primary issue of Heidegger's *Being and Time*.

It is in consideration of this guiding cognitive principle embodied
not only in Husserl's conception of "intuition" but also in Heidegger's
effort to "make known" two matters, "[1] the proper sense of *Sein* and
[2] the basic structures of Dasein's own *Sein*," that we can return to the
consideration of Heidegger's "hermeneutic" and begin to specify the
focus and aim of his investigation in distinction from Husserl's as well
as in the distinctive characterization of a "principle of all principles" for
his own progress, at least in the project of *Being and Time*.

As we would move from Part 1, Division I in *Being and Time* to Division II, we should be struck by the way we actually witness there the
interplay dynamic of what Fink finds as structuring Husserl's "system"
and his "way of working"—the interplay, namely, between guiding,
sketch-like anticipatory projections and investigative analyses such
that one advances the other, even while the advance has its grounding
source in the "phenomenon" in question—in *Being and Time*: human
being—under the guiding action of the "sketchy projection" of Dasein

9 My translation. For the concomitant feature of *Evidenz*, "evidentness," see
Husserl 1970a, (Prolegomena) §51.

as existence. We even see Heidegger drawing our attention to this—in his own distinctive fashion, of course—in the opening remarks before Chapter 1 of Division II. Note the phrasing: "Ontological inquiry is a possible kind of *Auslegung* ["interpretation," "laying out"] that was characterized as the working out and making one's own of an understanding." All the "preconceptions"—*Voraussetzungen*—all the "antecedent" takes on the matter of inquiry—*Vorhabe, Vorsicht, Vorgriff*—"that we have named the hermeneutical situation" have to be "clarified and secured beforehand from and within a fundamental experience of the object to be disclosed" (Heidegger 1963, 231-32, §45; 1996, 214. My translation). Here in these same paragraphs Heidegger emphasizes one ever-repeated necessity in the work of *Being and Time*, and gives technical designation to the way the "object to be disclosed" is got to in the inquiry situation. The constantly repeated need in *Being and Time* is to take the "idea of existence [*die Idee der Existenz*]" especially in the way existence is always a "can-be"—*Seinkönnen*—rather than as a mere "is," always as *mine* (Heidegger 1963, 232 §45; 1996, 214-15). It is never some genus or *kind* of being that is in question, but an individualized—ultimately personalized—being: human being as me. Along with this we see a second technical point, that terming my human being Dasein or existence is given methodological specificity by being called "formal indication" (Heidegger 1963, 231 §45;1996, 214,).

With these two notes we are already deep into the program of *Being and Time* in terms of the method for gaining access to that which is at issue, *Sein* as such, via that being for which being is the issue, human being as Dasein. It is in the analysis of the way human being as Dasein exists, in the integrated manifold of its constitutive structural complexity, that the "horizon [a very Husserlian term] for an interpretation [*Interpretation*] of the sense of being as such" is to be gained."[10] Otherwise put, it is via the laying out of the way Dasein exists that we shall be able to gain the proper setting for being able to catch sight of being as such. And here I wish to turn briefly to an effort of Heidegger's to lay out a proper approach to (re)thinking being, via the analysis of human being, that preceded *Being and Time* by a few years, and then to a retrospective on this same overall effort offered by him a few years before his death. These are, first, his lectures in the summer of 1923 initially entitled "Ontology," and secondly his remarks in the seminar conducted in his home at Zähringen in 1973.

10 Heidegger 1996, 13: title of §5 (1963, 15).

What is said about *Hermeneutik*—"hermeneutics"—so compactly at various points in *Being and Time* is given an earlier much more detailed characterization in the 1923 lectures on "ontology" that Heidegger renamed "hermeneutics of facticity" as soon as it had begun. Rather than a full reading, however, let me simply give the points I think are most pertinent to the overall aim of the present paper.

The first point is an observation about the fact that these lectures of Heidegger's lie within the whole series of studies on his part that stretch from his dissertation to *Being and Time*. Heidegger's effort to investigate the meaning of being had been under way for a long time, proceeding precisely in a repeated back-and-forth effort between a) conceptual formulations of what to focus on and b) what to look for in that focus. Moving back-and-forth here means simply constantly considering how the matter investigated in terms of guiding formulations leads to reassessing those same formulation in terms of what was found in the formulation-focused investigation; this in turn means looking at the same matter again under the reformulation, and so on. What we have here is actually neither a circle nor a back-and-forth movement, but something more like a spiral: a movement that changes with each return to modify, amplify, correct, and deepen an initial conception and question and the inquiry these spawn. It is clear that a process of this kind had been going on a long time before Heidegger sat down to put together the text of *Being and Time*. The way this book begins its inquiry is not the first beginning, but the <u>re</u>commencement that came after a number of renewed beginnings and that therefore can be better understood when the long process of earlier investigation is followed in its development. And, one has to add, the process did not and does not stop with *Being and Time*.

The second point, now, in taking a look at the 1923 lectures is that Heidegger's way of working there illustrates much that has just been said. In these lectures Heidegger makes clear that the decisive element in his program of inquiry is the "as what" in terms of which the matter to be inquired into is to be reached; and this "as what" is the very reason for his calling this inquiry *Hermeneutik* and the method it employs *Auslegung*. Here too, already, the matter to be inquired into is one's own being, already named Dasein; and in 1923 Dasein is the main focus of inquiry because it is the kind of being "out of which and for which philosophy 'is,'" in contrast to the way the approach to the problematic of being had been blocked by the work of previous ontology (Heidegger

1995, 2). Much in these lectures anticipates the analysis of Dasein in *Being and Time*, but in subtlety, comprehensiveness and complexity *Being and Time* goes much further than the 1923 lectures. For our purposes, however, what is methodologically important is the way these lectures emphasize the very special character of this "hermeneutics" and "interpretation" precisely because of the nature of the "as what" in terms of which Dasein is at issue.

The "as what" of this inquiry is "facticity [*Faktizität*]." More precisely, the facticity as which Dasein is to be approached means that my being *is mine*, and, again more precisely, *jemeinig*, in the sense that in its being (*seinsmässig*) my being, Dasein, is "there ['*da*']." This being of mine "is there to itself in the way it is its very own being to the utmost extent," in the concretely circumscribed being that is the only way of genuinely being "there."[11] This "ownness," *Eigenheit*, of facticity is not *Einzelheit*, isolated singleness, i.e., not *solus ipse*. It is rather the only "how of being" that is genuine to my being.

This ownness, now, is what the "hermeneutic" action is to get me to. "Getting to one's own being" is, in contrast to what hermeneutics earlier may have been, not a discussion of texts or propositions or any such complex of formulated meaning; its understanding is not a labor over generalities, but a *hermeneuein*, a *Mitteilen*—a communicating—an *Auslegung* (Heidegger 1995, 14) to myself of my own being as factic in my-ownness. It lives from, springs from, and draws from "a philosophical wakefulness [*Wachsein*] in which [my] being [*Dasein*] meets itself"; and this situation of "meeting" oneself in being "there" in the living sense of being-there, is what "interpretation" amounts to—that is, *self-interpretation*, *Selbstauslegung* (Heidegger 1995, 18 and 20). At the same time, the methodological complex of this "communicating" and "encountering" in which my-own-being "meets" my-own-being—my own Dasein—*as* factically there, *as* my very own in the fullest temporally fluid concreteness, by way of "laid-out" or "interpretive" specification of the "as-what," in sum, in its function the "laid-out," "interpretive" formulation itself of this "as-what" in conceptually laden specific delineation (*Darstellung*), is named "a formal indication" (Heidegger 1995, 51). Accordingly, to concentrate on the *content* of this delineating formulation as such would

---

11 "... sondern Dasein ist ihm selbst *da* im Wie seines eigensten Seins" (Heidegger 1995, 7). One should note that at this point Dasein can be simply rendered my *being*, in that "Dasein" is not yet designated the name to be henceforth *specific to* my being as human being.

be wholly to misunderstand things. That is not what "formal indication" is all about; it is not concerned with, as it were, mentally possessed knowledge *about* something. Instead, on the basis of the thus formulated indicative meaning, the functional point is "to bring understanding into the right line of sight (*Blickbahn*)" (Heidegger 1995, 80; also 18) via which to "meet" oneself experientially in one's own being "there," in one's own Dasein.

Summary as this restatement of one of the major points of the 1923 lectures is, it at least allows us to see what is at play in *Being and Time* in Heidegger's "hermeneutics" precisely via the analysis of Dasein elaborated through that book. It is the very special effort, via words and meanings offering delineations to guide, in *formal indication*, the achievement of a "meeting," under the guidance of a "seeing," specifically a "seeing-as" (in some sense of "seeing"), that will disclose for oneself both a) what constitutes my being in its utmost concreteness precisely as *my very own being,* and also thereby (eventually) b) the sense of *being as such.* This is in play in the enormously complicated analyses of Dasein that are so familiar to us in *Being and Time*.[12] And this programmatic aim, formulated so with greater care and precision in §7 C of *Being and Time*, is this methodology of "interpretation"—*Hermeneutik* and *Auslegung*—that distinguishes Heidegger's sense of "hermeneutics" from the many meanings of these terms that come into currency after *Being and Time*. It is this special sense of "interpretation" that Heidegger specifies to which I shall return for critical observations in the final part of my treatment. To serve that purpose, however, I want to turn to the remarks Heidegger makes on the problematic of philosophically disclosing Dasein and being as such fifty years after the 1923 lectures, namely, in his 1973 Zähringen seminar.

---

12 In the *Gesamtausgabe* edition the term Dasein gets hyphenated: Da-sein, a spelling that is followed in Joan Stambaugh's translation, which, given the sense the hyphenation can be taken to convey, to my mind only heightens the problem of the term that I shall briefly mention later in the third section. Indeed, in the "Translator's Preface," where Joan Stambaugh explains her following this practice in the *Gesamtausgabe* edition of the book (Heidegger 1977), she remarks that it was "Heidegger's insight that human being is *uncanny*: we do not know who, or what, that is, although, perhaps precisely because, we *are* it" (Heidegger 1996, xiv).

2. Retrospective upon the renewed beginning in *Being and Time*

Jacques Taminiaux, drawing from the transcript of the Zähringen seminar written in French by the French participants though Heidegger spoke in German, drew attention thirty-seven years ago to Heidegger's account of the crucial discovery he made on the basis of Husserls "Sixth Logical Investigation" (Taminiaux 1977). Heidegger realized that Husserl's "categorial intuition," intuition beyond, in *excess* of, the straightforward object-mode of givenness to take in the structural complexity of different kind of ensembles and wholes, whether entitative or situational, attested to a disclosure that could be taken as giving phenomenological validation of the "as it were" "givenness" status of being itself—as Heidegger terms it—namely, that beyond mere conceptual representation, being could be "made present, phenomenally present in the category" (Heidegger 1976, 315).[13] Husserl, however, so Heidegger explains, never inquired into what the sense of being as thus "phenomenally present" might be, taking for granted that being meant simply "object-being" for a subject.[14]

In the seminar, then, Heidegger recounts briefly the trajectory through the reading of Plato and Aristotle that led eventually to the transposition of Husserl's "givens in the dimension of sense" (*données sensorielles, sinnliche Gegebenheiten*) into the "givens" that matter in *Being and Time*. And in *Being and Time* what matters is the "given" of the *whole situation* within which a "consciousness" has its take on being, namely, the situation of the "*lumen naturale*" that in the first place allows any "looking (at)" something—*regarder* in the French, in the German version *anschauen*, which could also, in a less philosophically charged way, be translated *blicken (auf/nach etwas)*. Here Heidegger makes an etymology-like remark upon the sense of *re-garder*, that it is a doing,

---

13 The French transcript in Heidegger 1976 was subsequently translated into German for the *Gesamtausgabe* edition (Heidegger 1986). The German version here seems to diminish the force of the French in rendering "cette mise en présence de l'être, présent dans la catégorie" by "dieser Vergegenwärtigung des Seins, das in der Kategorie phänomenal anwesend ist," instead of a much stronger legitimate rendering, "Gegenwärtigung des Seins" (Heidegger 1986, 378).

14 This charge of Heidegger's against Husserl is criticized by Eugen Fink. See Bruzina 2004, 151.

a "*garder*" (presumably in the usual meaning: watching over), in a way that turns it "back" (*re-*)—which, therefore, allows him to paraphrase *regarder* as "bringing myself to be approached by what I look at" (Heidegger 1976, 317). Here, then, Heidegger points to what "grounds"[15] this *regarder*, this looking at: "the radical possibility for human being to cross an opening to reach things"; and this "being-in-an-opening" is precisely what is named Dasein—awkwardly named, Heidegger acknowledges, "but I did what I could" (Heidegger 1976, 317). Then, he immediately adds a second characterization of Dasein: "Dasein, one has to understand it as *die Lichtung-sein*: *être l'éclaircie* [being the clearing, the opening]. The 'there' is in actuality the word for the opening" (Heidegger 1976, 317).[16]

Now, leading up to this point—that Dasein is the "there" of the opening wherein "looking at" something can take place as reaching that something in its own being—this very "looking" is relegated to consciousness; for consciousness—*Bewußtsein*: conscious-being—is spoken of in terms of the power *to see*, vision being the paradigmatic action involved in "knowing [Wissen]." "Conscious-being moves in the dimension of seeing, where it is illuminated by the *lumen naturale*" (Heidegger 1976, 317). This is why *regarder*, looking (at) (*blicken, anschauen*), is spoken of as grounded by "being-in-an-opening," and this "being-in-an-opening," Heidegger points out, is what *Being and Time* names Dasein. Being-in-an/the-opening is what enables seeing and looking (at) to take place, but the opening itself is brought about in the very dynamic that constitutes Dasein, so that Dasein *is* also at the same time being the opening. In this way, too, Heidegger points out that "consciousness is rooted in Dasein, not the other way around" (Heidegger 1976, 317-18). But since seeing and looking (at) are so pivotal—and indeed they function in the very disclosure of being as the "excess" over object-like givens, not to mention (as we have seen) perhaps also in the very functioning of the hermeneutic/interpretive effort of the disclosure of being in Heidegger's lectures and writings—the relation between being-conscious, *Bewußtsein*, and the being of human being,

---

15 The French for Heidegger's word here is *fonde*, in the German translation, *gründet*.

16 The German expression given in the French transcript is presumably Heidegger's own.

Da-sein has to be examined, Heidegger admonishes. This is what the second session of the seminar takes up.

In the second session now, summarily put, Heidegger takes Husserl's consciousness (again, *Bewußtsein*) as "immanence" as if enclosure in a "box" and "without windows" (Heidegger's metaphors). Da-sein is completely different. The *Sein* in Da-sein, in contrast to the *Sein* in *Bewußt-sein*, "conscious-being," is not an interiorly held *Sein* but a *Sein* turned outward. "Da-sein strictly means: being ek-statically the there" (Heidegger 1976, 321-22).[17] And if one is going to consider the intentionality of consciousness, one has to "situate it in the ek-stasis of Dasein. In a word, it has to be recognized that consciousness is founded in Dasein"—to repeat a point already made, with the operative word again *fondée* or *gegründet* (Heidegger 1976, 322).[18]

To finish my reading of these first two sessions of the Zähringen seminar, I cannot omit bringing in one last consideration of Heidegger's, again from the second session, because it leads precisely to the problematic at the heart of my discussion. Heidegger adds a remark in which he says: "today I would formulate the relationship differently. I would not speak simply of ek-stasis, but of *Inständigkeit* in der *Lichtung*, [*instancy* in the *clearing* (or: opening)]," a turn of expression that Heidegger explains as "the unity of two meanings": "1) holding the three ek-stases in balance; 2) sustaining and enduring being across the entirety that is being-the-there." This *Inständigkeit* in der *Lichtung*, "instancy in the clearing (opening)," is a linguistic formula huge with implications that, so far as I know, are largely unsuspected;[19] and one should know that the term *Inständigkeit* occurs with some frequency in Heidegger's *Beiträge*, both in noun and adjective form (with variations).[20] The point, however, of

---

17 The discussion of *Bewußtsein* and *Dasein* running from pp. 318 to 325. The hyphenation of "Da-sein" is in the French text.

18 See the first mention of these terms in note 15.

19 In a sense developed rather differently, and apparently earlier—though not unrelatable to the one here—the German term, given in German in the French transcript, is in fact one of the principal expressions involved in Eugen Fink's "meontic" in the self-critical methodology of transcendental phenomenology. Rather than treat this point here, I have to refer to the full discussion of it in my book, section 5.1.1.2 (among others) and chapter 7 (Bruzina 2004)

20 The longest consideration is in number 174, which parallels the point made here in Heidegger 1976.

this phrase—*Inständigkeit in der Lichtung*—both in its context in the
1973 seminar and in Heidegger's *Beiträge* (Heidegger 1989), is the way
it affects how one considers, not simply the relation of consciousness to
Da-sein, but the relationship of *human being* and Da-sein.

This is something catching our notice when we see two closely related, but quite different statements. A little later in the second session
Heidegger remarks in regard to the "clearing," the "*Lichtung*," this "free
dimension [*diese Freie*]," that "man is not the creator of it, man is not it.
On the contrary, it is that which is destined for him, which addresses
itself to him: It is that which is consigned to him"—a clause that in
the French transcript is given in German: "*Es ist das ihm zugeschickte*"
(Heidegger 1976, 324-25). The other kind of remark follows shortly
after, when the discussion turns to Marx, whose main thesis in regard to
human being Heidegger puts as the idea that "the man who is his own
root to himself is indeed the man of production-consumption"—and
the process of production-consumption had just been discussed in
the seminar. To this idea Heidegger offers a counterpoint: "But man
understood as Da-sein, as ek-static instancy in the clearing of being, is
the opposite of the thesis Marx declares." Nor can one say, Heidegger
insists, that "Da-sein is the root of man" because the concept of "root"
is utterly incapable of conveying "the relationship of man to being"
(Heidegger 1976, 327). One may well suppose that here Heidegger
is also offering a corrective clarification in regard to his earlier remark
that "being-conscious, consciousness, is rooted in Dasein."[21] I shall be
returning to this seeming correction again, this caution and indeed rejection of "root"-terms for characterizing the place of Dasein in regard
to human being.

3. The difficulty of conceptually indicating—i.e., "*interpreting*"—the ontological structure of Dasein/Da-sein—or ultimately of being as such

We now have some basic elements for returning to the methodological
structure of Heidegger's *Hermeneutik* and *Auslegung* in *Being and Time*
in terms of 1) the issue: the sense of being, 2) the avenue of inquiry
for approaching this issue, namely, the ontological analysis of human
being as Dasein/Da-sein, and 3) the main problems lying in all this.

---

21 See the above reference on p. 14 to Heidegger 1976, 317-18.

To take all this up properly in such a way as to show both the continuity with Husserl's phenomenology and the transformation that this phenomenology undergoes in Heidegger's work on the one hand, and the methodological issues that similarly continue from Husserl and get transformed in Heidegger's investigations on the other—and my interest is really in these methodological issues—would require a close reading of a number of places in *Being and Time* that we simply could not do in the compass of this paper. As a result, at this point I shall have to offer an overview, a summary of what I see to be in play in this whole problematic.

Let me first speak again of the differentiation that the Zähringen seminar indicates between human being and *Da-sein*.[22] The differentiation emerges in the difference between speaking of Dasein as "*in*" the clearing, *in* the "there," and as unqualifiedly simply *being* the clearing, *being* the "there."[23] The first designation speaks of that which is enabled in the clearing to stand open to something standing forth to it therein as something-that-is, while the second speaks of the dynamic of opening the clearing as such, the "originative" factor enabling something-that-is to stand forth in disclosedness to that which is open to it. In *Being and Time*, Dasein is asserted as both, constitutively, unqualifiedly: Dasein is the kind of being that human being has precisely in deploying the "there" of disclosure in the dynamic of its temporalized existence, the disclosure both to itself of itself as Dasein in its being, and of all that Dasein in the dynamic of its existence brings to be as the complex of the sense-laden referential vectors that make up the world in the "there" of Dasein's engaged realization of its *Seinkönnen*—of its aiming ever forward into what it "can-be." In the Zähringen discussion, human being clearly has functions that are themselves directly *dependent upon* the "there" of the clearing, in particular the power of seeing—the mode of sensuous consciousness that we name *vision*, the intentional opening out into the clearing that envelops it and enables its intentional thrust,

---

22 It is a differentiation that is earlier explicitly indicated in Heidegger 1989, where *Inständigkeit* is itself focused on in number 174 and further discussed in the numbered sections that follow, 175 and 176. There are many other passages as well where more or less equivalent usages of noun or adjectival *inständig-* or *inständlich-*words occur.

23 This is what could make for a distinction between Dasein and Da-sein, partially at least disambiguating the ambiguity, but Heidegger's usage does not seem to allow any such clear contrast.

thereby to see what is there, in the "there."[24] We have to note too that
this parallels the 1923 lectures on "hermeneutics," where the forcefully
pronounced feature of facticity—the *this-way* in which an actual human being is contingently concrete at any time in its existence—is an
intrinsic feature in function of all the circumscribing particulars in play
right then in the field of being, namely, in the world. Yet, in contrast
to the Zähringen seminar, Heidegger in these 1923 lectures makes
explicitly clear that in the concrete this-way facticity of human being
in its constitutive placement in the field of being—the disclosure of
which becomes, in the project of *Being and Time*, the way to "make
show" being itself—human being *is* Dasein. For example, Heidegger
writes in italicized emphasis: "*Dasein (factic life) is being* [Sein] *in a
world*" (Heidegger 1995, 80).

This disaccord between a) Heidegger's 1923 lectures, along with
the continuing unqualified identity of Dasein with human being-in-
the-world in *Being and Time*, and b) Heidegger's partial decoupling
of Dasein and human being in the 1973 Zähringen seminar, relates
closely, now, to the second point that has to be raised about this whole
problematic: namely, regarding the nature of the investigational operation by which on the one hand the "there," the "clearing" itself, and on
the other hand the being that is this clearing—that is the world simply
put—are together brought to be "seen"; for seeing all this is the whole
point of the operation of "*Auslegung*," "interpretation." *Can* all this in
fact be "*seen*"? And in *what kind* of "seeing" (and disclosure, "showing")
is this to be done? Here precisely is where a joint reading of Heidegger
on "interpretation" and Husserl on "categorial intuition" would be both

---

24 The distinction I am pointing to in the Zähringen seminar (Heidegger
1976) no doubt reflects Heidegger's long, involved, fragmentary thinking in
Beiträge (Heidegger 1989), though it is also discernible earlier yet; but in *Beiträge*
Heidegger does not discuss vision as a power of human being that suggests
distinction from Dasein. The context of Husserl's *Logical Investigations* is what
in Zähringen leads to consideration of vision and consciousness. The 1923
lectures, however, are equally clear on distinguishing the cognitional character
of consciousness and intentionality (presumably as paradigmatically analyzed
by Husserl) from the ontological character of the very procedure of *Auslegung*
that Heidegger is setting out to practice; *Auslegung*, and the understanding that
is achieved in it, are themselves a form of the facticity that is characteristic of
the being of Dasein. Indeed, Heidegger speaks of *Auslegung* as an exceptional
form of this facticity (Heidegger 1989, 15).

interesting and helpful in its contrasts and similarities; but I shall not undertake that here. I shall have to restrict myself only to certain general remarks about it.

In the 1923 lectures the specific means for achieving this "seeing" is "formal indication [*die formale Anzeige*]"; and the paradigm case of "formal indication" is the sentence just quoted: "The anticipatory hold in which Dasein (at every moment one's own Dasein) stands in this investigation, can be expressed in formal indication: *Dasein (factic life) is being in a world*" (Heidegger 1995, 80). Heidegger is explicit about what formal indication is supposed to achieve in this seeing: "[This kind of] delineation is already a first indication that brings out the being-characteristic [of Dasein], or otherwise put a formal indicating for seeing ontologically" (Heidegger 1995, 51).[25] But this seeing is not supposed to be done in any way as a shift out of the "this-way" concreteness level of that which is thus "got" in "view" ontologically. Not long after beginning the lectures Heidegger writes: "Hermeneutics is really supposed to aim not at getting knowledge [*Kenntnisnahme*], but at existential recognizing [*Erkennen*], that is, [it aims at] a *being [ein Sein]*"; it is to be a "way of recognizing that is [itself] a way of being in factic life" (Heidegger 1995, 18).

Now, in *Being and Time*, we saw Heidegger in §7 C speak not of a "seeing," but rather of a "showing" of something that otherwise is concealed, a "showing" that is spoken of as the aim of the investigation in other terms as well, namely, as "making something known"—*kundgeben*. Nevertheless, there are clear parallels to such passages as the above cited from 1923. For example: Under the "interpretive" "laying out" in articulations meant to aim our inquiry into 1) "the proper sense of *Sein*" and 2) "the basic structures of Dasein's own *Sein*," Heidegger adds in the very same sentence in §7 C that this "making known" is to be provided "to the *Sein*-understanding belonging to Dasein itself." In other words, the understanding at work here is precisely the kind of understanding, the *Seinsverständnis*, that is constitutive of Dasein at the level of the existential dynamic that is being *described* in the book.[26] The problem is that I find disingenuous this insistence that the work of the

25 Supplementary phrases are my insertions from the context.

26 Parallel characterizations of it are given, for example, in Chapter 6, Part 1, Division I, especially §39 (especially Heidegger 1963, 181-82; 1996, 169-70), and in Chapter 3, Part 1, Division II, §65 (especially Heidegger 1963, 328; 1996, 301-2). One might add here that the insistence on Heidegger's part

"hermeneutic/interpretive/laying-out" of guidance for the situation of "making known" or "showing" and its corresponding "meeting" or "seeing" is itself without qualification operatively identical in its elements with the existential situation of existential *Seinsverständnis* being analyzed in that work. It is not because I think the structural whole of existential *Seinsverständnis* being analyzed in the analysis cannot be taken as absolutely fundamental to the analyzing task itself; it is rather that, however much the aim is "formal indication" for just this kind of existential "take" in existential understanding, there is an awful lot of consideration of the meaning of formulations going on, along with the right and the wrong of them, especially in regards to Heidegger's predecessors in philosophy, and I do not see sufficient consideration given to how all that conceptualizing itself has its efficacy for the guidance it offers to "formal" indicating—not to mention a role for perceptual orientations "in the clearing," of the sort that Heidegger, as we saw, allows for as the "intentionality" of ordinary modes of "consciousness," such as vision, in the "there" of the opening. Surely there has to be more analysis of how this all works, not as the *terminus ad quem*—a status clearly rejected by Heidegger—but as the register of the "*terminus per quem*" (if I may coin the term), that in terms of which to reach the *terminus ad quem*, factic Dasein, namely, the register of various existentials and of the totality of existential structure.

Actually there are hints of this in *Being and Time*, but I shall not be able to take them up here.[27] Instead, let me become even more summary in what I see to be the problem and its source, and what can be said in addressing it. For one thing, much turns on just how the distinction of human being from Dasein/Da-sein would be made, how the ambiguity

clearly implies that a distinction should be made between the *Verständnis* of *Seinsverständnis* and the *Verstand* of ordinary intellectual operations.

27 Adapting Heidegger 1996, 58 (Heidegger 1963, 62) to this issue, perhaps one could say that the conceptual work serving the formal indicative work of *Being and Time*, as a capacity for thematic, conceptually explicitated "knowing [*Erkennen*]," is "a new stance in being [*Seinsstand*] toward the world already discovered in Dasein." Heidegger seems to mean this new "stance of being" as a legitimating of scientific study, but *mutatis mutandis* there seems no reason why it could not cover also the thematic, conceptuality-governed cognition, as has been implemented in much of traditional philosophic method, including Husserl's, though this itself is not exactly traditional in many ways (as Heidegger himself allows).

of their identity and difference is to be resolved (if it *can* be resolved!) The close identity of the two in Heidegger's work does not seem to allow differentiating an ontological sense of understanding from a legitimate gnoseological sense for understanding.[28] It seems reasonable to think that legitimate operations of "being-conscious"—consciousness—would (as it seems it must) be admissible within the philosophic inquiry into Dasein (and the question of the sense of being) if human being did not so unqualifiedly have the duties of "being the there" in all one's existential performances. Are in fact all one's own efforts at understanding as a working, living philosophic scholar and thinker really and unqualifiedly ipso facto "acts" of Dasein/Da-sein within oneself in the capacity of the functioning projectionist of the "there" and the clearing? Can they not rather be a far more human occupation that, taking place *in* the realm—*in* the "clearing"—that Heidegger suggests is *enabled by* the "power" of Dasein/Da-sein, cannot be thought in terms of *being* that performing, enabling power?

Yet, whether this is the case or not—and in point of fact something like this is what I think in the end one must hold, on both Heideggerian "thinking-of-being" terms and Husserlian "transcendental phenomenological" terms—there is a problem relating directly to this same question that lies in the whole enterprise of Heidegger's project that I now finally want to pose. And I want to do so following upon Heidegger's own clarification that the relation of the realm of effort on the part of being-conscious to Dasein/Da-sein could not be properly put in terms of the language of "rooting." I shall not claim the credit for the critical point that has to be made here and that amounts to a radicalizing of the qualification Heidegger makes. And it doesn't come from Heidegger.

The critical point comes from someone who knew Heidegger very well, and Husserl equally well, and who to my mind grasped each better than either Heidegger or Husserl was capable of doing in regard to the other. The middle term in this philosophical situation, and history, is Eugen Fink, not so much because of his personal and philosophical involvement with both of them, quite different in each case, but because of the critical stance he was able to take on each, both from the standpoint of each with regard to the other and from a standpoint that developed out

---

28 I avoid saying "cognitional" simply because of Heidegger's near total dismissal of cognition as, in effect, unredeemable from its entrenchment in philosophy of reflection, most notably for him in Husserl, and certainly as having no place in the work of *Being and Time*.

of the inherent capacities of the two philosophical undertakings in their interplay. Already in notes from 1931 or 1932 Fink had observed what he called Heidegger's "luminary theory of subjectivity" in his conception of "transcendence." And the image for it is striking: "Only on the basis of light is there flame and is it seen. The flame becomes visible in its own light" There is a paradox, perhaps even an "internal contradiction," here in Heidegger's ontology that is formulated more technically in another of Fink's notes around 1931, as follows: if "transcendence' is the intrinsic essence of 'Dasein,'" and "transcendence as being-understanding makes possible the being of that-which-is," then, since "a human's relating to oneself as to something-that-is is grounded in transcendence," then "transcendence cannot be [itself] something-that-is." And yet in this ontology transcendence belongs constitutively to human being (Fink n.d., 1: Z-IX 31a, Z-XV 103a-b).[29] In a plainer way of putting it, if Dasein is the power the existential thrust of which sets up and deploys the world as the opening in which not only a being other than Dasein but Dasein itself are each something-that-is (*ein Seiendes*), then Dasein is the origination both of the condition of the clearing for the disclosure (manifestness) of any being as a being, and of the conditioned status in which it stands in its own being as set within that same disclosure clearing which it originates. It is both the ultimate ontological *condition for* being in the clearing of the world, and ipso facto a being *conditioned within* that clearing. Is there not, therefore, something incoherent, or at least methodologically problematic, about the analytic of Dasein that poses it as both a being—*Seiendes*—specifically human being, and the there for the disclosure of every being—of every *Seiendes*, including itself? How is it that the analytic terms for analyzing human being can in principle apply, even as "formal indication" (and not simply as adequate conceptualization), to that which is the *condition for* any such application, viz., for the disclosure of anything as anything? Here is the fundamental reason for rejecting the term "root" as simply inapplicable, but that reason holds as well as for such terms as "foundation," or "ground," used in the Zähringen seminar. These also really apply only to what is *within* the clearing and cannot express either *its* status or role or the factor of its origination.

---

29 Insertion in brackets mine. The folder Z-IX also contains as a point of reference notes on Heidegger's winter semester 1931-32 lectures "Vom Wesen der Wahrheit," (Heidegger 1997).

In point of fact, Fink posed the question analogously with equal trenchancy to Husserl for transcendental phenomenology, the statement of which, and Husserl response to it, is exhibited explicitly in Fink's *Sixth Cartesian Meditation: The Idea of a Transcendental Theory of Method*—with the difference that we know pretty well what Husserl thought about it. He saw the point, and he responded to it by integrating at least some considerations into his own thinking—but that is another story. It is not clear that Heidegger ever heard Fink offer his critique with equal explicitness, though in fact it is in play in the only recorded discussion involving both of them, the seminar in Freiburg from the winter semester of 1966-67 under the title *Heraklit* (Heidegger and Fink, 1970). But that, too, would merit another examination. Right now the point is this: There is serious question whether or not the status of Dasein in *Being and Time*, and beyond, is able to free itself from this difficulty—such as would be the case if there is a way to disclose how the "clearing" takes place other than in terms of an analysis of human experience in the world, precisely in its concrete facticity. Nevertheless, under the supposition that the conditioning-conditioned status of Dasein has central relevance—and I certainly have not given a full rendering of its legitimacy—one consequence is this: While the status and sense of being as such remains still unexamined as *Being and Time* comes to an end, to be taken up with strenuous, if not torturous subtlety and obscurity thereafter in *Beiträge*, Dasein seems to shift in sense only indirectly, by allusion rather than by way of reinvestigative elucidation. Yet on the other hand *Being and Time*, with Dasein in its ambiguous double status, remains a constant point of beginning and anchorage for Heidegger, and even more so for his ardent followers. In actuality I do not think this constancy is unmerited, but I also think the case for its entire legitimacy is yet to be fully made. Unfortunately I shall not be trying to make it today and must leave that for other work under way.[30] For now I want to turn to some final consequences of the validity, again supposed rather than demonstrated, of this last critical point I've been raising.

If this critique holds, then the idea that Dasein precisely as the "there" of the clearing, as the "originative" power (or if one wishes, the "deploying" power) that enables the opening to happen (perhaps conceived as the factor of a) Dasein/Da-sein in b) human being, if a distinction between

---

30 In particular it is part of the corollary considerations in my *Edmund Husserl and Eugen Fink*, especially Chapter 7 (Bruzina 2004).

these two is allowed) is precisely the sort of thing that defies adequate characterization, delineation, conceptualization, and indication; and, if so, it could be in no way analogous to Husserl's "categorial forms" that are givable in intentional, "intuitional" gnoseological grasp, in that all such grasp takes place in principle within the clearing, within the "there," within the horizon of the world. In what way, then, *could* any such thing as the being of Dasein as the being of the "there" come to be given, indicated, or thought of in specific meanings—on the principle that all such operations are intrinsically conditioned within the clearing, the "there," the horizon of the world?[31]

It seems to me that there is one feature of Heidegger's analytic of "formal indication" that, even under the supposition of the legitimacy of the critique I have just sketched out, might still have a role as a possible of addressing this. And it is this: The way *Seinsverständnis* works as an understanding is by a kind of existential operativeness, that is, by way of the movement of the dynamic of existing. It is not an intentional cognition or intentional thought or reflection; it is a thrust of existing that ipso facto makes sense to itself—perhaps in the manner in which Husserl's analysis of temporality shows its retentional-protentional structure as ipso facto a kind of self-awareness, conceivably of a performative-pathic sort. And given the role of temporalization as the very structure of the being of Dasein, it would not be implausible for this to be so for Heidegger, although he has not himself pronounced on it in these terms. But if this is so, then it makes sense for Heidegger to speak of the necessity for Dasein's "meeting" of itself in the philosophic "seeing" guided by the "formal indication" of hermeneutic procedure to remain in the mode of an *experience* of the factic being of Dasein.[32] It would be as if one doesn't "see" the structures that are given formulation to enable

---

31 Here one would have to return to the question whether indeed this is the very reason that Dasein has to be conceived in conditioning-conditioned ambiguity, for which a logic of intelligibility would need to be worked out.

32 This is the character of it in the 1923 lectures: "The how of being opens and delimits the 'there' possible at each moment. Being—transitive: be factic life!" (Heidegger 1995, 7). Or again, as quoted earlier, p. 22: "Hermeneutics is really supposed to aim not at getting knowledge [*Kenntnisnahme*], but at existential recognizing [*Erkennen*], that is, [it aims at] a *being* [*ein Sein*]"; it is to be a "way of recognizing that is a way of being in factic life" (Heidegger 1963, 18). And a bit later, beyond the lines quoted from the same text: "The wakefulness is philosophic, which means: it is living in an original self-interpretation

them to be "made known" to one's philosophic realization, so much as "sense" them, again, in the very operation of being—if one could allow this dangerous word "sense" into the Heideggerian linguistic economy. And yet, despite the standard renderings in English of *Sinn* as "meaning," which neutralize its otherwise constant sensuous connotation, Heidegger's regular use of this word *Sinn* and not *Bedeutung* in regard to what is to be "made known" via hermeneutic "formal indication" maintains a less optic and visual, a less intellectualistic connotation of the word "sense" that is diminished by translating it as "meaning". I do not think this use of *Sinn* is accidental, even if it may be out of familiarity with and sensitivity to language more than from an explicit philosophic conception.

The difficulty with this, however, is that Heidegger means the "experience" here to be *articulative*, that is, to be the grasp of something in the complexity of its structure; that is the whole point of "formal indication." But then here one has to distinguish between grasping the whole *as a whole*, complex as it may be, and grasping as such the *structural complexity* of the whole. This is analogous to the distinction in Husserl between perceiving a categorially structured object and perceiving the *structural categoriality* of the object. It seems to me Heidegger is ambiguous on this matter. It would be one thing for "formal indication" to lead to grasping the complex whole that is Dasein, and another to grasp the *structural complex* of the whole that is Dasein. Which it is that, for example, the *Augenblick*—the moment of (in)sight—in §65 of *Being and Time* is meant to grasp needs to be determined: Is making Dasein "known" *as* the full, temporally structured, complex wholeness of Dasein a matter of making "known" to myself my finite, factic Dasein grasped *globally as a whole*, or is the complex, temporally integrated *existential structure itself* of Dasein that which is to be "made known" as such? In the latter we have a clear analogue to Husserl's "categorial intuition," the point of which is precisely to grasp what Husserl calls a "higher order" of "object." But, again, under either answer, the question that has to be raised remains: how can this kind of "given" be construed as a being the very being of which *is the* "there" in which ultimately it is realized? It has to be either an achievement with a methodological character perhaps able to be made clear (perhaps along some of the lines outlined here),

---

[*Selbstauslegung*] that philosophy has given itself of itself ..." (Heidegger 1963, 18). Cf. also the opening paragraphs of Heidegger 1963, §65.

or it is an exceedingly elusive capability that seems to call for simple acceptance and belief.

As I leave the matter here in this form, what I hope is clear is that the issue that motivated Heidegger's distinctive "hermeneutics," radical as no other hermeneutic program is, remains very much an issue. I hope I have succeeded at least in showing how that issue can become more distinct in its important constitutive elements as we study it both in its development in Heidegger's texts, and in the context of the work of others closely associated with him.

Works cited

Bruzina, Ronald. 2004. *Edmund Husserl and Eugen Fink: Beginnings and Ends in Phenomenology, 1928-38*. New Haven: Yale University Press.

Fink, Eugen n.d. *Die letzte phänomenologische Werkstatt Freiburg: Eugen Finks Mitarbeit bei Edmund Husserl, Manuskripte und Dokumente*, Bd. 1-2, ed. Ronald Bruzina. Freiburg: Alber Verlag (forthcoming).

———. 1995. *Sixth Cartesian Meditation, the Idea of a Transcendental Theory of Method*. Trans. Ronald Bruzina. Bloomington: Indiana University Press.

Heidegger, Martin. 1963, *Sein und Zeit*. Tübingen: Max Niemeyer.

———. 1976. *Questions IV*. Trans. Jean Beaufret, François Fédier, Jean Lauxerois and Claude Roëls. Paris: Gallimard,

———. 1977. *Sein und Zeit*. Gesamtausgabe 2, ed. Friedrich-Wilhelm von Herrmann. Frankfurt: Vittorio Klostermann.

———. 1986. *Seminare*. Gesamtausgabe 15, ed. Curd Ochwadt. Frankfurt: Vittorio Klostermann.

———. 1989. *Beiträge zur Philosophie (Vom Ereignis)*, ed. Friedrich-Wilhelm von Herrmann. Frankfurt: Vittorio Klostermann.

———. 1995. *Ontologie (Hermeneutik der Faktizität*. Gesamtausgabe 63, ed. Käte Bröcker-Oltmanns. Frankfurt: Vittorio Klostermann.

———. 1996. *Being and Time*. Trans. Joan Stambaugh. New York: State University of New York Press.

———. 1997. *Vom Wesen der Wahrheit. Zu Platons Höhlengleichnis und Theätet*. Gesamtausgabe 34, ed. Hermann Mörchen. Frankfurt: Vittorio Klostermann.

Heidegger, Martin, and Eugen Fink. 1970. *Heraklit, Seminar Wintersemester 1966/1967*. Frankfurt: Vittorio Klostermann. Also published in Heidegger 1986, 5-266.

Husserl, Edmund. 1962. *Die Krisis der europäischen Wissenschaften und die transzendentale Phänomenologie; Eine Einleitung in die phänomenologische*

Philosophie. Husserliana 6, ed. by Walter Biemel. The Hague: Martinus Nijhoff.

———. (1970a) *Logical Investigations,* Vol. 1-2. Trans. John Findlay. London: Routledge & Kegan Paul.

———. (1970b) *The Crisis of European Sciences and Transcendental Phenomenology; An Introduction to Phenomenological Philosophy.* Trans. David Carr. Evanston: Northwestern University Press.

———. (1976) *Ideen zu einer reinen Phänomenologie und phänomenologischen Philosophie,* Erstes Buch:*Allgemeine Einfurung in die reine Phänomenologie.* Husserliana 3/1, ed. Karl Schuhmann. The Hague: Martinus Nijhoff.

Taminiaux, Jacques 1977. "Heidegger and Husserl's *Logical Investigations;* In remembrance of Heidegger's last seminar (Zähringen, 1973)." *Research in Phenomenology* 7. 58-83. Also published as "Le regard et l'excédent. Sur Heidegger et les 'Recherches logiques' de Husserl." *Revue philosophique de Louvain* 75 (1977). 74-100.

4

SAMUEL BECKETT: *WAITING FOR GODOT*: A PHENOMENOLOGICAL READING

Hans Rainer Sepp

First act, country road, "A tree. Evening." (6)[1] Estragon sits on the ground to lace his shoes. Vladimir appears. They rejoice seeing each other again. Estragon spent the night in a ditch and was again beaten. Vladimir bumps out his hat. Eventually, Estragon manages to remove his shoes. Vladimir once more wants to tell Estragon the often repeated story of the two butchers around Jesus on the cross. "It'll pass the time." (9) But Estragon constantly interrupts him with questions. They cannot leave this place. So Vladimir says, "We're waiting for Godot." (10) Even Estragon's attempts to tell Vladimir his dreams of anxiety come to naught and his request to Vladimir to tell the story "of the Englishman in a brothel" is not met (11). Eventually even Estragon's question "What about hanging ourselves?" ends up in playful arguments (12). Vladimir believes he heard a scream. Estragon asks him for a carrot, which he would prefer to the turnip. Then a loud scream is heard close by: Pozzo leads Lucky in a leash cracking his whip. Lucky has a rope around the neck and carries a suitcase, a stool, a picnic basket and a coat on his arm. Lucky falls to the ground. Pozzo screams at him and is given the coat, the stool, and the picnic basket. He sits down, eats a chicken leg and drinks wine. Vladimir and Estragon look at Lucky with curiosity, while Estragon contemplates with avidity the chicken bone Pozzo gnawed and threw away. After Lucky, for whom the leftovers were meant, as Pozzo explains, does not accept them, Estragon jumps to the bone. "It's a scandal," Vladimir immediately exclaims pointing to Lucky, "to treat a man ... like that." (18) Pozzo, who fills in his pipe for the second time, remains undisturbed. Vladimir wants to go, but Pozzo reminds him of what will happen with the appointment with Godot.

---

1 Pagination taken from *The Collected Works of Samuel Beckett*, vol. 5, *Waiting for Godot: a tragicomedy in two acts*. Translated from the French by the author. New York: Grove Press. Collected Works 1970, Originally 1954.

Vladimir asks him, "Who told you?" but Pozzo ignores the question.
Estragon asks why Lucky does not put the suitcase down. Stretching, Pozzo answers that Lucky wanted to impress him and he just
wants to wear him out. Pozzo explains that he wants to bring Lucky
to the fair and sell him. Lucky cries, Pozzo extends a hankerchief to
Estragon: "Comfort him, since you pity him." (21) Estragon wants to
wipe away Lucky's tears, but Lucky kicks him in the shins. Estragon's
pain leaves Pozzo undisturbed. Vladimir, turning to Lucky: "It's
abominable! Such a good master! To crucify him like that!" (23)
Pozzo continues, Lucky was nice to him, "and now ... he's killing
me!" (23) Vladimir withdraws and leaves the stage, but comes back
shortly after: "Will night never come? ... Time has stopped." (24)
Estragon examines his shoe, Vladimir his hat. Lucky is half asleep
and his hat falls down. With big gestures Pozzo describes the approach of dusk and the nightfall. When Estragon notes that "in the
meantime, nothing happens," Pozzo asks Lucky for some diversion
(26). "Shall we have him dance, or sing, or recite, or think, or —"
Vladimir wants to see Lucky think, Estragon wants to see him dance
(26). Lucky puts down his suitcase and dances. Pozzo wants to say
something and loses the thread of his thought. Then Vladimir and
Estragon take off their hats and concentrate. To Estragon's question
why Lucky does not put down the suitcase, Vladimir responds that
he has in fact put it down. Pozzo's further attempts to reflect remain
unsuccessful. Vladimir asks him to make Lucky think. After Vladimir puts the hat back on Lucky's head, as Pozzo asked him to do,
Lucky begins an incoherent monotonous talk. The unhappiness of
the audience increases until it finally lashes at Lucky. Vladimir takes
again Lucky's hat and Lucky keeps silent and drops to the ground. On
Pozzo's orders, Estragon and Vladimir help Lucky stand up. Pozzo
gives him the pieces of luggage and leaves the stage, cracking his
whip and driving Lucky by the rope in front of him. Estragon notes
that Pozzo and Lucky have changed each other quite a bit. "Only we
can't." (32) When Estragon wants to turn his attention to his other
painful foot, a boy breaks the news that Mr. Godot will not come
this evening, but certainly tomorrow morning. After the boy leaves,
the night falls quickly and the moon rises. Vladimir says: "At last!"
(34) Estragon has taken off his shoes; he could walk barefoot like
Jesus. Both look at the tree and regret not to have a rope. It would
have been better if each of them had gone his own way, but now it
is no longer worth it to leave each other.

Estragon: Well, shall we go?

Vladimir: Yes, let's go.

They do not move. (35)

Second act. "Next day. Same time. Same place." (36) Estragon's shoes lie on the forestage, Lucky's hat still lies on the ground. Vladimir enters the stage, walks around, looks at the horizon, starts singing, walks around. Estragon comes along barefoot. Vladimir asks Estragon whether someone has beaten him. Estragon responds that Vladimir has let him go. They hug. Estragon: "Another day done with." Vladimir: "Not yet." (38) Vladimir is satisfied today and he, Estragon, should also be satisfied. Vladimir points to the tree, but Estragon does not remember any more that they wanted to hang themselves from this tree the day before. Estragon has vague recollection of Pozzo and Lucky, but cannot remember having encountered them yesterday at the same place. It is not sufficient for dead voices to have lived: "they have to talk about this." (40) In order to think, Vladimir says, confront yourself with corpses, with a charnel-house. Estragon says: "We should turn resolutely towards Nature." (42) Vladimir shows Estragon again the tree which has since yesterday gained its leaves. Estragon denies that they are at the same place. He can only remember the leftovers of the meal and the kick, and the shoes are not his either. Estragon: "What'll we do, What'll we do?" (44) Vladimir gives Estragon a black radish, who besides carrots only like pink radishes. Vladimir helps Estragon to put on his shoes. They sit. Vladimir sings Estragon to sleep and then walks around. Estragon is frightened, both walk around the stage arm in arm. Vladimir sees Lucky's hat, he was thus not mistaken about the place. He takes Lucky's hat and gives his own to Estragon. Several times they exchange hats. Finally, Vladimir puts on Lucky's hat, throws his away and says they could play Pozzo and Lucky. But Estragon, for whom these names evoke nothing, only half plays. Estragon leaves. Vladimir orders himself to dance, sees that Estragon is no longer there and emits a heartrending scream. He runs on the stage, Estragon comes running along. Estragon, who had gone to the edge of the slope, calls that they come. Vladimir: "It's Godot! ... We're saved!" (47) Estragon walks to the other side of the stage, comes back, says that he has gone again to the edge of the slope. Vladimir concludes that they are on a plateau and are now encircled. Estragon walks to the back of the stage and falls against the scenery. Vladimir leads him toward the forestage. But Estragon does not want to flee beyond the forestage. Even the tree does not offer any cover to Estragon. Estragon on the left of the edge of the stage and Vladimir

keep watch. Both become angered, insult each other, and fall back
in each other's arms. Vladimir: "How time flies when one has fun!"
Estragon: "What do we do now?" (49) They make contortions, mark
the "tree." Estragon screams at the top of his voice: "God, have pity
on me!" (49) Pozzo, who has become blind, and Lucky, burdened as
before, appear. The leash is shorter, Lucky wears a new hat. Lucky,
under the stare of Vladimir and Estragon, stays there. Pozzo strikes
at him, both fall. Vladimir: "Now we're sure to see the evening out."
(49) Pozzo calls for help, Vladimir and Estragon debate and argue.
Vladimir wants to help Pozzo, but falls and calls Estragon for help.
Estragon extends his hand, pulls and falls down too: "Sweet Mother
Earth!" (53) Pozzo pleads again for mercy, Vladimir hits him, Pozzo
crawls away and collapses. Vladimir and Estragon call him. Estragon
believes that one should try with another name: "Abel! Abel!" (53)
Pozzo answers. Estragon: "Perhaps the other is called Cain," and calls,
"Cain! Cain!" (53) Pozzo answers again. Estragon: "He's all humanity."
(54) Vladimir and Estragon stand up altogether and help Pozzo, who
again calls for help, to stand up; but left alone, he falls again to the
ground. They make him stand up again and support him. Pozzo asks
where his slave is. Estragon kicks Lucky and hurts himself, Lucky
comes to consciousness, Estragon crouches down. Lucky stands up,
takes up his suitcase, gives Pozzo the whip and the ropes. He sets
out, Pozzo behind him. Still, as Pozzo comes to a halt and the rope is
stretched, Lucky falls to the ground; Vladimir hits Pozzo und kicks
Lucky. Lucky stands up, puts the rope back in Pozzo's Hand and
puts on the suitcase. Before Pozzo and Lucky leave, Vladimir wishes
that Lucky sings, thinks or recites. Pozzo answers that he is dumb.
Pozzo and Lucky leave the stage. Vladimir wakes up Estragon, who
had fallen asleep. "I was dreaming I was happy." (57) Estragon, busy
with his shoes and painful feet, falls again asleep. Vladimir ponders
what he will say tomorrow of this day. Estragon will know nothing.
But even himself, Vladimir, is looked at by another who tells himself:
"He is sleeping, he knows nothing, let him sleep on." (58) Vladimir
walks around excitedly and looks afar. The boy from yesterday appears.
He says that he does not recognize Vladimir. Mr. Godot will come
tomorrow. The boy runs away, the sun goes down, the moon rises.
Estragon wakes up, takes off his shoes. Vladimir: "Everything's dead
but the tree." (59) Estragon, later: "Why don't we hang ourselves?" (60)
They have no rope. Estragon's cord, which holds his pants, breaks up
as the two of them pull at it. Vladimir and Estragon fall down. They
want to bring "a good bit of rope" the next day (60). Vladimir: "We'll

hang ourselves tomorrow.... Unless Godot comes." (60) Vladimir takes off Lucky's hat and puts it on again.

Vladimir: Well? Shall we go?

Estragon: Yes, let's go!

They do not move. (60)

T he task I set for myself in what follows is to analyze the *structure* which builds the coordinates of the world, so to speak, presented in *Waiting for Godot*. A phenomenological reading can discover this structure. The result of such an analysis can be beneficial both for literature and philosophy. On the one hand, literary works are elucidated by phenomenological means and, on the other, philosophical experiences deposited in the work can be explicitly treated as philosophical problems. In my phenomenological reading I deal with the structural connections of such experiences.

I. Vertical + horizontal = crosswise

There are few *things* in this drama, but these few form a track to follow. They make apparent the structure in which the characters are involved. Three of these things seem particularly essential: shoes, hats, and the rope by which Lucky is led. "Shoe" and "hat" are among the most often mentioned real present things. Estragon is constantly busy putting on or taking off his shoes, because his feet hurt. Vladimir constantly occupies himself with his hat. The hat is also necessary for Lucky "to think"; Vladimir and Estragon take off their hat in order to concentrate and they exchange them, including Lucky's hat, back and forth. As the hat refers to the head wearing it, the shoes refer to the feet they are on. Head and foot form a polarity for which Vladimir and Estragon, even with their names, are accountable.[2] Their polarity encompasses the extremes that pertain to human existence: the earthly-natural and the spiritual-sacred, earth and heaven, ground and transcendence. Estragon is caught

2 'Vladimir,' the name of the Russian Grand Duke who is considered sacred in Orthodox Christiniaty, refers to the "higher," "heavenly" region of the sacred. "Estragon" refers to the taragon herb orginating from located in south Russia, Latin *Artemisia dracunculus*, and thus to the nether region of the natural.

in the earthly: he sits on the ground, constantly thinks of eating, easily
falls asleep, dreams and forgets. Human beings are natural, not only in
that they have needs, but also to the extent that their historical origin
can never be brought back into a present and thus remains foreclosed.
Vladimir is turned to the horizon. He moves around restless, stares in
the open, unremittingly combs the far away. Also with regard to what
is coming, human beings are not their own masters. Any search ends at
the point where what is alledgedly looked after is in reality something
yet to come. To be caught in the nature-like and natural and moving
forward into what is not yet are polarities in that they include a part
of what is their contrary. It is Vladimir who gives Estragon the paultry
meal, as Estragon from time to time contemplates the sky. The openness,
of itself relative to the ground, only exists for the possibility to set out;
conversely only an entity which can imagine and thus go beyond what
exists can come into relation with what exists. The polarity which is
embodied in Vladimir and Estragon, the polarity between ground and
transcendence, is a *vertical* one.

Pozzo leads Lucky around with a rope. Pozzo is the master and
Lucky the slave. But also for this polarity the following holds: Pozzo is
not simply the master and Lucky the slave. Pozzo as a master depends
on his being bound to his slave, who carries his belongings. Pozzo
has essentially internalized this relation of dependence with obvious
increasing intensity. In the first act the exploiter already appears spiritu-
ally depleted: he feels tricked by his slave. There is no way to find out
whether his feeling is the product of his imagination or is based on facts.
What is clear is that the master has mastery neither over others nor over
himself, over his own feelings. Vladimir's sympathy goes prima facie
only toward Lucky, but afterward also toward Pozzo. In the second act
the oppressor becomes completely oppressed when he becomes blind
and remains completely dependent on his slave. The master now does
not take the lead; the slave does. The master cannot keep up with the
pace and falls to the ground. The relativity of this polarity means that
on earth there are neither masters nor slaves, but everyone is both at
the same time, because nobody is able of himself to be only master or
only slave. The inability to be really a master is grounded in the twofold
uncertainty of not being able to avail oneself of one's own ground or
one's own future.

If the link to the ground and transcendence delineate human existence,
the relative opposition of the oppressor and the oppressed characterizes

the real form of this fundamental structure which appears as real where human beings live factually in the world, i.e., when they exist as social beings. The mode of existence of sociality is praxis. Pozzo manifests himself as a highly practical person. He is a member of society, while Estragon and Vladimir are *outlaws*, who embody the "naked" structure of existence itself and who have, so to speak, inhibited sociality. Even Pozzo has a link to heaven, but a determinate one: for example, he explains dusk. He has the need to eat too, but in the socially cultivated form of a picnic. However, he is interested neither in his shoes or feet as Estragon, nor only in his hat or the breadth of the sky as Vladimir. He is a practical person, because he is concerned with this or that. He has no time (and still he has), because he does not experience time, but counts it.[3] His existence is unstable like all praxis: Praxis has sometimes these interests and sometimes others. Hence, he forgets what no longer belongs to the direction of present interests. His business with numbers is the helpless attempt to counter what slips away with some stability. The unstable relationship between master and slave is reflected in the instability of the practical access to the world—in the occasional, in the forgetting, in being fixed on this or that and thus in the blindness not only toward everything that does not correspond to the present interest, but also and particularly toward everything else that does not have the structure of this being-fixed. Lucky appears as someone who is dependent. He is led by a leash. At the same time he is isolated, unable to communicate. In an autistic way he recites an incoherent conglomerate of texts. In his isolated dependence on Pozzo he reflects the theoretical position on the world that grows out of praxis: to make oneself independent as "theoretical praxis," and still to remain always dependent on praxis as "theoretical praxis" (Husserl).

If Vladimir and Estragon explore the vertical polarity of a possible human existence, Pozzo and Lucky are already in the horizontal polarity. The rope stretched horizontally binding them in their unstable master-slave relationship is the manner in which vertical possibilities of existence can be realized socially. Vladimir and Estragon, who as outlaws stand outside any real sociality, have only themselves; they are beaten by others or only come in loose contact with others. Obviously they had already met Pozzo and Lucky several times, but even these encounters

---

3 "Six hours"; "that was nearly sixty years ago"; "say ten o'clock in the morning." He also praises his watch: "A genuine half-hunter, gentlemen, with deadbeat escapement!"

build no relationship with one another. Estragon and Vladimir remain separated, lead an existence close to the margin of mere possibilities of existence, without actuality. The leash which horizontally binds Pozzo and Lucky also plays a role for them, but according to them a vertical one: as a rope from which to hang oneself in order to prepare an end to life. To realize existentially the mere possibility of existence Vladimir and Estragon talk about preparing an end to their life, but they do not manage to actually do it. They embody the *possibility* of existence and the structure of possibility cannot be eliminated. Since they *embody* such a possibility, they are by the same token concrete people who could also realize the possibility of dying. But they say: "Tomorrow." The temporal postponement still retains the possibility to end life and the possibility to break up the very possibility to live.

Estragon and Vladimir are thus not only outside the social integration, they also live an existential paradox: they exist and they constantly question the possibility of existence through the manner in which they realize their existence. They always want to "go away," but they cannot manage to do it. They stay in the "there." The fact that they are the "there" which can never be changed, not only represents a constant compared to the fundamental structures of human existence; they exist as the paradox that could cancel the conditions for authentic existence and still at the same time represents these very conditions. This means that they exist only as this paradox and as long as they exist as this paradox. The permanent postponement which maintains the paradox consists in *waiting*.

If the relation to the world is always practical, then master and slave, Pozzo and Lucky are "all humanity" (as Estragon says), since the master alone—as well as the slave—can be Abel and Cain, good and evil. "All mankind is us," claims Vladimir about himself and Estragon, and to be this means, as Vladimir continues, to wait, "waiting for Godot to come." (51) In order to be "humanity" the horizontal link of the practical, of the moral, of good and evil does not suffice. What needs to be added is the "vertical" urge to want the cancellation of one's own possibility of existence from the depth of the link to the earth and still to negate this will by oneself, thus *only* to wait. The "total humanity" as being human is thus this intermingling of praxis and naked link to existence, of the horizontal and the vertical. In Western culture this is expressed through the cross. Vladimir and Estragon twice allude to the carrier of this cross, which also carries its carrier, Jesus. But the cross formed by Pozzo/Lucky and Vladimir/Estragon does not manifest any more the failing of the son of God in the world. It is the cross, inherent in the being-in-the-world, which marks its outline and at the same time its being-surrendered to the world. The vertical polarity, the intermingled opposition of being confined to the ground and far-reaching transcendence, represents the essential structural axis which is inherent in all practical link to the world as a fundamental structure—like the body of Christ forming the vertical on the cross. At the same time the vertical axis only finds its full realization in the horizontal dimension of praxis—like the outstretched arms of the crucified on the cross, with his wide-open hands which are the tool at the beginning of all human praxis.

The "cross" of the being-in-the-world (Vladimir: "To every man his little cross") forms a circle in the dimensions of the temporal and spatial. Vladimir says, "at this place, at this moment of time, all mankind is us." (51) "Humanity" and the structure that constitutes it are not a form in which changing contents are poured. The structure as spatio-temporal only consists in being at each time a new realization. But the structures of time and space are not only always formed anew, they only unfold in a narrow reciprocal relationship. The fact that it is not possible to go away also means that in the world human beings are always assigned to a place ("there"), which at the same time allows for the experience of a temporality ("waiting"). Human beings are assigned to a time ("the same"), which opens a spatiality (transcendence). In the same way that waiting does not only refer to temporality, but also to the spatiality which forms itself in waiting, in the same way moving-beyond does not only refer to the place which is left and to the spatiality which opens up in the difference between the place left and the movement of moving-beyond; moving-beyond also refers to the temporality constituted with this movement. This intermingling of temporality and spatiality functions in every moment. All history is spatializing and all movement is temporalizing.

II. Jagged continuity

1. Spatio-temporal

As the fundamental structure-building axis, the vertical dimension delineates a spatio-temporality which lets its structure gleam through even in concrete forms like Vladimir and Estragon. Its structure is on the one hand the being-founded in a place and on the other its moving beyond which has always already been undertaken (being able to actually leave without doing it). This tension between remaining anchored and moving beyond constitutes the spatio-temporal field of existence. But it is constantly formed anew and in new styles which vary the fundamental schema or are superimposed on it. One of the fundamental styles consists in ending the *goal* of moving-beyond, to live such a moving-beyond as if it led to a goal. The ending can, even more objectively, be an objectification. The goal is tied to an end that is reachable as a goal, for example in a concrete representation of the divine—or in *Godot*. But in all these styles the fundamental schema remains. It shows itself not only in the mode of each style, but only has existence in the stylized concrete forms it takes and nowhere else. In these styles the spatio-temporal structures are concretized in a continuum of space and time. The continuous means a determinate rule-governed order in the interpretation of the spatio-temporal field of existence, an order of space and time which promises a certain permanence. It is what has been called, in a manner that is not satisfactory because linked to the domain of linguistic communication, "language games."

However, the constancy of this continuum is always threatened. The urge to break out causes an uncertainty with regard to the place where one is. Willing to move beyond, which gives existence its original spatio-temporal structure, also makes it the case, as a push into the u-topic, that the concrete forms of this structure always collapse, but can always be rebuilt. Being bound to the ground might well offer anchorage; it also leads to a fragility in time. The ground holds together, does not yield, is always threatening, so as to foreclose again everything that has been liberated in the undifferentiated of the unnameable. In the distanceless of what has been handed over to the ground, time intertwines itself. Human beings forget. The damage of spatial identity is met by action and the creation of a overarching view. The place is paced off. From it the open and the horizon are measured. Precisely in the moment of danger space (as space-time) is plumbed and the world of play is shown to be a "plateau." Even the restitution of time (as space-time) must always be mobilized anew through *counting* and preserving *memory*. To take place by acting and to carry the past through language attempt to stretch anew the tension of the fragile continuum.

2. Living bodily

The intermingling of temporality and spatiality is grounded in the body. The vertical polarity itself is bodily formed from "head to toe." The spatio-temporal stretching of transcendence is constantly a bodily taking of space (and time): the space of play is always paced off so that it can be plumbed. If the appearance of Pozzo and Lucky all too often stays in the mere crossing of the world of play, in a linear way, Vladimir's and Estragon's movements regularly measure them in all directions. Similarly the spatio-temporal breaking up of the ground through reminiscing talks are always bodily to the extent that all language not only presupposes a body endowed with language, but is founded in the body and has as its immediate foundation the "living physical body" (*Leibkörper*, Marc Richir).

If all movements of actions and all speaking are attempts to preserve the threatened existential spatio-temporal continuum against total disintegration, and if these attempts are grounded in the living body, this embodiment is first of all threatened by the possible rupture of the continuum. *Pain* is the great indicator of such an hiatus, always reappearing, in the continuum. Pain occurs at the beginning of all existential spatio-temporal tension at birth and the unfolding of the ground: Estragon's feet constantly hurt. The fact that the push forward in the u-topic establishes continuities, but at the same time causes them to founder, has its basis in the fact that the spatio-temporal stretching of human existence is grounded in the body—being able is freedom in an original sense and conceals in itself the moment of risk, the danger of disintegration. Vladimir shouts: "The air is full of our cries." (58) Transcendence is medium and addressee of a bodily wound. This means that the danger arises out of the same domain for which it is a danger: for what is not fixed, for the fundamental possibility that individual existences can make decisions in this or that way. Scream[4] is the expression of this split which in this way is integrated in a continuity. Scream, like laughter, represents a limit point of linguistic expression (where language itself comes to an end) and refers to the embodi-

---

4   The appearance of Pozzo and Lucky is announced by a twofold scream: as a reaction to Lucky's talk the others burst into shout; in the second act Vladimir screams because he believes that Estragon has tried to abandon him. And Estragon screams from pain because Lucky has kicked him. Pozzo emits screams of pain when Vladimir and Estragon attack him.

ment of language. The result of such ruptures, which establish pain, is separation, isolation, but also violent clash. Vladimir and Estragon measure out their world also through the fact that they (want to) leave each other and reunify again. In the social domain individual separation, individual will, leads to conflict of interests and violence. Where the vertical dimension meets the horizontal dimension, in the middle point of the cross we have a scuffle among all. Paradoxically it is only pain and thus the unceasing rupture of continuity causing it which promises continuity: "The tears of the world are a constant quantity," Pozzo says in the first act. But this continuity only gives parallels and superimpositions of continuities, for "for each one who begins to weep, somewhere else another stops. (22)

3. Transfinite

The threat against continuity, the threatening disintegration of the world is structurally possible from two sides. The violent confrontation gathers a world in which several particular worlds encounter each other. There in the center, at the crosspoint of the violent encounter all spatio-temporality, all freedom as possibility to move and to speak vanishes. Praxis itself is a non-place of the constant reciprocal space- and time-consumption. Hence Pozzo learned to count with time and he has eventually become blind. With his blindness he lost his freedom of movement and his spatio-temporality for action. If entering praxis (and theoretical praxis) has a tendency toward apathy and violence from apathy, the outsider runs the risk of becoming mad: to fall away *from* the world *in* the world. This threatens the fundamental coordinates of a spatio-temporal continuity. Estragon who is the properly uprooted, although not in a fixed way, walks around the stage and hits the absolute limits of his world against the scenery and the light and is almost beyond himself. Violence out of apathy and collapse in madness mark two poles of how the limits of the world of meaning, of the fragile spatio-temporal continuuum, can be touched. Both forms of such a limit experience lie on the withdrawal of meaning. In both cases the screen of meaningful relations or of a complete meaningful world has withdrawn. And it is such a screen that offers possibilities.

There is also an experience of the limits of the relations to the world or of the connection of meaning on the basis of what is opposite: on the basis of meaning. The simplest form to reach the limit of a determinate totality of meaning is reflection. It repeats a connection of meaning on the path of meaning, it reproduces it in the totality of the proper sense of reflection and thus takes the measure of its breadth. Vladimir advises Estragon that they should play with Pozzo and Lucky. In the real encounter with them Vladimir and Estragon are participants until the conflictual confrontation. In the playful repetition of this encounter and in its playful duplicity, the egos of Vladimir and Estragon break down: Vladimir becomes Vladimir/Lucky and Estragon becomes Estragon/Pozzo. Precisely then and only then, when Vladimir and Estragon play the roles of Pozzo and Lucky (and not in the cases in which they encounter each other and are involved in a real situation) can they "look" at each other. This reflective reflecting game is an increase in freedom. Vladimir and Estragon are not only free to be in the game different from what they are, with regard to the practical Pozzo they are already distinguished in that they are free from his involvement in the praxis (and free from the practical taking at one's service in the case of Lucky) and can take the full measure of existence bound to the earth until the experience of the breadth of the heaven. They become free now in that they can even choose to represent bound forms of existence for the duration of a game.

A play can be repeated: "I play that I play that I play..." Just a reflection: "I reflect that I reflect that I reflect, etc." In such a movement there is no end point. As in a whirlpool the meaningful experience of the limits of a connection of meanings is swept away in the meaninglessness of an infinite regress. Vladimir, the transcending, encounters such a meaninglessness as the extreme form of meaning twice: first, in the "transfinite" song, "The dog in the kitchen,"[5] which he recites at the beginning of the second act and, second, when he sees Estragon asleep and notes: "At me too someone is looking, of me too someone is saying. He is sleeping,

---

5   "A dog came in the kitchen
     And stole a crust of bread.
     The cook up with a ladle
     And beat him till he was dead.
     Then all the dogs came running
     And dug the dog a tomb
     And wrote upon the tombstone
     For the eyes of dogs to come:
     A dog came in the kitchen [...]." (37-38)

he knows nothing, let him sleep on."[6] The movement of the transfinite duplicity of meaning conceals in itself a pre-decision: people decide by and large not to tolerate a limit, but to transgress any delimitation with the help of the repeated relationship to meaning. What is not considered is whether this mode of transcendence through meaning with its implicit presupposition does not rather disclose a limit which not only is not transgressed, but does not even become visible. The transfinite relation of such a mode, of the "and so on and so forth," is the expression of *the finitude as termination of one's life.*

4. Finally

The example of "'The dog in the kitchen'" points to the finitude of the link to the transfinite to the extent that the carrier of the transfinite is a tombstone.[7] But this does not only mean that the carrier of the sense "transfiniteness" are human beings and specifically these mortals. Human beings are finite not only because they can imagine the infinite advance forward into the horizon of sense. They are finite precisely with regard to the transfinite, the proper meaning of which does not consist in the fact that situations continuously are left behind and thus provoke an infinite circle of meaning, but rather in the fact that to the contrary only *one* is exceeded: human existence, which limits itself with the apparent absence of all limits in the madness of the continuous. Only with this transfinite can existence grasp itself in its finitude in the fact that a limit is drawn for it and still grasps with and so to speak on the limit of its being-finite what transcdends this limit in its beyond itself. This me-ontic experience of the impression left by the beyond-itself as the not of the there *in the there* is the proper movement of transcendence. The tension that is immanent to such a movement cannot be cancelled at the ontic-existential or at the ontological level. The not of the there is in no way a not yet and no "anticipation" can ever recuperate it.

The unbridgeable chasm between the there and the not-there in the there which holds the transcending in its movement and which thus creates an essential condition for existence is also the moment which

---

6 The other in question here is par excellence the spectator of the play. The spectator of a play imagines that he knows more than the person acting in the play. But he forgets that he is also involved in a more encompassing play.

7 The French original says: "croix [!] en bois blanc".

also represents the first and last addressee for the attempt toward the self-elimination of existence. This chasm is a paradox: one wants to eliminate it but we are bound to it as a necessary condition for all action, even suicide. Apart from the alternative to confirm this chasm either in the dying out of existence or in ignoring it when people save themselves in busying themselves with things, there is only one way left to remain in the chasm in a paradoxical manner. If the permanent postponement in which this paradox is maintained consists in waiting, then the performance of the act of waiting is the only existential form of corresponding to the presence of the transfinite, to endure the chasm of the not-there in the there.

This enduring disrupts life, which in this manner hopes for the redemption of the principle of hope, and this hope can never find fulfilment. In this disruption, a spatio-temporal characteristic is constituted: of presenting the void. Anything particular, this and that, which lies in the practical interest is immersed for the ultimate interest in the chasm of the transfinite. The void is the spatio-temporal realm of a mere waiting which has no chance of redemption in this realm and the spatio-temporal realms associated with it. The void stands "above" this or that which can be hoped for and remains "below" what can never appear for human existence: below the closing of the chasm between what absolutely exceeds the there of existence. This void is felt in boredom which cannot be fought by any activity. Such a void can be fulfilled with this or that without really disappearing.

This void is for Vladimir and Estragon the fundamental mood of their existence. Any fulfilment is occasional and as a now already gone. For Lucky and Pozzo the fundamental mood of being fulfilled dominates. Lucky is in the truest sense filled with the data of his theoretical praxis and Pozzo presents himself as the "owner," manager of the fullness, of things, of numbers. But this fullness opens no spatio-temporal realm for movement and creates no freedom, to the contrary: It causes its owner to tumble, to fall to the ground. The suitcase Lucky carries (and which, as almost everything, belongs to Pozzo) is also filled: with sand. Sand, which is fullness, has no structure; it is thrown in the eyes and blinds; it runs through the fingers as through an hour-glass, which counts time only in the moment, but cannot stop it and eventually disavows any alledged gained true fullness. There is thus only one alternative for human existence: either giving up the attainment of fullness, i.e., the ideal of being-filled as a lasting state of happiness in which the difference between there and not-there is closed, and to transpose oneself in the void, or to immerse oneself in a finite fullness, in a fullness which can only be countability or mere materiality.[8]

However this is not really an alternative. Since both modes of existence would lead life so quickly to its end, there are not always breaking points which would always and again postpone an absolute immersion in the fullness—through the revolution of the master-slave relationship, through situations of conflict with others—as these breaking points prevent an oblivion of oneself in the unarticualted void. What pertains to the latter, the fullness is not only broken up through implanted fullness of time, through "pastime." Waiting also contains happy dreams[9] or even short real moments of content at hand,[10] so much that existence is always motivated toward a waiting. The strongest motivation results from hope that the gap between there and not-there could be closed. This hope is nurtured by a revelation which goes beyond the proper spatio-temporality, the actual relation to the world irrupting in it from the outside. The young man—a Hermes, the messenger of the gods as "sent" by the transfinite—always brings over the news that Mr. Godot will come not today, but tomorrow. This revelation is at each time constraining, since the messenger himself does not stand in any continuity to previous revelations. He himself has no recollection of a previous appearing and thus establishes no connection with his previous epiphanies or with the situation of those to whom the message is brought. For the spatio-temporal continua (already broken up) in which the revelation penetrates on the basis of the absence of connection between the revelation and the continua, revelation becomes the greatest stabilizer of the attitude of the void, of "waiting." For revelation articulates the void, makes in it always breaking moments, limits which motivate the waiting, to the extent that they make waiting realistic. Whereas oblivion within a continuum constantly threatens the continuum and finds in waiting a salvation (Vladimir must always encourage Estragon to wait),

---

8   "True" fullness only owns the un-conscious. Vladimir says: "Everything's dead but the tree." Nature knows, differently from humans with their "dead voices." Nature has no temporal unfolding, no conscious preservation of the past.

9   Estragon: "I was dreaming I was happy."

10 Estragon: "We are happy.... What do we do now, now that we're happy?" Vladimir: "... we were happy ... [...] what do we do now we're happy ... go on ... waiting ..."

the message reappearing as always new reinforces from the outside the power of waiting, which is always threatened from the inside in its establishment of continuity. Revelation and faith in revelation exercise the central function that life does not despair of permanently enduring the difference between there and not-there.

The experience of the limit breaks up the current spatio-temporal order, while also establishing a new order—the night falls quickly, time goes by faster. Waiting receives a new impulse. This impulse always carries something that has come to an end, an image, a concrete goal (and establishes anew a style of waiting): that Godot will certainly come tomorrow, and thus the certainty that life can be fulfilled. If the belief in this image is also the engine for the waiting itself, there is a final irony of existence in that precisely the belief in fulfilment is what guarantees the acceptance that fulfilment is impossible; or that the last confirmation of the finitude of existence produces the belief that the intent to actually lead to a goal (Godot) at the same time manifests and supports the infiniteness of existence (waiting).

The fact that the transfinite does not come to an end in the transfinite circle of situations, but in the belief in its recuperation is not in contradiction with its remaining open. This coming to an end rather maintains open the chasm of the not-there in the there, since this belief remains a belief and can never find fulfilment. Accordingly this "coming to an end" is "providing an end": leading existence back to the limit of its being-finite, as well as trans-finite, in making arrive in a finite way what exceeds the finite. The "figurative sense" of this pure experience of the impossibility of fulfilment on earth is the *eikon* as the image of the absolute remaining transparent and not *eidolon*, which captures the gaze and corresponds to the current coming to an end.[11]

Estragon and Vladimir embody a relation to the world the carriers of which do not fall from the world, but plumb the link of the world to its extreme. Phenomenologically speaking, this extreme includes in itself an *Epoché*, which dispenses not only of the style of being involved in practical and practical-theoretical attitudes, but maintains open the tension to the excess of the transfinite.

Translation edited by Kyle McNeel

---

11 See Jean-Luc Marion, "Fragments sur l'idole et L'icone", in: *Revue de Métaphysique et de Morale* 84, 1979, 433-445.

5

ENGAGING ACROSS TRADITIONS:
ROYCE & GADAMER ON INTERPRETATION

David Vessey

The canons of diverse traditions may share texts, figures, and questions, but that doesn't necessarily make communication across traditions any easier. The figures and texts, while shared, are often not shared in the same way. To know Karl Marx's *Capital* belongs to a thinker's tradition is not yet to know if that thinker is an economist or a social theorist. But to know the thinker works in the tradition of Marx and Theodor Adorno is to know the thinker most likely does not work in the tradition of Marx and Adam Smith, or Marx and Mao Tse-tung, for that matter. The Marx embraced by the economist is often not the same Marx embraced by the social theorist or the political revolutionary—for one the theory of capital is the central guiding principle of Marx's other views, for another it's the historical materialism, and for a third the theory of alienation. In this example, all lay claim to the "real" Marx; as a result the debates between them rarely constitute a genuine engagement but instead devolve into turf battles. Their first priority is claiming the figure or text as their own, not coming together to appreciate the complexity of the figure's views.

In the case of shared questions the situation is not as bad. A tradition's strength and staying power lies in its ability to pose relevant questions, to resolve those questions in compelling ways, and to show why other questions are not worth asking. When traditions intersect on a question the occasion arises for each tradition to take up the task of defending its answer. Engagement across traditions should follow. Of course, it may be that what looks like the same question being asked by two different traditions is actually two separate questions that appear united only when expressed in the most generic terms. Confucius and John Dewey both ask the question, "What is the relation between an individual and society?" but the simplicity of the formulation hides enormous differ-

ences. Also, it is not always clear whether the disagreements belong to
the question or to the answer. When Thomas Hobbes and Immanuel
Kant present divergent answers to the question, "What is one's duty
to the state?" are they asking different questions—they share neither
the same notion of duty nor the same of state—or is it that they are
offering complicated answers to the same question, answers that require
specifying what we mean by "duty" and "state"? To settle such questions
is to settle the debate itself, and that cannot be done without genuine
engagement across traditions.

All this is to point out that engagement across traditions on shared
questions is quite different from engagement across traditions on shared
texts and shared authors. When others disagree with us we need to see
if they are asking the same question, and, if so, why they answer the
question differently than we do. If they are asking a different question,
we need to know how we would answer that question as well as why
that question isn't ours. Hans-Georg Gadamer, the main figure in the
hermeneutic tradition, is right to say that to engage others requires seeing
how they could be right, which is to say that to engage others requires
seeing how they could be providing a plausible answer to a legitimate
question.

In *Truth and Method* and elsewhere Gadamer has articulated the
canonical history, figures, and texts of hermeneutics.[1] Needless to say
American pragmatism is not included in the canonical history, and
appropriately so. However, Josiah Royce—a canonical figure in the
pragmatist tradition—in the second part of his 1913 book *The Problem
of Christianity* takes up in detail the question, "What is interpretation?"
and in doing so crosses paths with one of the central questions in the
hermeneutic tradition. My task here will be to look carefully at how
Royce formulates and answers the question in order to see what hermeneutics can learn from Royce. The hermeneutic tradition as articulated
by Gadamer is my starting point and ending point, so the answer will
not be to abandon hermeneutics for pragmatism, nor will it be that the
answers Royce provides are so embedded in his tradition that engagement is impossible. As hermeneuts, we are committed to the denial of

---

1   His account has been reproduced in a number of histories of hermeneutics:
Palmer 1969, Grondin 1994, and Ferraris 1996 are three key examples.

radical incommensurability and to the hope of a fusion of horizons.[2] We are also committed to revising our views in dialogue with others.

First, a few words as to why Royce takes up the question of the nature of interpretation in such an unusual place as a discussion of the nature of Christianity. Royce lays out what he saw as the three essential features of Christianity—the importance of belonging to a spiritual community, the inescapable moral burden of every individual, and the need for atonement; the question then was how these three features manifested themselves in actual Christian communities and this required reflection on the general organization of communities. Royce concludes that a community gets its identity from the shared interpretations of the members of the community.

> A community as we have seen, depends for its very constitution upon the way each of its members interprets himself and his life. For the rest, nobody's self is either a mere datum or an abstract conception. A self is a life whose unity and connectedness depend upon some sort of interpretation of plans, of memories, of hopes, and of deeds. …Were there, then, no interpretations in the world there would be neither selves nor communities (Royce 1968, 274).

Two things will immediately endear themselves to hermeneutics. First, we interpret things when we need to understand them. All understanding is interpretive. Moreover, in some cases (and I'll leave it open whether this is true in all cases) it's the interpretation that acts to bring about the object of the interpretation. Interpretation doesn't just reveal something already waiting, but constitutes it. In Royce's case, interpretation is the means by which the self is constituted as a unified self. It connects not just to how we understand ourselves, but also to what we are as selves. Second, interpretation has social implications. In the case of the self, the same activity that individuates us socializes us. As we interpret we locate ourselves within various communities of interpreters who share our interpretation. This sociality may not exhaust the social dimensions of interpretation, but it serves our purpose here of highlighting two themes in Royce amenable to hermeneutics. Royce goes on to say

---

2 Properly understood, that is. A fusion of horizons is not the same as agreement, rather it is an increased understanding of the preconceptions that lead one to accept one view over another and an understanding of how those preconceptions need to be revised to integrate together the legitimate insights from both views.

that "to inquire what the process of interpretation is, takes us at once to the very heart of philosophy [and] throws light both on the oldest and latest issues of metaphysical thought" (Royce 1968, 274); this is hermeneutic gospel. So even though he belongs to a different tradition, those of us in hermeneutics can see Royce as "one of us." But perhaps that is because we have yet to look at his views in any depth of detail. It's easy to generate agreement by leaving out the details.

Royce contrasts the process of interpreting with the processes of conceptualizing and perceiving. Generally the latter two are thought to be sufficient for an account for the mental life of a person. We get universals from our conceptions and particulars from our perceptions, and we may even develop sophisticated theories about how they are related through successful action (i.e., that the content of the concept is just that which would appear to perception were the concept given power to guide action). The classic debate of empiricism versus rationalism swings on which of the two ought to be understood as taking precedence in the production of knowledge.

But Royce thinks interpretation constitutes a third, entirely distinct cognitive process best exemplified through our awareness of other minds. We are aware of other minds, but how? It couldn't be that we have a conception of the other mind, for conceptions only provide universals and we are aware of particular other minds. Yet we never have sense perceptions of other minds either. We can speculate about the contents of another's mind, but we lack the perceptions to trigger or confirm our speculations; without the perceptions, the conceptions have no place to lead, no cash value, and must remain empty, speculative, and incapable of generating awareness. There must be another kind of awareness. Royce takes up the metaphor of perceptions being the cash value of conceptions (thought of as credit) and points out that converting currency as we cross a border is always a different kind of transaction than simply providing cash for credit. There is an interpretation—an exchange rate—and actions based on this interpretation. He writes,

> Each of us, in every new effort to communicate with our fellow-men, stands, like the traveler crossing the boundary of a new country, in the presence of a largely strange world of perceptions and conceptions. Our neighbor's perceptions, in their immediate presence, we never quite certainly share. Our neighbors conceptions ... are so largely communicable that they can often be regarded as identical, in certain aspects of their meaning, with our own. But the active syntheses,

the practical processes of seeking and of construction, the volitions, the promises, whereby we pass from our own concepts to our own percepts, are often in a high degree individual.... Therefore, in our efforts to view the world as other men view it, our undertaking is very generally analogous to the traveler's financial transactions when he crosses the boundary. We try to solve the problem of learning how to exchange the values of our own lives into the terms which can hope to pass current in the new or foreign spiritual realms whereto, when we take counsel together, we are constantly attempting to pass (Royce 1968, 283–84).

Perceptions are individual and similar, but not the same due to differences in perspective. Conceptions are universal, and communicable for that reason, but fail to tell us about the other's particularity. The key to differences across traditions (across boundaries) has to do with the different ways that universal conceptions get "cashed out" by particular perceptions. How conceptions are connected to perceptions has to do with the actions and instincts of the individual and these vary from individual to individual (and from tradition to tradition). So when it comes to understanding one another in communication, we are not simply looking for confirming connections between perceptions and concepts. We are looking for new ways of associating concepts and percepts; we are coming to understand differently. This process is the same one that occurs when we try to understand ourselves across periods of time (though in such a case the boundary is not cultural but temporal).[3] Understanding ourselves and others, then, is never simply a matter of conceptions or perceptions alone, rather we need a third distinct cognitive process to explain how this is possible—interpretation.

At this point Royce introduces what might seem like a truism, but it will lead us to see what hermeneutics can learn from Royce. He argues that interpretation always relates three things: the interpreter, what is being interpreted, and that for whom the interpretation is taking place. Interpretations are always by someone of something for someone. For example Royce (by someone) interprets the "problems of Christianity" (of something) for a 1913 philosophical audience (to someone). This threefold structure applies to self-understanding too: we interpret our-

---

3   As in hermeneutics, for Royce self-understanding is not a special kind of understanding but operates in just the same way by which we come to understand others. Royce quotes Charles Sanders Peirce: "there is no royal road to self-knowledge" (Royce 1968, 285).

selves for ourselves; "through the present self the past is so interpreted that its counsel is conveyed to the future self" (Royce 1968, 288). But this is a special case of the more general fact that interpretation always happens with an audience in mind. According to Royce, the person for whom the interpretation exists is traditionally neglected from theories of interpretation.

Royce then connects the triadic structure of interpretation to the argument that interpretation is a unique kind of knowledge, typified by knowledge of other minds.

> Psychologically speaking, the mental process which thus involves three members differs from the perception and the conception in three respects. First, interpretation is a conversation, and not a lonely enterprise. There is someone, in the realm of psychological happen-ings, who addresses someone. The one who addresses interprets some object to the one addressed. In the second place, the interpreted object is itself something which has the nature of a mental expres-sion. Peirce uses the term "sign" to name this mental object which is interpreted. Thirdly, since the interpretation is a mental act, and is an act which is expressed, the interpretation itself is, in its turn, a sign. This new sign calls for further interpretation. For the interpretation is addressed to somebody. And so,—at least in the ideal,—the social process involved is endless (Royce 1968, 289–90).

Interpretation differs from perception and conception in virtue of always invoking an audience for the interpretation. In addition, perception and conception are solely directed at objects—perception at perceptual objects, conception at conceptual objects—and thus have a natural terminus in the object of perception or conception. Interpretation has no such terminus. Neither perception nor conception introduces the cycle of sign relations, as interpretation does. Gadamer too holds that all interpretation is modeled on conversation, and that interpretation can itself become an object of interpretation. He will disagree, how-ever, that everything interpreted "has the nature of mental expression," but it would take us too far afield to compare Royce's idealism with phenomenology's attempt to move beyond the debates between idealists and realists. Gadamer will also disagree, as we will see, with the view that perceptions and conceptions exclude interpretations.

Let's look more closely why Royce thinks interpretation is an infinite process while the other two are finite. Royce points out that when we are interpreting something for someone, in order for that person to understand our interpretation he or she must *also* engage in an interpretation. Since interpretation is the activity of being aware of other minds, a conversation requires interpretations of interpretations. One person authors an interpretation for another, interpreted as the recipient of the interpretation. That recipient interprets the author as the source of an interpretation and then interprets the interpretation presented by the author. It is not just that the conversation is a kind of interpretation, nor is it just that the conversation is an exchange of interpretations. Both of these are true. In addition, however, the conversation is a series of interpretations ending only in parting. In interpreting I interpret for someone, who then interprets my interpretation, again for someone (perhaps me), which then requires another interpretation and so on; "discoveries [of interpretation] are constantly renewed by the inexhaustible resources of our social relations, while its ideals essentially demand, at every point, an infinite series of mutual interpretations in order to express what even the very least conversational effort, the least attempt to find our way in life that we would interpret, involves" (Royce 1968, 290). All interpretations are like the number line: infinitely dense and infinitely extended.[4]

We should put out an example here on Royce's behalf or we may get led along by mathematical metaphors and lose track of what exactly is being argued for. Consider a road sign, such as a sign for deer crossing. The sign itself is a sign, put up by an interpreter who both recognizes the meaning of deer tracks and knows the road sign vocabulary so as to be able to convey that meaning to travelers. The traveler then sees the sign as an interpretation, and interprets the interpretation by grasping the interpreter's interpretation. The traveler understands what the sign-poster had in mind when placing the sign. In analogous fashion, we use language to interpret, creating an interpretation that is then shared with others. Others interpret our interpretation and in doing so grasp, though language, the interpretation we had in mind prior to our presentation in language. This mutual grasping of each other's minds is what Royce has in mind when he distinguishes the object of interpretation from the object of conception and perception. He writes, "metaphysically considered, the world of interpretation is the world in which, if indeed we are able to interpret at all, we learn to acknowledge the being of the inner life of our fellow-man" (Royce 1968, 294). Since interpretation is connected to intersubjective relations, it is always a

4 Here the influence of Peirce on Royce shows itself again.

constituent of community—recall our very first point that Royce sees questions of the nature of interpretation central to understanding the nature of a Christian community.[5]

Although I've made comments along the way about how Royce's views compare with Gadamer's, we need to make a more careful comparison to appreciate how Gadamer's views should be modified in light of Royce's views. Fortunately, our work may already have been done for us. In a recent article Kenneth Stikkers argues that "Royce calls into question at least three central features of Gadamer's hermeneutics" (Stikkers 2001, 16). Stikkers argues that there are severe limitations in Gadamer's account of interpretation and that putting Royce and Gadamer in dialogue brings these limitations to light. Stikkers's central concern is that Gadamer takes too strongly the paradigm of interpreting a text as the model for all interpretation. As a result, Gadamer takes the pre-interpretive unity of the tradition and of the self for granted and misses how interpretation is intersubjectively constitutive of both of these. Gadamer prioritizes reading over community building. Royce, on the contrary, views interpretation as essentially tied to, indeed conceptually subordinate to, community formation. In his summation Stikkers writes,

> I have suggested, first, that traditions and communities are taken for granted by Gadamer, as part of the backdrop, the fore-structure, of interpretive understanding, while for Royce, they are constituted though interpretation. Second, while "self" appears within Gadamer's hermeneutics as already given and present in a more or less unified way, "self," too, in Royce is co-constituted in relationship to texts and a community of others. And third, while texts are central to Gadamerian hermeneutics, they are instrumental and subordinate to the constitution of communities and selves in Royce (Stikkers 2001, 18).

Stikkers gets Gadamer wrong on all counts, but the way he gets him wrong is insightful for what it means to read across traditions and what hermeneutics can learn from Royce.

---

5 Royce also discusses the role of a third in adjudicating interpretations. For reasons of space I have not included that discussion here, but in a longer version I explore how Royce's argument has changed from his early essay "The Possibility of Error" and how Gadamer's account of interpretation needs to be clarified to both appreciate Royce's insight and avoid Royce's absolute idealism.

Stikkers's first objection is that Gadamer takes traditions for granted, while Royce sees them as "constituted through interpretation." What Stikkers means by saying they are taken for granted is that they are taken as given, and indeed this is true, traditions are taken as given by Gadamer. In fact, the case could be made that all Gadamer ever means by tradition are those things that are always taken as given—those implicit and explicit beliefs and practices that provide the background conditions for the intelligibility of a text or an action. We can with fairly loose and broad strokes distinguish traditions by their differences of interpretive priority, but, in fact, Gadamer has nothing to say about the necessary and sufficient conditions for something being a tradition or about the identity conditions of a tradition. It's a placeholder in his theory for those things operating behind the scenes. Royce would not want to deny that there are beliefs and practices operating behind the scenes that make interpretation possible, so the real issue becomes Stikkers's second point: that for Royce a tradition is "constituted through interpretation." The same, however, holds for Gadamer as well. Traditions only exist to the extent they are maintained, and they are only maintained to the extent they remain operative in interpretations. So interpretations are necessary conditions for the existence of traditions, and the way that the interpretations unfold give the explicit character to the tradition. To consciously come to understand a tradition always requires interpreting the way the tradition is active in interpretation and actions. This interpretation itself functions to affect the role of the tradition in the interpretation and, as a result, constitutes the tradition.

Take as an example the intellectual tradition of liberalism. Those operating under the effects of that tradition are likely to respond positively to some texts and negatively to others. For example, they may find John Rawls's political liberalism as a viable suggestion for how one might justly establish the basic political structure of a well-ordered society. They may not agree with it in its entirety, but they recognize it as sharing sympathies and concerns they have as liberals. However, say in the context of the ongoing debate about what constitutes liberalism—about how to understand the tradition of liberalism, its commitments, and its proper trajectory—they come to the conclusion that at the core of liberalism is the acceptance of a conception of the subject as a bearer of universal rights. This is explicitly marginalized in Rawls's account of justice as fairness, so they may come to have new-found suspicions about Rawls and about his position in, much less his contributions to, liberalism. In fact, such a decision about the nature of the tradition of liberalism may provoke a hostile reaction against Rawls as a dangerous pretender to the title of "liberal." We witness this in the strong pragmatist reactions against Richard Rorty out of concern that the tradition is being usurped or corrupted. So the tradition itself exists to the extent it persists in interpretive practice and takes on an explicit character only through interpretation. On this point, contrary to Stikkers's claim, Gadamer and Royce seem to be on par.

We could have come to this conclusion through other means: for Gadamer, the only way anything becomes present to consciousness is as interpreted. This is the shift that occurs from descriptive phenomenology to hermeneutic phenomenology. So to the extent a tradition is thematized, it is thematized through interpretation, though we still need to distinguish the tradition as thematized from the tradition operating to shape our interpretive thematizations, including that one. To the extent a tradition is consciously present, it is interpreted.

Given the general principle of interpretive awareness, we should expect Stikkers is mistaken on his second objection too: that "the 'self' appears within Gadamer's hermeneutics as already given and present in a more or less unified way." It does not take long to find examples where Gadamer says things contrary to Stikkers's interpretation. For example, "the essence of the realization of life is still being at one with another, whether the otherness of things or other people. This is true of seeing and perceiving, thinking and knowing. In this self-realization of life, moreover, one's own self is discerned and felt along with the other thing. ... Via another, a person becomes one with himself" (Gadamer 1999, 138). Gadamer also accepts Hegel's account of the origin of self-consciousness as laid out in the master/slave section of the *Phenomenology of Spirit*: we only become self-conscious through the recognition of another. This should shed new light on the passage in *Truth and Method* on which Stikkers bases his argument: "History does not belong to us; we belong to it. Long before we understand ourselves through a process of self-examination, we understand ourselves in a self-evident way in the family, society, and state in which we live" (Gadamer 1991, 276). Stikkers objects to the self-evidence claim, but that is because he takes this to be equivalent to being consciously self-aware with certainty. In fact, for Gadamer, following Heidegger, understanding as a mode of being is broader than understanding as a conscious state. So the understanding that manifests itself through our relations to our family, society, and state are likely to be understandings embodied in habits and practices. We are first and foremost our habits, so our identity is mediated through our traditions; as our traditions are reflected in our family, society, and state, they are the means by which we come to understand ourselves. The self-evidence of ourselves in our social relations stems not from certainty, but from being constituted by those relations. Stikkers provides Royce's view that the "'self', too, in Royce is co-constituted in relationship to texts and a community of others" as a contrast to Gadamer, but given Gadamer's emphasis on our embeddedness in tradition (a term Stikkers takes to be equivalent to community, but in important ways they are not equivalent), the self is not only co-constituted by its relation to tradition, it is almost *fully* constituted by its relation to tradition. As he says, and as Stikkers repeats, "history does not belong to us; we belong to it."

Stikkers's final argument is that "while texts are central to Gadamerian hermeneutics, they are instrumental and subordinate to the constitution of communities and selves in Royce." It's not entirely clear in what Stikkers means by subordination. His evidence for Royce's view comes from *The Problem of Christianity*—"inquiry concerning the nature and reality of the community is still our leading topic. To this topic, whatever we shall have to say about interpretation is everywhere subordinate" (Stikkers 2001, 16)—though that can't be the only support for his view. The fact that Royce, in a book about community, investigates interpretation as a means to better understand community is not evidence of an overall subordination of interpretation to community. Royce's statement, also quoted by Stikkers, that "were there, then, no interpretations in the world there would be neither selves nor communities" (Royce 1968, 274) seems to suggest an inverse priority, though I think we all expect the proper relation to go both ways: no interpretations without selves and communities; no selves nor communities without interpretations.

Still, we have two different ideas of subordination at work here. In one case we subsume our investigations of interpretation to our investigations of community. The relation is methodological given the goals of the project. In the other case, there is an ontological relation between interpretations and communities (and selves): interpretations depend on communities for their existence. There are other possibilities, all signaled by Stikkers. He says that "for Gadamer interpretation is foremost a matter of getting at, or laying out, the meaning of a text. ... For Royce, by contrast, interpretation is first and foremost the constitution of community, and hence community's traditions, for which texts being interpreted are instrumental" (Stikkers 2001, 16). The question of super and sub-ordination seems to be what is the paradigm instance from which we are going to best understand interpretation. For Gadamer, it's the interpretation of a text; for Royce it's the interpretation of communal signs. If this is the kind of subordination Stikkers is referring to in his objection, I agree with his interpretation of Gadamer, but how it constitutes an object is no longer so clear. At least in *Truth and Method*, Gadamer is concerned with rehabilitating the claim of truth in the humanities, so texts, and artworks, are the natural objects of inquiry since they are the focus of the humanities. But Gadamer goes on to extend the category of text to anything that can be interpreted, so it includes signs and actions, for example. It's not clear that there is a significant difference here.

Stikkers also writes, "for Royce, what one desires from interpretation is not to be alone, communion with others ... 'Love' is thus the central motive for interpretation in Royce's hermeneutics" (Stikkers 2001, 16). For Gadamer, in contrast, the point of an interpretation is achieving understanding.[6] It's hard to see how this is a criticism of Gadamer as opposed to a concern about Royce's goal of interpretive accuracy. It might be taken as a matter of personality, but perhaps more accurately it should be taken as a matter of their divergent interpretations of human nature. Royce thinks we are by nature seekers of community, and this is a, if not the, fundamental motivating feature of action. Gadamer believes we are interpreting beings—he embraces Aristotle's characterization of humans as *zoon echon logon*, as long as *logos* is interpreted as "linguistically disclosive"—and this is the fundamental motive for action. Stikkers's argument is that it follows from this difference that Royce sees textual interpretation as always being a kind of relation between two people. We interpret texts with others, or by ourselves because of our relations to others, as an explicit expression of that relation. (Recall that the other person for whom the text is interpreted can be future manifestations of our selves). We've seen something like this in Royce's

---

6 Stikkers claims that a discussion of love is "conspicuously absent from Gadamer's [hermeneutics]," but he would be well directed to Gadamer's writings on Plato (from his dissertation, *Das Wesen der Lust nach den Platonischen Dialogen*, to "Amicus Plato Magis Amica Veritas" and "'Logos' and 'Ergon' in Plato's *Lysis*") and his late writings on friendship, such as "Friendship and Solidarity" and "Friendship and Self-Knowledge."

suggestion that interpretation picks out a distinct form of cognition that is always at work in understanding other minds. Stikkers invokes the claim that interpretation always involves a three-fold relation: the interpreter, the interpreted, and that being for whom the interpretation is presented. He claims this is different from Gadamer in that Gadamer focuses primarily on "receptively listening to the 'voice of the other' as manifested in and through the text" (Stikkers 2001, 17). Royce focuses on the recipient of the interpretation.

This difference we will have to explore in detail for it is here that the relationship between Royce's hermeneutics and Gadamer's becomes most nuanced and we have the most to gain from close comparison. Let me first present briefly why Stikkers is mistaken in his Gadamer interpretation here as well. Stikkers misses three crucial features of Gadamer's account of interpretation. First, for Gadamer all interpretations involve three parties: the two interlocutors, and the subject matter of the interpretation. This is not quite the same as Royce's trinity, and I will unpack the differences below, but nonetheless interpretation for Gadamer is never simply a relation between a receptive reader and a text. Second, for Gadamer reading is not a passive activity of receiving the meaning of the text. We understand when we are able to interpret the text, which means to restate the meaning of the text, in effect to translate the text. We learn from being forced to become articulate anew in the presence of the interlocutor, not by simply listening to difference. Gadamer makes this point most clearly in his discussion in *Truth and Method* where he compares the interpretation of a text with the experience of Thou (Gadamer 1991, 358–62). He points out there that we only properly encounter texts when we take seriously what they reveal to us and that requires putting the views expressed there in ways that allow them to engage us. This is not a passive listening, but an often difficult reconstruction. Third, the alterity of the voice of the other is the alterity of the *view* of our interlocutor about the subject matter. Just because it is someone else making a claim doesn't mean the claim embodies some form of alterity. It is the relation to the subject matter that establishes alterity, not the mere presence of another person. So listening to the alterity of the other is, for Gadamer, actively trying to understand what the other person has to teach us about the subject matter, no more and no less. It is a social act seeking to understand a shared meaning.

Like Royce, then, Gadamer sees all interpretation as including three elements, the two interpreters and the object (or subject matter) of the interpretation. A is always engaging B about X. This is why all interpretation, whether of a text of another person's views, is a dialogue. Whether we are reading Ralph Waldo Emerson on how to best live one's life, or talking to a friend about how to best live one's life, in either case there is an exchange of views about a subject matter in such a way that new insights arise. We are guided in our understanding of the other person by our preliminary understanding of the subject matter—the principle of charity requires us to see how the other person is providing an answer to a legitimate question about the subject matter—and we revise our understanding of the subject matter through engaging the other's opinion. How this engagement plays out can vary, but it always includes an attempt on our part to rearticulate our understanding in such a way to take into consideration the concerns, ideas, or questions raised by our interlocutor about the subject matter. For Gadamer, then, it is not that every interpretation is *for* someone, but rather that every interpretation is *with* someone. How does this compare to Royce's trinity?

According to Royce there is the interpreter, the interpreted, and that for whom the interpretation is made. But interpreting for someone and interpreting with someone are very different activities. In the first case the audience is kept in mind, but the interpretive process is a singular activity, not a shared activity. Interpreting with someone, in dialogue with someone, is irreducible to explanation in terms of alternating interpretations for one another and for that reason is a genuinely shared activity. Thus Royce's account of interpretation is less intersubjective than Gadamer's; for Royce, interpretation is not an actual dialogue between two persons, it is an act of one person attempting to establish a relation with another person. Since it is a singular act (for another), we can see how the (absent) other plays such an important role in the motivation of the interpretation. For Gadamer, interpretations aren't for the sake of establishing community, as community is a condition for an interpretation to take place to begin with.

We can understand a little better why Gadamer has to argue that incommensurability is impossible and why he connects interpretation, dialogue, and friendship so closely. If Royce is presenting interpretation as an attempt to regain community it is because he sees interpretation as a distinctive type of intellectual activity that occurs in the wake of crisis. Consider his example of exchanging money. We need to exchange money because we are no longer able to use our currency; the conditions of normal social interaction have broken down and we need to go through the process in order to reestablish them. Royce introduces the "for whom" as part of the interpretive process and he sees interpretation as an attempt to re-establish community because he has a good, pragmatist appreciation for the conditions of interpretation. Throughout most of his career Royce embraced the pragmatist principle that all judgments are constructive responses to a situation.[7] Since interpretation is the key intellectual process whereby we are aware of our minds or other minds, the situation requiring a constructive response is a situation of intersubjective breakdown. We need to interpret because the meanings are unclear. This is not to say we are interpreting as *isolated* individuals; we are always interpreting given our intersubjectively established intellectual resources, our awareness of socially shared signs, and our metaphysically established desire for community.

Understanding Royce's emphases on the breakdown of social conditions that calls for interpretation helps us to see Stikkers's points in a better light. Although Stikkers consistently misinterprets Gadamer, we can appreciate some general concerns grounded in his Roycean spirit. Stikkers emphasizes that Gadamer takes our traditions and our self as if they are firmly in place unconstituted by the interpretations. In fact, Gadamer doesn't see them as unconstituted by our interpretations, but he does see them as in place, certainly in the sense that he doesn't discuss any crises that would lead us to engage in interpretation to begin with. Since interpretations, for Royce, deal with relations to others and self-understanding, the crises would be crises of community or crises of self, and thus the role the interpretation plays in reconstituting community and self is all the more apparent. Gadamer's examples of interpretation in contrast are particularly academic; he is concerned above all with the proper interpretation of the Greeks. We can see how Stikkers would be tempted to argue that, for Gadamer, interpretation is a purely intellectual activity, a relation between reader and text, rather than a communal activity. While Gadamer talks about an interpretation as answering a question, he doesn't consider the activity of interpreting itself as necessarily arising out of a lived dissatisfaction, a question generating crisis.

---

7 He says just this in a 1903 version of his argument for error, "Error and Truth," in Royce 2001.

Is Gadamer so oblivious to the contexts that call for interpretation? Since Gadamer considers all intellectual activity, perception and
conception included, as interpretation, he doesn't focus on the specific
case of social crisis. Since what counts as an interpretation is broader,
the motivation for interpretation must likewise be much broader than
social crisis. Nonetheless, in one sense Gadamer does preserve the
insight that all calls for intentional interpretation arise out of a question (on this point he is sometimes compared to John Dewey). He
argues that all interpretations involve application, which is the same
as saying all interpretations respond to questions in such as way as to
allow us to move forward differently afterward. Application is his term
for the practical consequences of the completion of inquiry. Since all
intellectual activity is interpretation, application is not merely a social
moving forward, a reestablishment of community and self, it includes
all comportment. According to Gadamer the virtue associated with
application is *phronesis*—a moral and intellectual virtue guiding action.
Stikkers's point that "the absence of the other to whom one's interpretation is addressed is especially conspicuous in Gadamer's explication of
interpretation as application" only makes sense in the context of Royce's
restricted understanding of interpretation where interpretation is clearly
distinguished from perception and conception.

So the difference between Royce and Gadamer has become focused
on their disagreement about the scope of interpretation. Royce holds
that interpretation is a special kind of knowledge distinct from perception and conception. Gadamer disagrees with Royce in holding that all
perception and conception are also interpretations; all understanding is
interpretive. Yet, when Gadamer claims interpretation is a dialogue with
someone he is clearly only talking about explicit, intentional interpretations of a subject matter with a text or another person, not perceptions
or conceptions. Royce therefore has a point. Even if we were to grant
that Gadamer is correct in following Martin Heidegger and arguing
that we are fundamentally interpretive beings and that not only all our
intellectual activity, but all our actions, are only properly understood as
interpretations, this should not preclude us from distinguishing those
interpretations that belong to our everyday, unreflective activities from
those that are conscious and explicit. When a person walks into a room
and sits in a chair, that person is expressing an interpretation of his or
her surroundings and his or her place in those surroundings. But that
activity is different from the one that occurs when a person walks into a

foreign space and has to think about where to sit, and both are different from the activity of interpreting a confusing text (or interpreting what someone else means) when the meaning isn't apparent. Interpretation as a conscious, deliberate activity is what occurs when meanings come up short, and these meanings are always social meanings. So explicit, intentional interpretation is a social activity geared toward the rehabilitation of a disrupted sense of community or self. Gadamer should be completely amenable to this differentiation, as it would square with what he has to say about friendship and community. Moreover Gadamer can explain, perhaps better than Royce, how it is that the community is re-established since his account of interpretation is explicitly dialogical. It needs to be pointed out, however, in contrast to Royce, that just because intentional interpretation is irreducibly social that doesn't mean that everyday interpretation is not. Our actions, perceptions, and conceptions are themselves intersubjective in the sense that they are conditioned by and express the traditions out of which we live. In the end, Royce is right to isolate interpretation as a class of intellectual activity with a uniquely social nature; hermeneutics should embrace this distinction and work to show its consequences.

Traditions are always intersubjective. Conflicts between traditions are thus social conflicts; they are the kinds of crises that Royce would put forward as inspiring the need for interpretation. To do that, however, requires careful reading and articulating of both traditions in such a way that they can be seen at some juncture as addressing similar questions. How they answer the questions differently then becomes the key for seeing how their other differences play out and what we have to learn from them.

Works cited

Ferraris, Maurizio. 1996. *History of Hermeneutics*. Atlantic Highlands: Humanities Press.

Gadamer, Hans-Georg. 1991. *Truth and Method*. New York: Continuum.

———. 1999. *Hermeneutics, Religion and Ethics*. New Haven: Yale University Press.

Grondin, Jean. 1994. *Introduction to Philosophical Hermeneutics*. New Haven: Yale University Press.

Palmer, Richard. 1969. *Hermeneutics: Interpretation Theory in Schleiermacher, Dilthey, Heidegger, and Gadamer*. Evanston: Northwestern University Press.

Royce, Josiah. 1968. *The Problem of Christianity*. Chicago: University of Chicago Press.

———. 2001. *Josiah Royce's Late Writings: A Collection of Unpublished and Scattered Works*, vol. 1. Ed. Frank Oppenheim. Bristol, England: Thoemmes Press.

Stikkers, Kenneth. 2001."Royce and Gadamer on Interpretation as the Constitution of Community," *The Journal of Speculative Philosophy* 15 (1): 14-19.

6

RICOEUR'S NARRATIVE HERMENEUTICS IN RELATIONSHIP WITH GADAMER'S PHILOSOPHICAL HERMENEUTICS: CONTINUITY & DISCONTINUITY

KEITH D'SOUZA

In this essay I attempt to show how the 'triple-mimesis' of Ricoeur's *Time and Narrative*[1] may be understood to be a reappropriation as well as a reformulation of allied concepts in Hans-Georg Gadamer's *Truth and Method*. I do not claim that Ricoeur's triple-mimesis is a conscious and systematic development of allied concepts within *Truth and Method*. Instead, I make the weaker claim that each of the elements of the triple-mimesis may be seen to be in continuity with key elements of Gadamer's hermeneutical theory as spelled out in *Truth and Method*, albeit reformulated in the context of narrative hermeneutics.[2] While there are many dimensions of continuity between these related concepts, we shall see that there are also significant strands of discontinuity. This will help to highlight the manner in which Ricoeur advances the project of philosophical hermeneutics in a narrative, methodological, critical and normative direction.

---

1 *Temps et récit* (*Time and Narrative*) is Ricoeur's trilogy on narrative theory. The first volume was published in French in 1983 and translated into English in 1984. The second was published in French in 1984 and translated into English in 1985. The third was published in French in 1985 and translated into English in 1988. Hayden White, himself an expert on literary and historical theory, describes *Time and Narrative* as, "the most important synthesis of literary and historical theory produced in our century" (White 1987, 170).

2 Ricoeur does not explicitly use the expression 'narrative hermeneutics' to refer to his project in *Time and Narrative*. However, he does use the expression 'narrative theory,' on occasion. I will use the term 'narrative hermeneutics' to represent the specifically hermeneutical features of Ricoeur's narrative theory.

I will first point out the significance of the triple-mimesis for narrative hermeneutics, and then indicate why I choose to relate this complex concept within *Time and Narrative* with allied concepts in *Truth and Method*. I will then proceed to an analysis of the nature of the relationship between these respective concepts.

The significance of the triple-mimesis within narrative hermeneutics

Ricoeur adopts Aristotle's treatment of mimesis in the *Poetics* as a starting point for his own narrative analysis. Aristotle uses *mimesis* in connection with the construction of a *muthos* or plot of a narrative (especially a tragic narrative). Ricoeur's narrative hermeneutics originates with a creative synthesis of this Aristotelian understanding of the plot (*muthos*) in the construction of narratives with the Augustinian understanding of the subjective distention of the soul (*distentio animi*) to account for the paradoxes (*aporias*) of temporal understanding. It is this creative synthesis that leads Ricoeur to conclude that,

> Between the activity of narrating a story and the temporal character of human experience there exists a correlation that is not merely accidental but that presents a transcultural form of necessity. To put it another way, *time becomes human to the extent that it is articulated through a narrative mode, and narrative attains its full meaning when it becomes a condition of temporal existence* (Ricoeur 1984, 52, original italics).

In this essay, we will only focus on the *narrative* dimension (and not on the *temporal* dimension) of this equation between time and narrative. Ricoeur highlights three key elements or moments of narrative activity, viz., the triple-mimesis, that have to do with the condition, the act and the consequence of narration, respectively. In doing so, he has provided us with a far more complex understanding of narrative theory than that presented by Aristotle.[3] First of all, what is presupposed in narrative activity (in the reporting, writing, reading, acting, viewing and living of narratives) is a shared understanding of different facets of human action. This is what Ricoeur identifies as the level of the 'prefiguration' of narratives (or mimesis$_1$). Secondly, Ricoeur examines the nature

3 In *Time and Narrative*, Vol.1, Ch.3, Ricoeur provides us with a detailed overview of this notion of the triple-mimesis.

of both historical and fictional narratives, distinguishing between the hermeneutical features of these two modes of narrative discourse. This is the level of the 'configuration' of narratives (or mimesis$_2$). Finally, Ricoeur explores the manner in which narratives can have an impact on human action via the act of 'reading.' This is the level of the 'refiguration' of human action on account of a productive encounter with narratives (or mimesis$_3$). I consider these three concepts to be the formal principles of narrative hermeneutics.

The triple-*mimesis* does not designate three separate *types* of mimeses, but rather three different *moments* of one complex mimetic activity, even though for Ricoeur, "'configuration' constitutes the pivot of this analysis" (Ricoeur 1984, 53). 'Prefiguration' thus constitutes the condition of the possibility of 'configuration,' 'configuration' constitutes the condition of the possibility of 'refiguration,' and 'refiguration' constitutes the condition of the possibility of a new order of 'prefiguration.' This would be the equivalent of the hermeneutical circle or the hermeneutical spiral in Ricoeur's narrative theory. Furthermore, between 'prefiguration' and 'configuration,' and between 'configuration' and 'refiguration,' *imagination* plays a very significant role. This is because the same set of facts or events at the stage of 'prefiguration' could lead to different narrative configurations at the stage of 'configuration,' while any given fictional or historical narrative could lead to quite different types of appropriation and human action at the stage of 'refiguration.'

Why is this notion of the triple-mimesis so fundamental to Ricoeur's narrative theory? First of all, there is a *methodological* value in an examination of the triple-mimesis in terms of the larger thesis of *Time and Narrative*, viz., the resolution of temporal paradoxes at the practical level by narrative. Ricoeur methodologically reduces the larger speculative problem of time-analysis to the more focused and practical analysis of the experience of time at the level of narrative mimesis.[4] Furthermore,

---

4 In *Time and Narrative*, Vol. 3, Ricoeur systematically discusses the contributions of the different philosophical approaches towards time. His main contention is that while each of these approaches has something positive to contribute, it does not by itself resolve all of the paradoxes (*aporia*) connected with time. For example, Aristotle focused on the cosmological understanding of time, while Augustine focused on the subjective or psychological understanding of time. Kant demonstrated the transcendental nature of the possibility of understanding temporal concepts, but not cosmological time itself. Husserl's phenomenological *epoché* does not help explain objective time. Heidegger's

he affirms that, "to resolve the problem of the relation between time and narrative I must establish the mediating role of emplotment between a stage of practical experience that precedes it and a stage that succeeds it" (Ricoeur 1984, 53). Secondly, there is a *phenomenological* value in the triple-mimesis. Like Augustine's *distentio animi* (distention of the mind or soul), Husserl's *intentio animi* (intention of the mind) provides an account of the subjective nature of temporal consciousness. However, unlike Ricoeur, Husserl does not employ Aristotle's notion of the *muthos* (plot) in order to provide a *narrative* foundation for the phenomenological experience of temporal consciousness. By providing this narrative framework, Ricoeur complements and completes the study of temporal consciousness which Husserl inaugurated from a phenomenological perspective. Thirdly, there is a *theoretical* value of the triple-*mimesis* in terms of literary and historical theory. Ricoeur borrows liberally from historical and literary theorists in the development of his narrative theory in *Time and Narrative*. But his detailed analysis of the triple-mimesis from a phenomenological and hermeneutical perspective is a unique and significant contribution to literary theory. Finally, there is a novel *hermeneutical* value of the triple-mimesis. For unlike any other hermeneutical theorist, and unlike any of his own previous reflections over hermeneutics, Ricoeur for the first time provides us with the rudiments of a new type of hermeneutical theory, viz., narrative hermeneutics. Heidegger provided an analysis of *Dasein* which was largely future-oriented, while Gadamer, influenced by Heidegger's ontological hermeneutics, adopted an approach that was fundamentally past or tradition-oriented. Ricoeur synthesizes these approaches within his narrative hermeneutics by working out the categorical framework through which we experience temporal and narrative intentionality, viz., the triple-mimesis. In the presentation and discussion that follows, I will focus mainly on this last *hermeneutical* dimension of the triple-mimesis.

---

analysis of *Dasein*, following Husserl, does not help explain objective time. Neither of these approaches helps to resolve the paradox of time. One of the primary theses of *Time and Narrative* is to propose narrative intentionality as the resolution of the primary paradoxes connected with time, albeit on the *practical* level of human action, and not on a theoretical or discursive level *per se*.

The rationale behind relating the triple-mimesis with *Truth and Method*

The reasons for choosing *Truth and Method* as representative of Gadamer's hermeneutical position with regard to its narrative development in the thought of Ricoeur are manifold. It is true that Gadamer has written much more on hermeneutics since *Truth and Method* was first published. Especially after his debates with Habermas and Apel in the 1960s and 1970s,[5] he has refined some of the themes and epistemological claims in *Truth and Method*, especially stressing the theme of *phronesis* or practical wisdom.[6] However, *Truth and Method* continues to be generally recognized as his *magnum opus* in the field of hermeneutical theory, and to a large extent Gadamer has not substantially distanced himself from its major hermeneutical claims in a systematic manner. Ricoeur himself, in an autobiographical essay which features the many philosophers who have had an influence on him, states quite plainly that "the hermeneutics illustrated and brilliantly renovated by

---

5 For a concise presentation of the development of this debate, see Graeme Nicholson, "Answers to Critical Theory," in Silverman 1991. For a more detailed presentation, see Teigas 1995, and How 1995. Also, for a succinct presentation of the objections raised by Gadamer and Habermas with respect to each other's positions, see Gorner 2000.

6 See the Section entitled 'Truth and Method Reconsidered,' in "Reflections on my Philosophical Journey," for the more important of these intellectual developments since *Truth and Method* was published (Gadamer 1997, 40-57). This essay is the inaugural autobiographical essay in the book devoted to Gadamer in the 'Library of Living Philosophers' Series, edited by Lewis Edwin Hahn. In this essay, Gadamer himself largely focuses on *Truth and Method* as the locus of his hermeneutical thought—most later developments are viewed with reference to this foundational work. Writing thirty-seven years after *Truth and Method* was first published, Gadamer somewhat regrets both his polemical approach against the natural sciences and his lack of appreciation of the achievements of the social sciences in terms of adopting a methodological approach towards the truth. However, he has not attempted to substantially and methodically revise his hermeneutical theory in the light of these advances in the human sciences.

Gadamer, whose great work *Truth and Method* ... became for me a privileged reference" (Ricoeur 1995, 22).[7]

For the purpose of this essay, however, there is no major need to go much beyond *Truth and Method* in order to be able to relate Gadamer's hermeneutics with Ricoeur's narrative theory. For in *Time and Narrative*, Ricoeur explicitly mentions the correspondence between the stage of the 'refiguration' of human action and Gadamer's notion of 'application' (Ricoeur 1984, 70). Gadamer considers the dimension of 'application' to be an intrinsic part of the hermeneutical process, besides the more obvious roles of 'explanation' and 'understanding' in the act of interpretation (Gadamer 1989, 307ff.). 'Application' is the practical consequence of the process of interpretation via a 'fusion of horizons' with the object of interpretation. Both the interpreter and the object of interpretation (a text, a work of art) have their own 'horizons of meaning.' After an encounter, the 'horizon of meaning' of the interpreter is widened. As a result, new possibilities of meaning unfold in terms of the interpreter's own life situation. We shall see how this concept of 'application' is narratively analogous with Ricoeur's notion of 'refiguration.'

Starting with this most obvious correspondence pointed out by Ricoeur himself, I have attempted to identify two other concepts within *Truth and Method* that best correspond to the other stages of the triple-mimesis, viz., 'prefiguration' and 'configuration.' The concept that I best associate with Ricoeur's notion of 'prefiguration' is Gadamer's notion of *Wirkungsgeschichte* or 'effective history.'[8] 'Effective history' is the principle of historical efficacy, and represents the cumulative effect of historical consciousness, i.e., the operative effect which the history of one's tradition has had on one's consciousness. Together, 'effective history' and its resultant 'horizon of meaning' constitute the hermeneutical condition of the possibility of knowledge in the human sciences and the humanities. Finally, the concept that I best associate with 'configuration' is the notion of mimesis as presented in *Truth and Method*. While discussing

---

7   This is from Ricoeur's autobiographical essay in the 'Library of Living Philosophers' Series, edited by Lewis Edwin Hahn, published two years before the one on Gadamer (Ricoeur 1995).

8   Joel Weinsheimer and Donald Marshall, in their translation of *Truth and Method* (Gadamer 1989; which I use throughout this work) use the term "history of effect," as a translation of *Wirkungsgeschichte*. I much prefer "effective history," however, used in the first English translation of *Truth and Method* by Garrett Barden and John Cumming (Gadamer 1975).

the nature of the creation and presentation of a work of art, Gadamer borrows the notion of mimesis from Aristotle's treatment of the subject in the *Poetics*. However, for Gadamer, the phenomenon of creative representation does not just involve the activity of imitating human action, but rather constitutes the activity of grasping the essence (or the truth) of the subject matter being portrayed or enacted. Participation in the process of representation reveals the truth of the subject matter under consideration. The resultant 'understanding' is not objective but participatory in nature.[9] In the following section, I intend to demonstrate that there is continuity between these respective concepts as well as change, within the context of narrative hermeneutics.

Continuity and discontinuity between *Truth and Method* and the triple-mimesis

1. 'Prefiguration' and 'effective history'

Gadamer's notion of effective history' and Ricoeur's notion of prefiguration' (or mimesis$_1$) both have to do with the conditions of the possibility of knowledge—knowledge in the human sciences and humanities, and a more specific knowledge concerning human action, respectively. Accordingly, for Gadamer, 'effective history' constitutes the condition of the possibility of understanding 'being-in-the-world,' while for Ricoeur, 'prefiguration' constitutes the condition of the possibility of understanding 'doing-in-the-world.' The concept of 'effective history' is fundamental to Gadamer's project in *Truth and Method*, for in keeping with the project of Heidegger, he wishes to demonstrate the fact that the process of understanding transcends the traditional epistemological opposition between a knowing subject and a known object. But Gadamer further refines Heidegger's project in terms of traditional and historical parameters. In his Foreword to the Second Edition of *Truth and Method*, Gadamer states,

---

9 See Schweiker 1990, where the author relates the mimetic aspects of the thought of Gadamer, Ricoeur and Kierkegaard. Schweiker argues that Gadamer focuses on 'understanding' as the mimesis of the 'world,' while Ricoeur focuses on 'narrative' as the mimesis of 'time,' and Kierkegaard focuses on the 'self' as mimesis of 'life.'

The purpose of my investigation is not to offer a general theory of interpretation and a differential account of its methods (which Emilio Betti has done so well) but to discover what is common to all modes of understanding and to show that understanding is never a subjective relation to a given 'object' but to the *history of its effect* [*Wirkungsgeschichte*]; in other words, understanding belongs to the being of that which is understood (Gadamer 1989, xxxi, italics mine).

Understanding is thus constituted by an ontological relationship between subject and object which is influenced by historically influenced cultural and linguistic practices.

Similarly, Ricoeur lays down the conditions for the possibility of understanding 'human action' in terms of "a semantics of action," "symbolic mediations of action" and "temporal elements" (Ricoeur 1984, 54). For Ricoeur, the world of temporal objects of investigation (i.e., specific data of historical or fictional human action) can only be understood depending upon these prior conditions of the possibility of temporal understanding: "whatever the innovative force of poetic composition within the field of our temporal existence may be, the composition of the plot is grounded in a pre-understanding of the world of action, its meaningful structures, its symbolic resources, and its temporal character" (Ricoeur 1984, 54). While Ricoeur does not explicitly relate 'effective history' with 'prefiguration,' he seems to affirm this relationship when he states that, "the possibility of historical experience in general resides in our capacity to remain exposed to the effects of history, to borrow Gadamer's category of *Wirkungsgeschichte*" (Ricoeur 1991, 181). From a temporal perspective, human action will necessarily have a narrative structure (i.e., a beginning, a middle and an end), in some cases explicit, in others implicit. Also, actions take place within social contexts and hence assume their meaning from such contexts. For Gadamer, the 'horizon of meaning' that results from the process of 'effective history' constitutes the specific condition of an act of knowledge. Likewise, for Ricoeur, we already live personal and collective narratives (by way of personal and social projects), know what it is to engage with narratives (e.g., historical, legal, fictional, scriptural narratives), and know what factors go to make up a narrative (a beginning, a middle, an end; the development of characters, causal connections between events, subplots, etc.). 'Prefiguration' thus constitutes the matrix of preconditions for narrative understanding in general.

Where both Gadamer and Ricoeur are in agreement is the fact that they conceive 'effective history' and 'prefiguration' as *pre-conscious* conditions of knowledge and consciousness. *Wirkungsgeschichte* ('effective history'), for Gadamer, is different from *wirkungsgeschichtliches Bewußtsein* ('consciousness of effective history'). That is why he prefers *wirkungsgeschichtliches Bewußtsein* to be considered as "more being than consciousness" (Gadamer 1976, 38; 1997, 47).[10] Ricoeur too considers 'prefiguration' to be at a pre-conscious or existential level rather than at more reflective levels of narrative consciousness such as 'configuration' or 'refiguration.' 'Prefiguration' is more of an ontological understanding of temporality, i.e., the manner in which an understanding of 'doing-in-the-world' takes place spontaneously and unconsciously. Ricoeur specifically uses the Heideggerian expression 'being-in-the-world' to refer to 'prefiguration' (Ricoeur 1984, 81).

Furthermore, both Gadamer and Ricoeur presuppose a *common* world of meaning and reference. For Gadamer, consciousness and subjectivity are a function of a shared 'linguisticality' which has its roots in traditional practices. So also, for Ricoeur, we share a common understanding of the semantics of action, of cultural symbols, of temporal terms, and of a general understanding of time itself at the level of *Innerzeitigkeit*. Gadamer's presupposition of a common 'being-in-the-world' is echoed in Ricoeur's presupposition of a common 'doing-in-the-world,' which is the mimetic condition of the possibility of temporal consciousness. The phenomenological analyses of Gadamer and Ricoeur do not begin with individual consciousness in a Cartesian or Husserlian manner, but instead presuppose a Heideggerian 'being-with' another (*Mitsein*).

There are indeed many similarities between 'effective history' and 'prefiguration' in terms of how they function as conditions of the possibility of knowledge and consciousness. However, the primary difference between these two concepts—besides the more obvious difference in emphasis between the realms of 'being' and 'doing'—is that 'effective history' entails the positing of more *material* claims with regard to the conditions of understanding, as compared to 'prefiguration.' The implicit

---

10 In "On the Scope and Function of Hermeneutical Reflection," in *Philosophical Hermeneutics*, while discussing the nature of hermeneutical reflection, Gadamer states, "reflection on a given preunderstanding brings before me something that otherwise happens *behind my back*. Something—but not everything, for what I have called the *wirkungsgeschichtliches Bewußtsein* is inescapably more *being* than consciousness, and being is never fully manifest" (Gadamer 1976, 38).

narrative 'givenness' of consciousness at the *formal* level is the condition through which human beings understand the phenomenon of time at the practical level. 'Prefiguration' serves as a correlate of 'effective history' primarily at the *formal* level of 'understanding,' because it provides a specifically *narrative* dimension of understanding, i.e., a sense of what it means to engage in human action with a complex set of goals, purposes, causal sequences, temporally relevant terminology, etc.

At the *material* level, however, this 'givenness' is the result of specific temporal terms and traditional and cultural practices, as well as the influence that past narratives have on consciousness. Ricoeur explains 'prefiguration' in terms of semantic, symbolic and temporal features which constitute a "storehouse of those expressions that are most appropriate to what is properly human in our experience" (Ricoeur 1984, 62). While 'semantic' and 'temporal' features of 'prefiguration' have to do with the way in which we understand actions temporally, the only element that has material dimensions to it is the area of symbolic patterns of behavior which are culture-dependent, as it constitutes "signs, rules and norms" (Ricoeur 1984, 57). However, unlike Gadamer, who is averse to methodological inquiry and analysis in general (at least in *Truth and Method*), Ricoeur allows for the possibility of a 'hermeneutics of suspicion,' or a moment of reflective and critical *distanciation* from these cultural "signs, rules and norms." The three 'masters of suspicion' whom Ricoeur has in mind are Marx, Nietzsche and Freud, because they attempt a radical questioning of socially constituted prejudices: "the *Genealogy of Morals* in Nietzsche's sense, the theory of ideologies in the Marxist sense, and the theory of ideals and illusions in Freud's sense represent three convergent procedures of demystification" (Ricoeur 1970, 34). In line with this hermeneutics of suspicion, Ricoeur recognizes the validity of the critique of hermeneutical prejudice as expressed by the critical theorists Apel and Habermas. In one of the key articles representing the debate between Gadamer and Habermas, the latter argues that "in grasping the genesis of the tradition from which it proceeds and on which it turns back, reflection shakes the dogmatism of life-practices... A structure of preunderstanding or prejudgment that has been rendered transparent can no longer function as a prejudice" (Habermas 1977, 357-58). By subscribing to the notion of a moment of critical distanciation from texts in general—and by implication, narratives in particular—Ricoeur would be in agreement with Habermas, with regard to this moment of reflective and even methodological analysis. Ricoeur largely adopts a mediatory and dialectical position between Gadamer on the one hand and Apel and Habermas on the other.[11] For Gadamer, 'effective history' is "the history within whose effects we all exist. It is something that we can never completely go beyond" (Gadamer 1997, 47). That is why, for him, "historical consciousness is itself situated in the web of historical effects" (Gadamer 1989, 300), and *"the prejudices of the individual, far more than his judgments, constitute the historical reality of his being"* (Gadamer 1989, 276-77, original italics).[12] Ricoeur's understanding of 'temporality' or 'narrativity' however, does not include an understanding of 'historicality' in this determining manner, because of his willingness to employ *critical* criteria as part of the interpretive process. This is where the notion of 'prefiguration' clearly has far less of a material foundation to it as compared to 'effective history.'

In addition to this critical dimension, Ricoeur also incorporates a distinctly *moral* dimension within hermeneutical theory, whereby 'signs,' 'rules' and 'norms' at the level of 'prefiguration' may be in need of evaluation by using criteria stemming from moral reflection.[13] Follow-

---

11 For Ricoeur's reconciliatory position between hermeneutics and critical theory, see "Ethics and Culture. Habermas and Gadamer in Dialogue" (Ricoeur 1973) and "Hermeneutics and the Critique of Ideology" (Ricoeur 1981).

12 Georgia Warnke points to three important dimensions of Gadamer's rehabilitation of prejudice as a condition of the possibility of knowledge (Warnke 1987, 75-82). First of all, influenced by Husserl, Gadamer stresses the intentionality or anticipatory dimension of consciousness: "'the very perception of objects involves projections of meaning, or interpretations" (Warnke 1987, 76). This entails that "pure seeing and pure hearing are dogmatic abstractions which artificially reduce phenomena. Perception always includes meaning" (Gadamer 1989, 92). This is the phenomenological equivalent of the hermeneutical circle, wherein the part (the abstracted phenomenon) can only be understood in terms of the whole (the background phenomenon), and vice versa. Secondly, influenced by Heidegger, Gadamer claims that interpretation is rooted in the particular situation of the interpreter (and in the fore-structure of understanding): "Even before I begin consciously to interpret a text or grasp the meaning of an object, I have already placed it within a certain context (*Vorhabe*), approached it from a certain perspective (*Vorsicht*), and conceived of it in a certain way (*Vorgriff*)" (Warnke 1987, 77). Finally, though, Gadamer adds something original and quite distinct from the subjective and personal approaches of Husserl and Heidegger, viz., a historical or traditional dimension of understanding.

13 I will follow Ricoeur's general distinction between *ethical* and *moral* dimensions of normativity. 'Ethical' principles represent teleological, culture-specific

ing Aristotle, Gadamer largely conceives of normativity in terms of a
teleological 'ethics' inbuilt into traditional practices, rules and goals.[14]
However, in *From Text to Action* and *Oneself as Another*, Ricoeur recognizes the necessity for a Kantian deontological moment which would
serve to critically evaluate these practices, rules and goals:[15]

---

or contextual rules for human action, whereas 'moral' principles represent universal, reflective principles for human action. Aristotelian teleological principles
would thus constitute an 'ethics,' for Ricoeur, whereas Kantian deontological
principles constitutes a 'morality.'

14 For a short presentation of Gadamer's ethical position—which is largely
influenced by the *Nicomachean Ethics*—see Georgia Warnke, "Hermeneutics,
Ethics and Politics" (2002).

   In the section titled, 'The hermeneutic relevance of Aristotle' in *Truth and
Method*, Gadamer agrees with Aristotle that the teacher of ethics (and indeed
every ethical person), "is always already involved in a moral and political context
and acquires his image of the thing from that standpoint. He does not himself
regard the guiding principles that he describes as knowledge that can be taught.
They are valid only as schemata" (Gadamer 1989, 320). Thus, for Gadamer,
there can be no certainty in *phronesis* as there is in *theoria* and in *techne*: "Even
if we conceive this knowledge in ideal perfection, it is perfect deliberation with
oneself (euboulia) and not knowledge in the manner of a techne ... There can
be no anterior certainty concerning what the good life is directed toward as a
whole" (Gadamer 1989, 321).

   This ambiguity with respect to the moral realm arises because of the nature
of moral law itself, which does not have the certitude that natural law possesses. Instead, the guiding principles of moral law are "not norms to be found
in the stars, nor do they have an unchanging place in a natural moral universe,
so that all that would be necessary would be to perceive them. Nor are they
mere conventions, but really do correspond to the nature of the thing—except
that the latter is always itself determined in each case by the use the moral
consciousness makes of them" (Gadamer 1989, 320). The reference to 'norms
to be found in the stars' is a likely caricature on the part of Gadamer of the
Kantian image of moral law, which, for Kant, was as certain and definite as
that of the stars above.

15 In a rare instance, Gadamer admits of the significance of Kant's deontological approach to practical action, but in order to bolster his own distrust of
enlightenment rationality: "in Kant's *Foundations for a Metaphysics of Morals*
I believed I had found, and I still believe this today, what is, within limits, an
unshakable truth ... It is that the impulses to enlightenment should not lead
to a social utilitarianism" (Gadamer 1997, 56). Georgia Warnke argues that
Gadamer provides a critical form of ethical reflection "in the move he makes

> Kantian morality ... constitutes the moment of interiorization, uni-
> versalization, and formalization with which Kant identified practical
> reason. This moment is necessary, for it alone posits the autonomy of
> a responsible subject, that is to say, a subject who recognizes himself
> capable of doing what at the same time he believes he ought to do
> (Ricoeur 1991, 200).

However, unlike Kant's duty-oriented approach to practical action, Ricoeur takes the comparatively more affective principle of the 'Golden Rule' as his primary deontological principle. The positive (obligatory) formulation of the rule is expressed by Luke as "treat others as you would like them to treat you" (Luke 6:31), while the negative (interdictory) formulation is expressed by "Hillel, the Jewish master of Saint Paul (Babylonian Talmud, *Sabbath*, 31a): 'Do not do unto your neighbor what you would hate him to do to you'" (Ricoeur 1992, 219). By identifying the primary deontological principle as the 'Golden Rule,' Ricoeur retains the formalism and universality of the second of Kant's categorical imperatives (viz., to treat others as ends and never only as means), as well as its affective (or 'inclinational') dimensions. The formal, universal and rational dimension of the principle derives from the conviction that no one would like to have something done to himself or herself that is hateful, and everyone would like something done to himself or herself that is desirable or loving. The inclinational or affective dimension of the principle has to do with the emotions of hate and love, thus enabling a moral system to combine rectitude with an inclination towards what is emotionally attractive and an overcoming of what is emotionally repulsive.[16]

On account of this possibility of a critical and moral distanciation from the effects of the past, Ricoeur does not harbor an attitude of

---

from Aristotle to Kant and to what he calls the moral experience of the 'thou,'" in *Truth and Method*, 358-61 (Warnke 2002, 91). However, unlike Ricoeur, Gadamer does not seem to systematically develop this moment of autonomous moral reflection which would serve to reflectively transcend tradition-based practical action.

16 See "Practical Action" in *From Text to Action* (Ricoeur 1991) and "The Self and the Moral Norm" in *Oneself as Another* (Ricoeur 1992) for Ricoeur's critique of the Kantian deontological position with regard to practical action. See John Wall, William Schweiker, and W. David Hall, eds. *Paul Ricoeur and Contemporary Moral Thought* (2002), for a discussion of different aspects of this specifically moral dimension within Ricoeur's thought.

conservatism with regard to the construction and interpretation of foundational events and texts of the past. While he does speak specifically of a "narrative tradition" that bears the marks not only of a general narrative theory but also of seminal works in particular, e.g., the *Iliad* and *Oedipus Rex*, it is quite clear that he makes room for both a 'sedimentation' and an 'innovation' of this narrative tradition, and by extension, of social values and norms (Ricoeur 1984, 69-70). Gadamer also allows for innovation in understanding, but he would be hesitant in employing a 'hermeneutics of suspicion,' as this entails a methodological process of suspicion and domination of the text rather than a submission to what the text proposes. Ricoeur, however, terms innovation as a "counterpoint to sedimentation" (Ricoeur 1984, 70). By consciously emphasizing the role of 'innovation' in the construction and interpretation of texts and narratives, Ricoeur clearly does not consider 'prefiguration' to be such a limiting and determining condition of the possibility of narrative consciousness. While it may be argued that Gadamer's concept of 'tradition' is not static but instead open to change, it seems to me that Ricoeur provides us with a more dynamic understanding of 'traditionality,' in terms of his proposal of a constant dialectic between the 'sedimentation' and 'innovation' of a narrative tradition. This is because, for Ricoeur, it is the past, present and future that are connected by this semantics of desire—present action is rooted in the past, but must be evaluated in terms of methodological, critical and normative criteria, so that it can bear positive consequences in the future. The future is more important for Ricoeur than for Gadamer, because of the former's emphasis on the conditions and consequences of practical action. Ricoeur's notion of narrative consciousness is thus a fecund combination of Heidegger's focus on the future and Gadamer's focus on the past as the locus of authenticity, based on an Aristotelian notion of the 'plot' in terms of constituting mimetic activity. Heidegger understood 'Care' to function at the most primordial level of temporality, i.e., *Zeitlichkeit*, in terms of a 'being-towards-death.' Gadamer took '*Bildung*' based on a rootedness in tradition to represent authenticity. Thus, for him, the values and desires of the past are given priority over the values and desires of the present or the future. That is why Gadamer criticizes Habermas, because the latter focuses on a future that we do not know (i.e., that which represents a 'utopian' situation) rather than finding worth in a traditional reality with which we are already familiar. For Ricoeur, however, 'Care' is manifested even at the level of

Innerzeitigkeit, the realm of ordinary time, which includes the past, the present and the future (Ricoeur 1984, 60-64).

2. 'Configuration' and the 'mimesis' of *Truth and Method*

'Configuration' (or mimesis₂) has to do with the construction of fictional and historical narratives, and entails numerous constraints that govern the formulation of a meaningful plot (or *muthos*). 'Configuration' imposes consonance (a complete plot) on dissonant components (discrete events). Every fictional and historical work involves the construction of a plot which holds together different characters, causal connections, sub-plots, etc. This is primarily a work of imagination, as one has to construct a meaningful plot from the myriad events that have taken place (in a historical work), or that one imagines to take place (in a fictional work). But 'configuration' also presupposes a shared participation in creative activity, because a work of history or fiction is a public work, i.e., a work that is created to be read, heard, viewed or enacted. This understanding of 'configuration' shares features with Gadamer's understanding of mimesis in *Truth and Method*, as both concepts deal with the activity of the representation or reproduction of human action in a narrative form.[17] Ricoeur would be in agreement with Gadamer when the latter points out that there are limits to creative expression in mimetic activity:

> for the writer, free invention is always only one side of a mediation conditioned by values already given. He does not freely invent his plot, however much he imagines that he does. Rather, even today the mimesis theory still retains something of its old validity. The writer's free invention is the presentation of a common truth that is binding on the writer also ... The player, sculptor, or viewer is never simply swept away into a strange world of magic, of intoxication, of dream; rather, it is always his own world, and he comes to belong to it more fully by recognizing himself more profoundly in it. There remains a continuity of meaning which links the work of art with the existing

---

17 Gadamer discusses the theme of mimesis in *Truth and Method*, Part I, Section II.1.D. This sub-division ('The Example of the Tragic') falls within the larger section on 'play', entitled, 'Play as the Clue to Ontological Explanation.' Gadamer begins the analysis of mimesis with tragic drama, but extends his mimetic theory even to the plastic arts (sculpture and architecture), and to literature in general, for all of these involve some form of participation.

world and from which even the alienated consciousness of a cultured
society never quite detaches itself (Gadamer 1989, 133-34).

The obvious element of continuity between the notion of mimesis
in *Truth and Method* and that of 'configuration' in *Time and Narrative*
stems from the fact that both concepts are derived from Aristotle's
presentation of mimesis in the *Poetics*. Both concepts cover the activity of creative representation in terms of specific 'figurations' of human
action. However, the primary difference between Gadamer's treatment
of mimesis and Ricoeur's treatment of 'configuration' is that the former
is influenced by a Platonic epistemology, while the latter is influenced
by a temporal appropriation of the Aristotelian treatment of dramatic
presentation. Thus, for Gadamer, the construction and presentation
of narratives is intended to communicate a truth whose *essence*, once
appropriated, would lead to a better understanding of 'being-in-the-
world.' For Ricoeur, however, mimetic construction and presentation
is intended to lead to a better temporally related understanding of
'doing-in-the-world.'

In order to present his own understanding of aesthetic truth, Gadamer reinterprets Plato's approach to art in a unique and productive
manner, viz., as an important medium through which truth may be
communicated:

> What we experience in a work of art and what invites our attention
> is how true it is—i.e., to what extent one knows and recognizes
> something and oneself ... In recognition what we know emerges, as if
> illuminated, from all the contingent and variable circumstances that
> condition it; it is grasped in its essence. It is known as something. This
> is the central motif of Platonism (Gadamer 1989, 114-15).

Ricoeur, however, reads Plato in the more conventional fashion as one
who is dismissive of the cognitive and revelatory function of art, and
he accordingly takes objection to this assessment of art:

> Far from producing only weakened images of reality—shadows,
> as in the Platonic treatment of the *eikon* in painting or writing (*Pha-
> edrus* 274e-77e)—literary works depict reality by *augmenting* it with
> meanings that themselves depend upon the virtues of abbreviation,
> saturation, and culmination, so strikingly illustrated by emplotment
> (Ricoeur 1984, 80, original italics).

For this reason, Ricoeur prefers to adopt Aristotle as his mentor, especially in the production of works of dramatic configuration. That is why Aristotelian concepts such as *poiesis, mimesis, phronesis* and *praxis* play a significant role in Ricoeur's narrative theory. For Aristotle, "poetry is something more philosophic and of graver import than history, since its statements are of the nature rather of universals, whereas those of history are singulars" (*Poetics* 1451b5-7). Gadamer tends to apply this Aristotelian estimation of poetic works to art in general, and hence considers all creative activity as mimetic. This is largely because of his adoption of Platonic essentialism in his hermeneutical theory.[18] That is why he uses mimesis in art to arrive at truth. However, he does recognize that mimesis in a strict sense in the form of drama (as depicted in Aristotle's *Poetics*) is the *most* representative of a form of art that leads to truth, because of its participatory nature and the evocation of powerful emotions that lead to a change of 'being' on the part of those who participate in a dramatic presentation. For Ricoeur too, all creative activity (*poiesis*) is mimetic or metaphorical in a loose sense, and he would agree with Gadamer that mimesis leads to a new way of 'seeing-as,' which leads to a new way of 'being-as.' But Ricoeur adopts the more specific sense of mimesis which Aristotle adopts, viz., tragic works that best represent a narrative form, because there is a clear beginning, middle and end. This is because Ricoeur is not as much driven by the *ontological* concerns of Gadamer, as much as he is by *practical* and *temporal* concerns which Gadamer does not seem to take as seriously. However, unlike Aristotle, Ricoeur does not believe that historical works are merely descriptions of *particular* events rather than universally meaningful events. Instead,

---

18 However, Gadamer interprets Plato's metaphysical realism in a non-conventional dialectical fashion: "Plato does not have a doctrine that one can simply learn from him, namely the 'doctrine of ideas.' And if he criticizes this doctrine in his *Parmenides*, this also does not mean that at that time he was beginning to have doubts about it. Rather, it means that the acceptance of the 'ideas' does not designate the acceptance of a doctrine so much as of a line of questioning that the doctrine has the task of developing and discussing. That is the Platonic dialectic … The work that goes on in a Platonic dialogue has its way of expressing this: it points towards the One, towards Being, the 'Good,' which is present in the order of the soul, in the constitution for the city, and in the structure of the world" (Gadamer 1997, 33). Gadamer's interpretation of this dynamic realism of Plato is largely based on the contents of the Seventh Letter, the criticism of the 'doctrine of ideas' by Plato in the *Parmenides*, but most especially by the role and function of Socrates in the Dialogues.

Ricoeur insists that historical works not only serve to describe particular episodes, but in the manner of fictional narratives, serve to inspire people to action, based both on the debt we owe to the past and the desire to construct a new social order on the basis of the positive or negative lessons we may learn from the past.

This difference between the emphasis on *ontological* and *epistemological* concerns between Gadamer and Ricoeur is reflected in the manner in which they appropriate Kantian elements in their respective philosophies. Gadamer takes recourse to Kant's *third* Critique (the 'Critique of Judgment') to justify his account of the truth of a work of art, but Ricoeur takes recourse to Kant's *first* Critique (the 'Critique of Pure Reason'), to illustrate his claim pertaining to the transcendental schematism that lies at the foundation of temporal and narrative consciousness.[19] While in both cases there is a transcendental principle involved, in the case of Gadamer, it is more of a subjective one, because it involves *aesthetic* consciousness, whereas for Ricoeur it is more objective, because it involves the *epistemological* foundation of narrative structure, for the claim that the plot makes is commonly accessible and understandable to all who encounter the narrative. Thus, a judgment regarding the hermeneutical status of the narrative is not just a matter of subjective taste, but rather a process that involves an objective assessment of facts, and how these facts are articulated within a coherent and complete plot. In this regard, Ricoeur makes room for a distinctly *explanatory* moment in the process of interpretation, which Gadamer in general consciously avoids. Consequently, Gadamer's relatively unconstrained notion of 'play' is hermeneutically more liberal as compared to Ricoeur's more

19 Commenting on the nature of 'configuration,' Ricoeur invites us, "not to hesitate in comparing the production of the configurational act to the work of the productive imagination. This latter must be understood not as a psychologizing faculty but as a transcendental one. The productive imagination is not only rule-governed, it constitutes the generative matrix of rules. In Kant's first *Critique*, the categories of the understanding are first schematized by the productive imagination. The schematism has this power because the productive imagination fundamentally has a synthetic function. It connects understanding and intuition by engendering syntheses that are intellectual and intuitive at the same time. Emplotment, too, engenders a mixed intelligibility between what has been called the point, theme, or thought of a story, and the intuitive presentation of circumstances, characters, episodes, and changes of fortune that make up the denouement. In this way, we may speak of a schematism of the narrative function" (Ricoeur 1984, 68).

constrained notion of 'emplotment,' with regard to both historical and fictional narratives. Historians simply cannot 'play' with the truth, but are expected to represent it appropriately in their narrative account, however creatively. Also, the 'play' involved in fictional narratives is similarly constrained by factors such as semantic and temporal coherence, linguistic and symbolic meaningfulness, inner consistency of the depiction of characters and event, and the presence of a coherent and complete plot.[20] In *Interpretation Theory, The Rule of Metaphor, Hermeneutics and the Human Sciences, Time and Narrative* and *Oneself as Another*, Ricoeur advocates the methods of structuralism, and is open to the contributions of the social sciences and historical-critical research in general in order to provide an explanatory account of texts and narratives.[21] That is why, for Ricoeur, a narrative configuration may be the object of structural analysis or any other form of systematic investigation, as part of the moment of 'explanation' of the historical or fictional narrative in question. Gadamer proposes that Aristotelian *phronesis* be used as a model for explanatory procedures in the human sciences and the humanities (i.e., he recommends that *Wahrheit* be appropriated via the method of *phronesis* rather than *theoria*), but Ricoeur uses *phronesis* not at the level of 'explanation' but rather at the level of 'understanding' and 'application,' when it comes to the interpretation of narratives. However, unlike the mainstream structuralist approach to texts, Ricoeur is ultimately interested in how the text relates to, or ties in with trans-textual personal and social reality. In this regard, he

---

20 According to Schweiker, Gadamer's notion of 'play' (*Spiel*) has its roots in festive celebration and traditional religious cultic activity (Schweiker 1990, 45 ff.). While this creative approach towards 'emplotment' may be employed in the composition of fictional narratives, this approach does not manifest the gravity of the process of 'emplotment' Ricoeur seems to demand of historical narratives.

21 A study of the semiotic and semantic structure of the text would include the discipline of structuralism as well as historical-critical methods such as form criticism, rhetorical criticism, redaction (editorial) criticism, canonical criticism, source criticism, narrative criticism, etc.—methods which Ricoeur is open to and employs in his biblical interpretation. A text could also be explained from the point of view of the social sciences such as psychology, sociology, anthropology, archeology, etc. Also, a study of the economic, political, religious, and cultural influences that may have influenced the formulation of the text could also help provide a more comprehensive 'explanation' of the text.

is much closer to Gadamer than to the structuralists, for even though he allows for the role of method in interpretation, his primary dictum is, 'explain more in order to understand better.' The dichotomy of 'truth versus method' is thus a false one for Ricoeur. For in opposition to the structuralists, he would say, 'be more methodical *so that you can be more truthful*,' while in opposition to Gadamer, he would say, 'be more methodical so that you can be *more truthful*.'

When it comes to fictional works, Gadamer is influenced by the ontological stance that Heidegger adopts towards the phenomenon of art. Art (especially poetry) for the later Heidegger is the privileged medium through which truth becomes unconcealed.[22] But this revelation of truth which art brings to consciousness is a participatory revelation. There is no subject-object dichotomy while encountering a work of art. This is because the nature of a work of art is such that it makes sense only when one participates in it (e.g., when one listens to music; when one reads or listens to a story, when one sees a drama being enacted): "'presentation' is the mode of being of the work of art" (Gadamer 1989, 115). Ricoeur, on the other hand, seems to affirm the position of a personal, responsible and subjective creativity on the part of the author of the historical or fictional narrative. While he does insist upon general semantic, symbolic and temporal rules that constrain the construction of the narrative, the origin of the work of art or the narrative 'configuration' for Ricoeur is the artist himself or herself, and not 'art' in the abstract. The individual artist has to assume responsibility for the specific 'configuration' which is created, and not attribute what is produced to an impersonal entity, viz., 'art.'

This matter of assuming moral responsibility for creative production does not seem to be systematically developed by Gadamer, and is in keeping with the reluctance on the part of Heidegger to work out an explicitly moral component within his ontological hermeneutics. Unlike Ricoeur, Gadamer does not consciously adopt any *moral* criteria to determine the course of narrative production or interpretation. As

---

22 In "The Origin of the Work of Art," Heidegger says, "*Beauty is one way in which truth essentially occurs as unconcealedness* ... Art then is the becoming and happening of truth ... All art, as the letting happen of the advent of the truth of beings, is as such, in essence, poetry ... The origin of the work of art ... is art. This is so because art is in its essence an origin: a distinctive way in which truth comes into being, that is, becomes historical" (Heidegger 1977, 178-87, original italics).

pointed out earlier, in *Oneself as Another*, Ricoeur explicitly develops the moral features of creative and interpretive activity within the context of narrative hermeneutics. Ricoeur appeals to an interpretation of the moral universalism found in Kant's *second* Critique (the 'Critique of Practical Reason') as the foundation for the possibility and necessity of employing moral norms in narrative hermeneutics. Accordingly, for Ricoeur, it would be imperative for both fictional and historical narratives to be subject to moral scrutiny, if they are intended for a public audience. Fictional works more obviously aim at changing narrative consciousness, especially at the level of 'refiguration.' Even if a fictional narrative is constructed purely or largely for entertainment, it still needs to meet minimal moral standards before it is published, so that it does not have a morally deleterious effect on the audience. This is usually the social responsibility of the publisher, and in the world of the audiovisual media, the responsibility of an official censor board. However, the authors of narrative texts to begin with need to recognize that they are subject to the critical and moral standards that we have discussed earlier. Even in the construction of historical narratives, the point is not merely to provide an objective account, but to engage in a creative and responsible reconstruction which is meant to communicate a message and bring about a change of perspective. Especially with reference to tragic historical episodes, Ricoeur calls our attention to the fact that, "fiction gives eyes to the horrified narrator. Eyes to see and to weep" (Ricoeur 1988, 188). Ricoeur is especially sensitive to the past and the debt we owe the past. When talking about the transition from inchoate narratives to articulated narratives, he speaks of "the necessity to save the history of the defeated and the lost. The whole history of suffering cries out for vengeance and calls for narrative" (Ricoeur 1984, 75). Thus, the historian needs to make claims that are not only true but also morally responsible, even though these claims will inadvertently be couched in terms borrowed from the field of fictive expression.

Finally, both Gadamer and Ricoeur share in Hegel's dialectical disposition towards the construction of historical narratives, albeit in a phenomenological rather than a systematic or metaphysical manner. This is because both Gadamer and Ricoeur rightly stress hermeneutical *finitude* rather than omniscience in the construction of historical narratives, for it is hermeneutically impossible to entirely overcome one's finitude and to attempt to conceptually grasp the nature of absolute historical development. Commenting on the influence of Hegel on Gadamer,

Domenico Jervolino states, "the appeal to Hegel does not imply a 'return' to Hegel in the sense of a retrieval of his system, but rather, we feel, a reappropriation of the spirit of dialectics beyond any possibility of a system" (Jervolino 1996, 66). While this refusal to adopt Hegel's system (or indeed any system at all) matches Gadamer's suspicion of 'method' at arriving at truth, Ricoeur complements this Hegelian dialectical and historical phenomenology with the epistemological foundation of a Kantian and transcendental understanding of narrative structure. Hence narrative construction is not only dominated by a synthetic 'plot' as the condition of the possibility of narrative rationality (the Kantian element of the narrative construction), but also by an ongoing development of the plot, or a process of 'emplotment' (the Hegelian element). Historical description lends itself to a continual interpretation and reinterpretation of human action. That is why Ricoeur may be considered to be a 'post-Hegelian Kantian.'[23] David Pellauer glosses this expression: "there are structures that organize human experience, but they are to be understood to change over time and hence themselves to be marked by the historicity that characterizes hermeneutic consciousness and self-understanding" (Pellauer 1997, xviii). Thus, like Gadamer, Ricoeur too does not attempt to propose a meta-temporal or a trans-historical account of historical reality, as Hegel attempted to do in his systematic philosophy, by way of positing a historical metanarrative or 'absolute plot.'

3. 'Refiguration' and 'application'

For Gadamer, the moment of 'application' cannot be separated from 'explanation' and 'understanding,' in terms of the whole dynamics of the process of interpretation (Gadamer 1989, 307 ff.). Indeed, for him, the fruit of the interpretive process is the resultant increase in consciousness or being of the interpreter, as a consequence of engaging in dialogue with the text. In the realm of narrative hermeneutics, 'refiguration' (or mimesis3) has to do with the process of prudential deliberation between the imaginative variations that are inspired by a productive encounter with a narrative. Ricoeur clearly states, "this stage corresponds to what H.-G. Gadamer, in his philosophical hermeneutics, calls 'application'" (Ricoeur 1984, 70). Ricoeur also links 'refiguration' with Gadamer's

23 Ricoeur himself uses this term as a self-definition (Ricoeur 1974, 412 ff.). See Pamela Sue Anderson (1993, 21-32) for a fuller explanation of this term.

thesis of the 'fusion of horizons' (Ricoeur 1984, 77). 'Refiguration' takes place via a fusion between the horizon of the 'configured' narrative and the 'prefigured' horizon of the reader, or via a 'fusion of horizons' of one's world of meaning with the world of meaning of a text or a narrative. Consciousness and activity gets 'refigured' or transformed as a result of a productive 'reading' of narratives. This is because a narrative has the power to open up new worlds or new possibilities of meaning and action, and to 'refigure' old worlds of meaning and action. A productive encounter with a narrative is thus an important condition of the possibility of the transformation of narrative consciousness. It is Ricoeur's explicit mention of 'refiguration' as the correlate of 'application' that led me to search for similar concepts in Gadamer's thought which could serve as suitable correlates to 'prefiguration' and 'configuration.'

In contradistinction to Romantic hermeneutics, Gadamer and Ricoeur contend that the act of reading or participation in a creative work is not meant to arrive at the original intention of the author or his or her original affective state of consciousness when the work was composed.[24] Rather, participation is in its own right another act of creation, based on the interrelationship that one has with the work of art itself. For Gadamer, this involves a participatory 'play,'[25] whereas for Ricoeur this involves 'emplotment,' or a temporal refiguring of a course of action. 'Emplotment' is manifested in the construction of narratives, by way of the creation of a synthetic plot that holds together elements that could have been held together by quite different means (at the level of 'configuration'). But for Ricoeur, a 'configuration' also takes place via the act of reading, when the reader attempts to make sense of the plot, char-

---

24 See the section entitled, "The questionableness of romantic hermeneutics …" in *Truth and Method* (pp. 173 ff.) for Gadamer's position with regard to this issue of the significance of arriving at the author's intention in the process of interpretation. For Ricoeur's analysis of this problem, see "What is a Text? Explanation and Understanding" (Ricoeur 1981, 145-164), and "The Model of the Text: Meaningful Action Considered as a Text" (Ricoeur 1981, 197-221). In the second article, Ricoeur not only explains the major features of a text and how it differs from discourse, but even how actions or social phenomena may be considered to be texts.

25 Accordingly, for Gadamer, "Reading with understanding is always a kind of reproduction, performance, and interpretation … Thus the reading of a book would still remain an event in which the content comes to presentation" (Gadamer 1989, 160-61).

acters, theme, etc., being proposed in the narrative. Thus 'emplotment' takes place at different levels: at the level of the creative 'configuration' performed by the author of the historical or fictional narrative; at the level of 'configuration' performed by the reader of the narrative; and at the level of 'refiguration' performed as a result of a productive act of reading of the 'configured' text. Imaginative variations that come into play at the level of 'refiguration' enable one to posit and choose between different alternatives of human action that result from a productive reading of the narrative.[26]

In spite of his insistence on the need for explanatory moments in the process of interpretation, Ricoeur does not abandon the basic *ontological* dimension of 'application,' because a 'refigured' 'seeing-as' leads to a 'refigured' 'being-as,' on "the deepest ontological level" (Ricoeur 1984, xi). However, Ricoeur is not just concerned about the existential enhancement of 'being' brought about by such a 'fusion of horizons,' but with clearly more practical interests, and concomitantly, with clearly more critical and normative dimensions of human action. Gadamer's concern about 'truth and being' or 'tradition and being' is reappropriated and enhanced by Ricoeur in terms of a more practically oriented 'being and acting' or 'being and doing.' Here too, this difference of hermeneutical concern between Gadamer and Ricoeur may be demonstrated in the way they understand 'play' in the process of 'application,' and 'emplotment' in the process of 'refiguration,' respectively. The choice of the term 'emplotment' itself reveals a far more serious concern for social and personal change on the part of Ricoeur than the word 'play,' chosen by Gadamer. That is why, for Ricoeur, the criteria employed in the process of 'understanding' and especially 'application' within narrative hermeneutics would necessarily have *structural, critical* and *morally normative* components.

To begin with, the 'refigured' narrative needs to be subjected to *structural* investigation, before being personally 'appropriated' and applied in terms of the possibilities of human action which the text inspires. Without subjecting the creative work to a minimal moment of objective scrutiny (or 'distanciation'), the chances for mis-interpretation and thus

---

26 Ricoeur deals with the issue of productive reading in the Chapter titled, "The World of the Text and the World of the Reader," in *Time and Narrative*, Vol. 3. His presentation of this encounter between text and reader is influenced by a number of works on the theme of reader-response criticism, including Iser 1978, Ingarden 1973 and 1974.

for mis-figuration or dis-figuration (of human action) are much more possible. While Gadamer is generally reputed to give priority to the claim that the text makes on the interpreter, in this sense (of providing for a necessary explanatory moment), it is Ricoeur who seems to take the text far more seriously. This moment of explanatory 'distanciation' would result in a more careful and studied scrutiny of the text in terms of historical-critical and structural methods of investigation. In terms of the appropriation of a text, Ricoeur's dictum of 'explain more in order to understand better' can equally well be translated into a similar dictum of 'explain and understand more in order to apply better.'

Secondly, for Ricoeur, any reading would need to take into account a *critical* analysis of the text. Gadamer is averse to such analysis. Rather, for him, a participatory reading of texts contributes to a project of a continual *Bildung*, or educational and cultural development. Gadamer advocates an engagement with classical texts, because of the perennial and substantive values such texts represent, thereby deepening the values of culture and tradition. Ricoeur would agree with the basic premise that if one is exposed to comparatively more sublime texts, this increases the likelihood of being well-directed in one's practical life-world. However, unlike Gadamer, Ricoeur would maintain that any narrative should in principle be open to a critical assessment, allowing for a 'hermeneutics of suspicion,' so as to expose possibly unhealthy ideological elements within the text. These elements may be psychological (following the critique of Freud), economic (following the critique of Marx), or political (following the critique of Nietzsche)—the three figures that Ricoeur designates as the 'masters of suspicion' of critical hermeneutics. Gadamer rejects these attempts to explicitly explain texts in terms of critical inquiry, as for him texts may not be treated as objects to be analyzed but rather the repository of wisdom with which to dialogue. Of course, unlike the general trend within the field of critical hermeneutics, Ricoeur shares Gadamer's interest in a 'hermeneutics of retrieval,' or a positive appropriation of the text. For the task of understanding cannot appropriately terminate with merely a hermeneutics of suspicion, which is only a means towards a deeper end of the interpretive process, viz., an appropriation that is at the level of 'belonging' rather than that of critical distanciation.[27]

---

27 There are a number of expressions in the literature which indicate a position contrary to the 'hermeneutics of suspicion,' viz., 'the hermeneutics of disclosure,' 'the hermeneutics of retrieval,' 'the hermeneutics of trust,' 'the hermeneutics

Thirdly, the appropriation of the narrative text needs to be governed by *morally normative* criteria. Following Heidegger, Gadamer does not seem to pay as much attention to—or at least does not systematically develop—distinctly moral dimensions within hermeneutical theory. While Ricoeur does not develop an explicitly moral dimension to narrative theory within *Time and Narrative*, he systematically devotes attention to moral concerns in *Oneself as Another* and *From Text to Action*, complementing teleological (ethical) normative criteria with necessary moments of deontological (moral) reflection that would help to govern interpretation and human action. For Ricoeur, the act of 'refiguration' shifts the locus of attention from the past to the future. This is in keeping with his general interest in the philosophy of the will and of human action, rather than merely a philosophy of the understanding. That is why he is not interested in a mere 'fusion of horizons' leading to a better understanding of a text or narrative, but instead in a '*fission* of narrative figurations'—to coin a new expression—resulting in the momentum to transform the world of human action by following through on one or more of the imagined figurations. A 'fusion of horizons' is more in keeping with Gadamer's strategy to reappropriate the past and its values, while a 'fission of figurations' would be more oriented towards transforming the world of action by introducing refined values into the world, based on morally normative criteria. In this regard, Ricoeur sees the reading of even historical texts as important from the normative and practical point of view, as such texts have a bearing on how we decide to act in the future. Unlike Gadamer who largely restricts himself to works of art as bearers of 'truth,' Ricoeur believes that *poiesis* is "a function of both revelation and transformation ... one may say both that *poiesis* reveals structures which would have remained unrecognized without art, *and* that it transforms life, elevating it to another level" (Ricoeur 1991, 182). Following Heidegger, Gadamer stresses the *revelatory* function of a work of art. What is deficient in such a disposition towards texts is the *transformative* function, and in Habermasian terms, an *emancipatory* function of a work of art. Thus, a 'refiguration' of action would entail not just a 'redescription' of the narrative form of action, but a 'represcription' of *values* that undergird action. This 'refiguration' would take place not

---

of affirmation,' and 'the hermeneutics of reenactment.' According to Richard Kearney, e.g., "the hermeneutics of affirmation emphasizes our *desire to be* open to an irreducible 'surplus of meaning' (*surcroît de sens*)" (Kearney 1998, 449, original italics).

only in the act of understanding, but also, as a consequence, in personal and social action and personal and social narratives as well.

Conclusion

Both Gadamer and Ricoeur view an encounter with narratives as a participatory and not an object-oriented or speculative activity. Whereas Aristotle adopts a largely *psychological* approach to participation in a tragic drama, Gadamer adopts a largely *ontological* approach to it, while Ricoeur adopts a largely *practical* approach not only to drama, but to narrative works in general. Where Ricoeur clearly takes the Gadamerian project to a new hermeneutical level is in working out a comprehensive analysis of mimesis that takes into account not just an existential manner of 'being-in-the-world,' but a dynamic, practical manner of 'acting-in-the-world' or 'doing-in-the-world,' subject to methodological, critical and morally normative considerations.

We have seen that Ricoeur's notion of 'prefiguration' shares a number of features associated with Gadamer's 'effective history,' albeit in a narrative mode, and bereft of the constraints of a commitment to tradition-based prejudice as the condition of the possibility of knowledge. As regards 'configuration,' Ricoeur places far more emphasis than Gadamer on the dimensions of methodological 'explanation,' here applied to historical and fictional narratives. Finally, in the area of 'application,' Ricoeur takes structural, critical and morally normative criteria associated with practical action far more seriously than Gadamer, for the latter is more interested in existential appropriation as the fruit of interpretation.

Ricoeur's hermeneutical theory complements and advances the project of Gadamer's philosophical hermeneutics in significant directions. By proposing that narratives are the framework through which we interpret human action, Ricoeur has taken hermeneutical theory to a new and practically relevant level. Coupled with this narrative dimension to hermeneutics, Ricoeur's sympathetic approach towards methodological, critical and moral criteria serves to provide a nuanced, balanced and comprehensive understanding of contemporary hermeneutical theory.

Note

I wish to thank Pol Vandevelde and Bradford Hinze for their guidance and valuable suggestions connected with an earlier work on narrative hermeneutics from which this essay has been constructed, viz., my doctoral dissertation (Marquette University, 2003).

Works cited

Anderson, Pamela Sue. 1993. *Ricoeur and Kant: Philosophy of the Will*. Atlanta: Scholars' Press.

Apel, Karl-Otto. 1997. "Regulative Ideas or Truth-Happening?: An Attempt to Answer the Question of the Conditions of the Possibility of Valid Understanding." In *The Philosophy of Hans-Georg Gadamer*, ed. Lewis Edwin Hahn. Chicago: Open Court.

Aristotle. 1984. *The Complete Works of Aristotle* (2 Vols), ed. Jonathan Barnes. Princeton: Princeton University Press.

Gadamer, Hans-Georg. 1975. *Truth and Method*, trans.of second ed. (1965) by W. Glen-Doepel, ed. Garrett Barden and John Cumming. New York: Seabury Press.

———. 1976. "On the Scope and Function of Hermeneutical Reflection," trans. G. B. Hess and R. E. Palmer. In *Philosophical Hermeneutics*, trans. and ed. David Linge. Berkeley: University of California Press.

———. 1989. *Truth and Method*. 2nd revised ed., trans. revised by Joel Weinsheimer and Donald G. Marshall. New York: Continuum Publishing Company.

———. 1997. "Reflections on my Philosophical Journey." In *The Philosophy of Hans-Georg Gadamer*, ed. Lewis Edwin Hahn. Chicago: Open Court.

Gorner, Paul. 2000. *Twentieth Century German Philosophy*. Oxford: Oxford University Press.

Habermas, Jürgen. 1977. "A Review of Gadamer's *Truth and Method*." In *Understanding and Social Inquiry*, ed. Fred R. Dallmayr and Thomas A. McCarthy. Notre Dame, IN: University of Notre Dame Press.

Hahn, Lewis E, ed. 1995. *The Philosophy of Paul Ricoeur*. Chicago: Open Court.

———, ed. 1997. *The Philosophy of Hans-Georg Gadamer*. Chicago: Open Court.

Heidegger, Martin. 1977. *Basic Writings*, ed. David Farrell Krell. New York: Harper & Row.

How, Alan. 1995. *The Habermas-Gadamer Debate and the Nature of the Social*. Brookfield: Avebury Press.

Ingarden, Roman. 1973. *Cognition of the Literary Work of Art*, trans. Ruth Ann Crowley and Kenneth Olson. Evanston: Northwestern University Press.

———. 1974. *The Literary Work of Art: An Investigation on the Borderlines of Ontology, Logic, and Theory of Literature*, trans. George Grabowicz. Evanston: Northwestern University Press.

Iser, Wolfgang. 1978. *The Act of Reading: A Theory of Aesthetic Response*. Baltimore: Johns Hopkins University Press.

Jervolino, Domenico. 1996. "Gadamer and Ricoeur on the Hermeneutics of Praxis." In *Paul Ricoeur: The Hermeneutics of Action*, ed. Richard Kearney. London: Sage Publications.

Kearney, Richard, ed. 1996. *Paul Ricoeur: The Hermeneutics of Action*. London: Sage Publications.

———. 1998. "Ricoeur." In *Companion to Continental Philosophy*, ed. Simon Critchley and William R. Schroeder. Malden, MA: Blackwell.

Pellauer, David. 1997. "Foreword: Recounting Narrative." In Morny Joy, *Paul Ricoeur and Narrative: Context and Contestation*. Calgary: University of Calgary Press.

Ricoeur, Paul. 1970. *Freud and Philosophy*, trans. Denis Savage. New Haven, CT: Yale University Press.

———. 1973. "Ethics and Culture. Habermas and Gadamer in Dialogue." *Philosophy Today* 17: 153-65.

———. 1974. *The Conflict of Interpretations: Essays in Hermeneutics*, ed. Don Ihde. Evanston: Northwestern University Press.

———. 1981. *Hermeneutics and the Human Sciences: Essays on Language, Action, and Interpretation*, ed. and trans. John B. Thompson. Cambridge: Cambridge University Press.

———. 1984. *Time and Narrative*. Vol. 1, trans. Kathleen McLaughlin and David Pellauer. Chicago: University of Chicago Press.

———. 1985. *Time and Narrative*. Vol. 2, trans. Kathleen McLaughlin and David Pellauer. Chicago: University of Chicago Press.

———. 1988. *Time and Narrative*. Vol. 3, trans. Kathleen Blamey and David Pellauer. Chicago: University of Chicago Press.

———. 1991. *From Text to Action: Essays in Hermeneutics, II*, trans. Kathleen Blamey and John B. Thompson. Evanston: Northwestern University Press.

———. 1992. *Oneself as Another*, trans. by Kathleen Blamey. Chicago: University of Chicago Press.

———. 1995. "Paul Ricoeur: Intellectual Autobiography." In *The Philosophy of Paul Ricoeur*, ed. Lewis E. Hahn. Chicago: Open Court.

Schweiker, William. 1990. *Mimetic Reflections: A Study in Hermeneutics, Theology and Ethics*. New York: Fordham University Press.

Silverman, Hugh, ed. 1991. *Gadamer and Hermeneutics*. New York: Routledge.

Teigas, Demetrius. 1995. *Knowledge and Hermeneutic Understanding: A Study of the Habermas-Gadamer Debate.* Lewisburg: Bucknell University Press.

Wall, John, William Schweiker, and W. David Hall, eds. 2002. *Paul Ricoeur and Contemporary Moral Thought.* New York: Routledge.

Warnke, Georgia. 1987. *Gadamer: Hermeneutics, Tradition and Reason.* Stanford: Stanford University Press.

———. 2002. "Hermeneutics, Ethics and Politics." In *The Cambridge Companion to Gadamer,* ed. Robert J. Dostal. Cambridge: Cambridge University Press.

White, Hayden. 1987. "The Metaphysics of Narrativity: Time and Symbol in Ricoeur's Philosophy of History," In *The Content of the Form: Narrative Discourse and Historical Representation.* Baltimore: The Johns Hopkins University Press.

7

THE QUESTION OF (IN)TOLERANCE IN HEIDEGGER'S ACCOUNT OF WORLD-DISCLOSURE

PAUL R. GYLLENHAMMER

> And if he were forcibly dragged up
> the steep and rugged ascent of the cave
> and not let go till he had been dragged
> out into the sunlight,
> would he not experience pain,
> and so struggle against this
> (Plato)?[1]

> We experience at the same time
> *how* the liberator liberates.
> He does not liberate by conversing
> with the cave-dwellers in the language,
> and with the aims and intentions,
> of the cave, but by laying hold of them violently
> and dragging them away
> (Heidegger 2002, 62).

The possibility of *liberation* (*Befreiung*) is of paramount concern for Martin Heidegger. In his major work, *Being and Time*,[2] Heidegger attempts to liberate us from the blindness of the Western metaphysical tradition by setting before us a genuine understanding of

---

1   Quotation as it appears in Heidegger's 1931 lecture course on the allegory of the cave from Plato's *Republic* (Heidegger 2002, 30).

2   References to *Being and Time* appear parenthetically as (Heidegger 1962), with the English edition page numbers followed by the German. John Macquarrie and Edward Robinson's translation is used throughout except where

Being. Heidegger refers to this liberating project as *fundamental ontology* the beginning of which is an analysis of the human experience of the *question of being (Seinsfrage)*.

Humans question the meaning of existence because we are temporal and historical beings. As temporal beings, we are not only mortal but aware of our own mortality. Our attunement to death manifests itself in the general *care (Sorge)* we display for leading a meaningful life. As historical beings, we understand the limits which surround the choices we make in the pursuit of a purposeful life.

In spite of historical limits, there is a common goal for all humans. Heidegger identifies this pursuit as the struggle for *authentic resoluteness (eigentliche Entschlossenheit)*. I find a limit, however, in Heidegger's analysis of this notion. Underdeveloped in his account is the role an interaction with a foreign way of life (*Volksfremd*) plays in the possibility of being authentic.[3] I argue that an engagement with foreign ways of existing is a necessary condition for becoming aware of one's own historical limits and, consequently, for being authentic in Heidegger's sense. If this is the case, then tolerance—taken as the means for coping with otherness—can be seen as a fundamental virtue for accurately understanding and responding to the reality of our interpretive or hermeneutic nature.

To uncover the idea of authentic resoluteness, an exploration into Heidegger's account of world-disclosure (*Erschlossenheit von Welt*) is necessary. World-disclosure is closely connected to an awareness of contingency and carries with it the experience of *being unsettled* or *uncanniness (Unheimlichkeit)*.[4] Being-unsettled is a turning point for Heidegger because it prepares the individual for authentic resoluteness:

the reference is Heidegger 1996, which indicates the use of Joan Stambaugh's translation.

3 Wolin appropriates the term *Volksfremd* from an ominous source: Adolf Hitler's *Mein Kampf*. Wolin's point is to show that Heidegger is ultimately hostile toward the "intellectuals" who are alien to the spirit of true German culture (Wolin 1990, 95). I am using this term in a positive manner to show that the *alien other* is necessary for authentic action, which, in turn, requires a tolerance of the other's difference from our world.

4 Heidegger describes the ontological mood of *Anxiety* as the experience of *uncanniness*. I derive the notion of *contingency*—a term cautiously used in *Being and Time* (Heidegger 1962, 183/143)–from this fundamental experience of uncanniness.

the resolve, in the face of contingency, to choose among the possibilities handed down from one's *heritage* (*Erbe*). Again, I argue that the very awareness of the hermeneutic situation is made possible by an interaction with foreign ways of life and, so, requires the virtue of tolerance. Without tolerance, we may never hear the significance of otherness as a mode of disclosure of our own historical limits. Tolerance liberates us to the truth of existence.

The World

Heidegger's central concern, in *Being and Time*, is to account for the meaning of fundamental ontology. A key insight he draws upon is the failure of the Western metaphysical tradition to inquire into the *question of the meaning of Being*. Since humans are the ones who question being, an appropriate methodological starting point for doing ontology is with an analysis of human being. Heidegger enters, then, the *Analytic of Dasein*. Analogous to Immanuel Kant, Heidegger endeavors to uncover the structural conditions which account for the meaning of existence. Unlike Kant, Heidegger does not question into the mind's structure for such an approach presupposes an artificial subject-object duality. Heidegger uncovers a structure which is more primordial than the structure of the mind: *Being-in-the-world* (*In-der-Welt-sein*). Heidegger's structure of being reveals what Kant's does not, namely, why humans care about meaning at all.

As *Being-in* (*In-Sein*), human existence is grounded in the following notions: attunement, understanding, discourse, and falling (*Befindlichkeit, Verstehen, Rede,* and *Verfallen*, respectively). Given the complexity of Heidegger's analysis, each notion will be briefly discussed at an appropriate point below. For my purposes, the issue of the *world* (*Welt*) will take center stage.

Heidegger lays out four possible meanings of the word *world* in section fourteen of *Being and Time*. Each meaning points to the next in terms of a more fundamental ground. "World," in the first sense, "is used as an ontical concept, and signifies the totality of those entities which can be present-at-hand within the world" (Heidegger 1962, 93/64). In Heidegger's terminology, something is *present-at-hand* (*vorhanden*) when it is taken as a discrete entity abstracted from its context of involvement. To say that the world *is* the unity of discrete entities is simply to think of the world as being made up of the actual number of existing things.

The limit to this account is twofold. First, as an abstract way of dealing with things, we bracket the meaningful contexts in which things exist. Second, and following from the first, this account overlooks the *ontological difference* between things and world. Heidegger's philosophy is rooted in this ontological difference.

The world is not the entities themselves but that which *contains* a unity of things. Thus, the second meaning of the term: "'World' functions as an ontological term, and signifies the Being of those entities which we have just mentioned. And indeed 'world' can become a term for any realm which encompasses a multiplicity of entities" (Heidegger 1962, 93/64). The *being* of entities is synonymous with *world* insofar as the world refers to the *regional ontologies* within which entities are gathered, for example, mathematics, physics, anthropology, psychology, etc. At this level, we have a less abstract and more meaningful account of world/being given this level of categorization. Entities have meaning through a context. There is, nevertheless, a shortsightedness to this more appropriate account of world. Heidegger develops a deeper sense of world from out of the ontic-ontological or thing-region distinction.

What is lacking in the prior two notions of world is reference to Dasein (human being). The ontic-ontological distinction remains abstract as long as Dasein is not developed *into* the account. So, in accordance with fundamental ontology, we have to consider a world as that *wherein* Dasein *exists*. In this case, world refers to a *practice* to which and within which individuals belong and live (Dreyfus 1994; Heidegger 1962, 93/65).

A practice is set apart from other practices by a distinct set of concerns and, of course, the things, instruments, and tools used in meeting those concerns. Worlds are *ontic-existentiell* at this practical level because each depicts a real, historically established *totality of equipment* (*Zeugganzes*) which circumscribes and gives coherence to an individual's action. Heidegger describes human engagement with a practice as a *totality of involvement* (*Bewandtnisganzheit*) where such involvement is understood by the one who actually belongs to the practice in question (Heidegger 1962, 116–18/84–6). Heidegger emphasizes the *existential understanding* or personal *belonging* to a practice as means to distinguish this notion of world from the former two. People are the *conduits* of a world because their actions bring to life this way of being. Through our actual involvement with things, we have the most intimate understanding of a thing's world.

The final sense of world relates to an *ontological-existential* insight. World, in this instance, can be understood in a structural or transcendental manner. As Heidegger explains, this more general awareness of world occurs when the individual recognizes his or her contingent relationship to all ontic-existentiell worlds. At such a moment the "world as world" discloses itself (Heidegger 1962, 232/187).

Our access to the ontological-existential sense of world is, oddly enough, through a breakdown of our meaningful relation to a practice. Heidegger describes two distinct levels of such a breakdown. The first level triggers a grasp of the world as a specific region or practice within which I live. The second level of meaning-breakdown triggers a genuine insight into the ontological-existential meaning of world.

The world is most meaningful to us when we are harmoniously engaged in a project. Like a master bicycle mechanic, who is intently slipping spokes through the holes of a hub and lacing them together onto a rim, the practice of bicycle maintenance is her ground for being-in-the-world. The entities which surround her take on meaning through this context of engagement. But no practice goes undisturbed. Heidegger discusses the privation of harmony in moments of *conspicuousness, obtrusiveness,* and *obstinacy* (Heidegger 1962, 102-7/72-6). Take the phenomenon of obtrusiveness as an example.

Something is obtrusive, in Heidegger's sense, when an object is *noticeably missing* for the project at hand. Imagine then, our bicycle mechanic, who is building a wheel, reaching for a spoke wrench but time and again grabs the wrong tool for the job. Each wrong tool is thrown back onto the bench in frustration. Each wrong tool stands in the way of, i.e., is obtrusive to, completing the project at hand. Now, one of the critical points Heidegger makes about such momentary breakdowns of harmony is that these ruptures allow room for reflection about the world in question. The ontic-existentiell world of involvement is *potentially disclosed* to someone in moments of disharmony because one's prior involvement with the world is broken. The breakdown of meaningful engagement with the world is a necessary condition for gaining a reflective apprehension of one's involvement with a world. Moreover, an individual's involvement in a world is the ground for any and all reflection about what *matters* to the person.

Although the ontic-existentiell world of involvement is disclosed through momentary breakdowns of harmony, we cannot conclude that the person understands the true significance of world-disclosure. In fact, when the harmony of my world is broken by something obtrusive, since I am so concerned with the project at hand, I remain focused on that task. How, then, do we gain an understanding of the *structural* difference between the ontic-existentiell and ontological-existential notions of world? Such an understanding becomes available, Heidegger explains, in those strange moments when a person feels totally disconnected or not-at-home (*Unheimlich*) in the task at hand. Humans have the capacity, in other words, to sense that their world, or actual practice, is not binding. The individual senses that she is *not* essentially tied to a particular way of life. This disconcerting attitude is brought about by the mood of *anxiety* (*Angst*). Anxiety is the source of the second-level breakdown of meaningful engagement with the world.

Within the *Analytic of Dasein*, anxiety is the fundamental mood which discloses to someone the reality of what it means to be human. By understanding anxiety, we become attuned to the very essence of human existence. And that essence is, for Heidegger, finitude. By finitude, Heidegger means more than just the fact that we are going to die. Humans are also limited in what they can do. As finite, we are limited in being, knowledge, and ability. Anxiety is a result of our intimate awareness of all three of these dimensions of finitude. Although I take issue with the power of anxiety later in the paper, for now I will focus on the least controversial dimension of finitude: the link between anxiety and death.

Anxiety is the mood which *takes us over* and draws us out of our intimate involvement with the world. Moments of anxiety re-awaken us to the fundamental truth of our finite or mortal being. Thus, we are reminded of our *being-toward-death* (*Sein-zum-Tode*). Far from being a negative experience, Heidegger sees such a reawakening to death as the very source of passion one has for life. We can see the awareness of death as a productive paradox: death is the most intimate of all certainties in life, and my awareness of it makes me concerned about being-in-the-world; however, the reality of death, although it brings about my meaningful orientation in the world, cannot be a reality of mine. The reality of *my* death is, Heidegger says, my "ownmost non-relational possibility" (Heidegger 1962, 294/250). By calling death a *non-relational possibility*, Heidegger highlights the alterity in this most certain of future events. It is an approaching possibility or reality but one which will extinguish all reality and possibilities for me. My death is an enigma. I cannot even *imagine* my own not-being since each scenario has me as the ultimate perceiver. The alterity of death draws me out of my harmonious involvements with the world.

When anxiety/death extracts me from out of the world, I reflect about my world in a way radically different from the way I do when something obtrusive stands in the way. Through anxiety, someone asks the *big question* about the meaning of life, e.g., "Is this really how I should be spending my time?" Anxiety reveals, then, a primordial kind of responsibility in that life demands a *response* to do something before it all ends. Here, we are on the threshold of understanding the ontological-existential meaning of world. When I recognize the freedom implicit in choosing to continue a way of life, I, thereby, recognize the fluidity of my own self and the world. Anxiety reveals, in other words, the intimate bond which exists between self and world insofar as they are *not permanent things*. Who should I be? To what world should I be committed? These are *angst* driven questions which reveal the world *as* a totality of involvement as well as the self *as* bound to such a world.

What is most important for my analysis is Heidegger's insistence that humans can understand the structure of being-in-the-world. In this case, we start to see that *I* am bound to a context or a world of possible engagement. Recognizing that *I* must be in a *world* is a structural awareness of being human. There are no autonomously thinking subjects because humans are always understanding and acting with the support of established practices (Heidegger 1962, 344/298). I am *nothing* without an actual world of possible engagement.[5] "In this, Dasein is taken all the way back to its naked uncanniness (*nackte Unheimlichkeit*), and becomes fascinated by it. This fascination... *takes* Dasein back from its 'worldly' possibilities" (Heidegger 1962, 394/344). Although anxiety dislodges us from the meaningfulness of our world, we recognize our intimate belonging to the world because it exposes the nullity of ourselves without the world. This is a fundamental insight into being human and as such it is an ontological insight. The individual grasps simultaneously these features of human existence: 1) the contingency of myself (death), 2) the necessity of being in a world (the nothingness

---

5   Stressing this dimension of self-nothingness, Heidegger says, "(T)here is ontologically a gap (*Kluft*) separating the selfsameness of the... Self from the identity of that 'I' which maintains itself throughout its manifold Experiences" (Heidegger 1962, 168/130). And again: "Anxiety discloses an insignificance of the world; and this insignificance reveals the nullity of that with which one can concern oneself" (Heidegger 1962, 393/343).

of the self without a world), and 3) the contingency of the world (the nothingness of the world without human action). Grasping the structure self-world is the experience of what Heidegger calls *formal indication*: a living experience of a structure of human-being. Heidegger refers to the fundamental structures of human being as formal indicatives (*formale Anzeige*), highlighting the fact that these structures can only be accessed by each Dasein in a moment of personal appropriation (Heidegger 1962, 362/315).

In the next section, Heidegger's account of authentic resoluteness is introduced. Before we proceed, I would like to highlight a problem. We have just explained that anxiety reveals to me my own contingency as well as my intimate connection to the world. Anxiety also reveals *the world's contingency*. Heidegger, I argue, does not offer enough insight into how this level of disclosure occurs. It will be shown that an awareness of historical contingency requires another triggering-event, e.g., a stranger to my world.

Authentic Historicity

The significance of the notion *world* is further developed when the ideas of authenticity and choice are developed. The question of authenticity is a hotly debated topic in Heidegger scholarship. On the one hand, there are those, such as Richard Wolin, who understand the issue of authenticity to be caught within an egocentric and/or decisionist account of human agency (Wolin 1990). On the other hand, there are those, such as Lawrence Vogel, who understand authenticity to be anything but egocentric and certainly more than mere decisionism (Vogel 1994). Contrary to the self-centered account, Vogel has the correct insight regarding the inherently social aspect of authenticity. And for the question of choice, the problem of decisionism is overcome by developing, beyond what Heidegger actually says, a social obligation regarding tolerance, which is implicit in Heidegger's account of authenticity. I now turn to the issue of authenticity in order to show its underlying social dimension. The problem of decisionism will be taken up in a later section.

A vast proportion of life is spent involved with the world(s) of daily concerns. When we are wrapped up in such concerns we are existing in an *inauthentic* (*uneigentlich*) mode. As inauthentic, we live as *fallen* among things and people within the world. Any course of action I take is not unique because the same practices circumscribe everyone's daily routines. As inauthentic, I exist as a one among the many (*das Man*).

Within this fallen state of being, although we have a *circumspective* (*Umsicht*) grasp of the concerns which govern our attention, we do not distance ourselves from such concerns to an extreme degree. Because of this lack of reflective distance, our capacity to choose is affected. Employing the term *expectation* (*Erwarten*), Heidegger describes what choice is like when we are tied so closely to the world.

> Expectation is not just an occasional looking-away from the possible to its possible actualization, but is essentially a *waiting for that actualization*. Even in expecting, one leaps away from the possible and gets a foothold in the actual. It is for its actuality that what is expected is expected. By the very nature of expecting, the possible is drawn into the actual, arising out of the actual and returning to it (Heidegger 1962, 306/262).

Expectation can be understood as the kind of awareness that anyone uncritically bound by context or factual circumstances may experience. People certainly choose what to do while existing inauthentically, that is, while consumed with the project at hand, but the *possible* future is actually quite routine and unquestioned. Expectation is correlated to a *closed* future insofar as what is possible is subsumed under the comforting grasp of the *actual realization* of the future.

Although Heidegger describes this level of pre-reflective involvement with one's surroundings as *inauthentic* we need not take this in a pejorative manner. In fact, Heidegger repeatedly claims that our state of fallenness is a descriptive, not an evaluative, mode of being. Indeed, human understanding (*Verstehen*) can only be grasped if we read this pre-reflective mode of *being-in* the world as ultimately positive. As the German word suggests, *uneigentlich* means to be *not* in possession of oneself; and this can simply point to the fact that we become *consumed* by our involvements in the world. When I am engaged in the world I am not reflectively aware of my own self as distinct from the things with which, and people with whom, I am interacting. The inauthentic mode of existing cannot be overcome in any ultimate sense for it is an existential-ontological structure of being-in-the-world.

Anxiety, as previously explained, draws us out of this pre-reflective state and delivers us over to a new kind of choosing. In such instances, a person opens up to the possibility for being authentic. Heidegger accounts for this level of choosing by employing the term *anticipation* (*Vorlaufen*):

> (B)y anticipation... one is liberated from one's lostness in those possibilities which may accidentally thrust themselves upon one; and one is liberated in such a way that for the first time one can authentically understand and choose among the factical possibilities (Heidegger 1962, 308/264).

When Heidegger speaks of anticipation, he points to the *openness* of the future given that the *possible* has been grasped by the concerned individual. Authentic choice relates to the kind of awareness which accompanies a critical grasp of a possible, i.e., open future. However, as Taylor Carman discusses, authenticity comes about not only from an awareness of the openness of a possible future; it arises from an awareness of the closing down of possibilities as well. When I choose, the possibilities available to me are limited by my past and present. Thus, I cannot do anything that is *logically* possible; rather, I am existentially limited. Furthermore, any step I take in the future will ultimately close off other real-world possibilities for me. The individual is, then, acutely aware of death in the choices made. We *are* death, in a certain sense, insofar as possibilities are constantly unavailable to and dying away from us (Carman 2003, 276-91).

At this point, we can easily misunderstand Heidegger's account of authenticity. There is no doubt that the issue of being-authentic is a

Authentic choice relates to the person's awareness that a world of practical engagement is a play of possibility/impossibility. Because of this, as stated previously, a sense of responsibility hangs over one's head regarding what choices are made. When someone becomes liberated from the chains of seeing the world as static (or expected), one is, thereby, opened to the personal freedom and responsibility inherent in the way life unfolds.[6] As authentic, one rises above one's own fallen self (*Man-selbst*) and encounters an intimate, *first-person* awareness of one's involvement in the world.[7]

At this point, we can easily misunderstand Heidegger's account of authenticity. There is no doubt that the issue of being-authentic is a

---

6   Cf. Heidegger 2002, 43-44. Heidegger, following Nietzsche, has an *inverted Platonism* since a static vision of reality is ultimately an illusion.

7   Carman explains the distinction between the first-person intimacy of authenticity and the mediate understanding of oneself as anyone (Carman 2003, 292 ff.). Arguing for the importance of a first-person responsibility in no way commits Heidegger to a theory of the *autonomous subject*.

matter of taking hold of oneself in contradistinction from just going along with the flow of *the they*. Authenticity is a liberation from my unreflective participation in the world. This does not necessarily indicate Heidegger's slide into an egocentric position, however. Even though he does describe the mode of inauthenticity as a state of self-alienation (Heidegger 1962, 164 ff./126 ff.), Heidegger's notion of authenticity cannot be reduced to a me *against* society type thesis.[8]

Heidegger certainly emphasizes the fact that the *I* or *individuality* is retrieved in moments of authenticity; however, this is in no way an endorsement of a retrieval of a *purely independent and autonomous subject.* We need only to recall what was said above about anxiety to understand why. Anxiety brings us face to face with the realities of 1) death and 2) the nullity of the *I* independent of the world. In reference to the latter, Heidegger says, "In clarifying Being-in-the-world we have shown that a bare subject without a world never 'is' proximally, nor is it ever given" (Heidegger 1962, 152/116). Heidegger recognizes, therefore, an intimate bond between the culturally established world and the self.

Heidegger is clear that Division II of *Being and Time* deepens the analyses given in Division I. There should be no question, then, that the *individualist* tendencies found in Division I, where there is a heightened sense of a person's fight to distance herself from the rest of society, is modified by the analysis of *historicity* (*Geschichtlichkeit*).[9] Within Division II, Heidegger explains that authentic choice is always tied up with one's historical community. We always choose from among those possibilities handed down to us from our *heritage* (*Erbe*). Heidegger goes so far as to discuss one's *fate* (*Schicksal*) and communal *destiny* (*Geschick*) given these historical limitations. Authentic choice is a matter of *repetition* (*Wiederholung*): "In repetition, fateful destiny can be disclosed explicitly as bound up with the heritage which has come down to us" (Heidegger 1962, 438/386).

---

8   Heidegger totally avoids the *egocentric* problem insofar as this relates to the issue of how the mind knows external reality. The egocentric problem, if there is one for Heidegger, is often related to a latent *Kierkegaardianism* detected in his notion of authenticity (Wolin 1990; Dreyfus 1994; Carman 2003).

9   Wolin reads Heidegger here as inconsistent or at odds with himself regarding the question of authenticity (Wolin 1990, 63). Vogel, in turn, divides his book into the *existentialist, historicist,* and *cosmopolitan* readings of Heidegger (Vogel 1994).

Fate and destiny are seemingly odd word choices given the emphasis Heidegger places on the openness of the future. He obviously wants us to take the notions of fate and individual responsibility as complementary notions. How can this be done?

Heidegger's sense of authenticity occurs within the horizon of a history, tradition, or heritage. Insofar as authenticity is the choice of an individual, however, it is more than just a renewal of a preestablished way of life. Heidegger emphasizes that *refiguring* the past into one's own is essential to being authentic.[10] Although our actions may be influenced by our *hero* (Heidegger 1962, 437/385), the path we assemble can be uniquely ours. The future is open, even if set on a course through the past, because Dasein can retrieve past *possibilities* unexplored by others. What someone assembles in her own practical comprehension of the world is certainly handed down from the past; yet, the individual can always assemble things in a new way. There can be, then, moments of discovery *by individuals*, e.g., Newton's laws of motion, within a distinct history of inquiry. Such individuals are rightly praised for their accomplishments even if their insights are not the product of sheer genius.

Heidegger's way of balancing fate and individual responsibility helps us avoid hypostatizing the existence of world/being. We must always remember that a world—no matter how much influence it has over us—does not exist in the way a thing does. There is an ontological difference between the world and thing. Worlds are maintained (or changed) only through the acts of people, whereas things exist independently of any such acts.[11] The world and, hence, meaning are fluid in a way things are not. Any world risks disappearing through a lack of participation and, so, the individual is responsible for how and what meanings are maintained.

Heidegger is, of course, not content with establishing the mere fluidity of a world. Our heritage adds a kind of ground to this openness. Heidegger even seems to indicate an interest in establishing and maintaining a particular kind of world. In other words, Heidegger offers a

---

10 Joan Stambaugh notes, in her "Translator's Introduction" to *Being and Time*, that a possible translation of the term *Wiederholung* is *recapitulation* "since that word is used in music to refer to what Heidegger seems to intend by *Wiederholung*. In music... recapitulation refers to the return of the initial theme after the whole development section. Because of its new place in the piece, that same theme is now heard differently" (Heidegger 1996, xv-xvi).

11 See Carman's notion of *ontic realism* (Carman 2003, 155-203).

vision of society which is itself authentic. An authentic society would be established around the bond which exists between people through their awareness of their historical destiny. Heidegger says,

> (I)f fateful Dasein, as Being-in-the-world, exists essentially in Being-with Others, its historizing (*Geschehen*) is a co-historizing (*Mitgeschehen*) and is determinative for it as *destiny* (*Geschick*). This is how we designate the historizing of the community, of a people. Destiny is not something that puts itself together out of individual fates, any more than Being-with-one-another can be conceived as the occurring together of several subjects. Our fates have already been guided in advance, in our Being with one another in the same world and in our resoluteness for definite possibilities (Heidegger 1962, 436/384).

Authenticity is, ultimately, based around a bond between people. As Heidegger implies in this passage, although this bond *already exists* between people, it is not necessarily *recognized*. With this in mind, I propose a distinct way of understanding personal responsibility in *Being and Time*. I suggest the authentic individual has a specific mission, viz., to help others understand the destiny of the community. The individual must become the *voice* of a community. From this perspective, the political dimension of *Being and Time* can be seen to have a rather specific goal. If this is the case, then the charge that Heidegger is caught within a form of decisionism is unwarranted. Let us now look into this charge.

Becoming an Other's Conscience

Authentic choice derives from an understanding of the human condition, particularly, one's responsibility for maintaining a world. Here, we can say that authenticity relates to the attitude one has toward *how* one acts in the world. However, insofar as authentic choice is guided by a *certain* (*gewiss*) understanding of the original truth of existence (*die ursprüngliche Wahrheit der Existenz*), *what* one does may be prescribed by fundamental ontology as well. Before we look into what this determinate content might be, we have to discuss the truth disclosed by Heidegger's inquiry.

Following Hubert Dreyfus, the basic truth exposed by fundamental ontology is the truth of *hermeneutic realism* (Dreyfus 1994, 253). Hermeneutic realism is a position which derives from Heidegger's awareness that any *situation* (Heidegger 1962, 346/299) within which one must choose is itself a mere one among many possible, existentially real worlds. The second and third senses of world, discussed in the first part of this paper, actually expose this reality because they show that, at any given time, a plurality of worlds are actually available to me. Thus, any world I may currently inhabit is but one possible horizon of understanding. Anxiety reveals this contingency to me insofar as I can choose to stop participating in a world in an attempt to change the meaning of my life.

The *hermeneutic* part of this way of thinking is simply an expression of an acknowledged *pluralism*. My world is just one interpretive nexus of meaning. The *realistic* aspect comes in because, when we recognize the plurality of worlds, we are also aware of the *independence* of things from our world. Since there are different ways of interpreting things, we know that our world—*as* an interpretive nexus of meaning—does not, once and for all, constitute the meaning of a thing.

However successful this claim to realism may be is beside the point of this paper.[12] Whether Heidegger's pluralism is best described as idealist, realist, or something in between is not particularly relevant for me at this time. What is significant is that our first real contact with the issue of tolerance arises with this *truthful* insight into pluralism. Thus, an essential part of being-authentic is to recognize the fact that any choice "cannot become rigid as regards the Situation" (Heidegger 1962, 355/307). The individual who makes a choice must respect the contingency implicit in the choice made. Any path that is taken has its rationale "in terms of the heritage" which the individual "takes over" (Heidegger 1962, 435/383). So, Carman states, even if living authentically means living for the sake of some particular thing, "(w)hat sort of thing that might be... can in no way be anticipated or prescribed by fundamental ontology. There is simply nothing to say a priori about what kinds of things are worthy of our wholehearted devotion" (Carman 2003, 296 fn. 34).[13] Hermeneutic realism, we might say, exposes

12 Carman provides an interesting critique of many attempts to *prove* realism (Carman 2003, 183-90).

13 In light of what Carman says, consider the following statements by Heidegger: "The Situation cannot be calculated in advance or presented like something present-at-hand which is waiting for someone to grasp it" (Heidegger 1962, 355/307); "If everything 'good' is a heritage, and the character of 'goodness' lies

the *true lack* of any *a priori* grounds for taking an interest in something. We could also conclude, as Carman implies, and Wolin clearly argues, that fundamental ontology leaves us with a mere decisionism. Wolin describes the problem:

> (W)hat might be described as the *normative impoverishment* of the Heideggerian category of "resolve" or "decisiveness" goes far toward explaining the failings of decisionism in all its forms. For when it is devoid of any and every normative orientation, "decision" can only be *blind* and *uninformed*—ultimately, it becomes a leap into the void. Without a *material criterion* for decision, it becomes impossible to distinguish an *authentic* from an *inauthentic* decision, *responsible* from *irresponsible* action–let alone on what grounds an individual would even prefer one course of action to another (Wolin 1990, 52).[14]

Wolin's point is compelling. The truth of pluralism could lead one to conclude that any way of life is as good as the next insofar as an individual's resolve to maintain a particular world is not supported by a priori principles. Certainly, Heidegger does not provide us with a *material criterion* for either governing our actions or as a norm for judging all cultures. Indeed, all moral principles are worldly, historically based, and not necessary to the being of a person. So, without a normative principle, the notion of authenticity only tells someone *how* to act but not *what* one should do. Heidegger even says that fundamental ontology reveals the truth of existence without "holding up to Dasein an ideal of existence with any special 'content', or forcing any such ideal upon it 'from outside'" (Heidegger 1962, 311/266). Is this the ultimate message Heidegger is offering through his inquiry? Is he trying to let us know that there are no a priori grounds for any action; thus, all we can do is go along with what history alone has conditioned us to respect? This is a plausible way of interpreting the notion of authentic resoluteness as guided by a sense of fate. Wolin goes so far as to charge Heidegger with supporting a vicious kind of *opportunism*, which allows people

---

in making authentic existence possible, then the handing down of a heritage constitutes itself in resoluteness" (Heidegger 1962, 435/383).

14 Similarly, Dreyfus describes the difference between inauthenticity and authenticity as a gestalt shift (Dreyfus 1994, 317). Dreyfus concludes that "there can be no meaningful differences among projects, and that therefore we must base the distinction between authenticity and inauthenticity on the form or style of activity only, not upon its content" (Dreyfus 1994, 328).

to go along with any kind of action a context may offer (Wolin 1990, 65).

I suggest that Heidegger leaves the door open for a more *principled* kind of action. When we develop Heidegger's philosophy beyond what he explicitly says, there is a way beyond the problem.[15] In particular, I want to look into his claim that an authentic person can help others become liberated. Then, in the following section, I discuss the limit to Heidegger's account of historical-disclosure. Once these issues are addressed, it can be shown that Heidegger's philosophy allows room for a kind of a priori obligation which derives from the truth disclosed by fundamental ontology.

Without denying Heidegger's understanding of pluralism, and the problem of decisionism which it introduces, I emphasize again the importance of truth in his philosophy. Although our choices are always based within a *hermeneutic circle*, our accurate understanding of this situation leads us to a positive appropriation of a world. In a rather famous passage, Heidegger says,

> In the circle is hidden a positive possibility of the most primordial kind of knowing. To be sure, we genuinely take hold of this possibility only when, in our interpretation, we have understood that our first, last, and constant task is never to allow our fore-having, fore-sight, and fore-conception to be presented to us by fancies and popular conceptions, but rather to make the scientific theme secure by working out these fore-structures in terms of the *things themselves* (Heidegger 1962, 195/153; emphasis added).

Heidegger is offering an important insight regarding authentic choice. We have a capacity to disclose a "primordial kind of knowing" which will liberate us from "popular conceptions" and "fancies". This is our "first, last, and constant task" as humans. On the one hand, Heidegger is asking us to be attentive to the temporal-historical ground of human being. Part of this understanding will be a recognition of our deep belonging to a heritage and, thereby, a communal sense of destiny. Wolin is rightly concerned with the problem of decisionism given the absence of a concrete criterion alongside the emphasis on destiny and fate.

---

15 Perhaps the most valuable aspect of Vogel's argument lies in his ability to work out a moral standpoint from the truths disclosed by Heidegger's analysis (Vogel 1994, 88-102).

On the other hand, Heidegger speaks of a *task* and, so, intends something more than just a mere readjustment of our attitude. Heidegger can be taken as expressing a political vision which draws an individual back into the world through this primordial kind of knowing. If this is the case, then Heidegger is advocating not just how one's attitude toward life should be but what one *should do* with the insights gained from grasping the reality of being human.

According to the passage above, we have the responsibility to make sure that the world we maintain is worthy of being handed down to others. We must ensure, in other words, that the tradition which will be inherited by others is in league with the *things themselves.*[16] One's choice is not, therefore, merely based upon an arbitrary or unfounded decision. The truth of existence is known with certainty (*Gewissheit*) for Heidegger. It is this insight which provides the passion for continuing with a particular world of meaningful engagement. More importantly, if one's tradition is not unified around a genuine understanding of human being, then there is a personal responsibility to begin such an awakening. Heidegger suggests this line of social transformation ever so briefly in *Being and Time.* If we go back into the issue of inauthenticity, we can see just how far Heidegger supports this level of social transformation.

Being-inauthentic means to live life within the confines of *expectation.* We are lost in *the they* insofar as we are consumed by our circumspective concerns. Living inauthentically can be so all consuming, however, that an individual, indeed, *an entire culture,* can spend the whole of life absorbed in this way of being.[17] Heidegger expresses this extreme level of blindness to the truth throughout the text. He speaks of the *dictatorship (Diktatur) of the they* (164/126) and of the *dominance (Herrschaft) of the public way in which things have been interpreted* (213/169). One can be so totally *seduced (Verführt)* by the public account of things that "(t)he 'they' prescribes one's state-of-mind and *determines* what and how one 'sees'" (Heidegger 1962, 213/170; emphasis added).

---

16 This sense of legitimacy/illegitimacy follows Heidegger into his later concern with our treatment of the earth as a *standing-reserve* (Heidegger 1977, 299).

17 For instance, Heidegger says that a true grasp of *anxiety* is rare: "Even rarer than the existentiell Fact of 'real' anxiety are attempts to interpret this phenomenon according to the principles of its existential-ontological Constitution and function. The reasons for this lie partly in the general neglect of the existential analytic of Dasein" (Heidegger 1962, 234-5/190).

Heidegger is describing a level of inauthenticity which is a *radical* kind of *alienation* (*Entfremdung*) from the reality of existence (Heidegger 1962, 222/178). It appears, then, that, like the lotus eaters in the *Odyssey*, Heidegger sees a possible situation in which almost everyone is *incapable* of gaining an authentic understanding of the world.[18] Here, Wolin sees an implicit elitism in Heidegger's analysis of authenticity and, consequently, political action: "The *de facto* separation of human natures into authentic and inauthentic is radically undemocratic. The political philosophy that corresponds to this ontological dualism suggests that human beings are divided by nature into leaders and followers" (Wolin 1990, 56).

I do not think Heidegger would support this claim. Heidegger clearly recognizes that there is no *natural* aptitude for understanding fundamental ontology. Fundamental ontology springs from out of a history of inquiry prior to which there was no such comprehension. Similar to the cave allegory which began this paper, even the liberator was once shown the truth of existence (cf. Heidegger 1962, 162/125). But *who* shows the liberator the truth? Heidegger's answer here is anything but clear. Because Heidegger never clearly works through this question, Wolin's charge of elitism cannot be easily countered. I will let this question lay idle for the moment.

Wolin's charge of elitism includes the point that Heidegger's notion of authenticity contains an evaluative component. Some people are better off than others. There is, then, a dimension to being-inauthentic which is distinct from the merely descriptive aspect of falling into a practice. Given this evaluative tone, a moral goal is part of what it means to be authentic. In other words, contrary to Wolin's argument regarding decisionism, a *specific what* is implied in Heidegger's account of fundamental ontology.[19] And that specific content is partly revealed by Heidegger's own account of authentically *being-with-others*. When Heidegger states that Dasein "can become the 'conscience' of Others" (Heidegger 1962,

---

18 In the lectures on technology, Heidegger discusses the issue of *enframing*, where the world-historical frame of the technological paradigm comes to dominate the whole of our thinking. Heidegger's concern with poetry is an attempt to bring to our awareness a perspective distinct from the technological frame (Heidegger 1977).

19 Even if Wolin's argument is correct, and Heidegger is an *opportunist*, there is still a moral message being advocated through fundamental ontology. I think there is a different moral message, however.

344/298),[20] we see a specific moral goal implied in a person's grasp of the truth. First, we need to say something about Heidegger's notion of *conscience (Gewissen)*.[21]

The notion of *conscience* is crucial to understanding the basis, and I would claim limit, of Heidegger's account of fundamental ontology. The *call (Ruf)* of conscience is a passive experience of being lifted out of the first level of inauthenticity (Heidegger 1962, 320/275; 322/277). It is a passive experience in that it *happens to* an individual through an attunement to the reality of one's own finite existence. "The call comes *from* me and yet *from beyond and over me*" (Heidegger 1962, 320/275). The experience of conscience is a kind of internal awakening to the reality of finitude, which does not allow me to remain blind to the limited time and responsibility I have for the meaning of existence. I cannot simply rest comfortably within the harmony of the world given the limited time there is to accomplish certain tasks in my life. The call of conscience is "unfamiliar to the everyday they-self; it is something like an *alien (fremde)* voice." Thus, Heidegger rhetorically asks: "What could be more alien to the 'they', lost in the manifold 'world' of its concern, than the Self which has been individualized down to itself in uncanniness and been thrown into the 'nothing'?" (Heidegger 1962, 321-322/277). Conscience *is* the anxious state whereby I am open to my own existential-historical limits.

We cannot overstress the importance of conscience within Heidegger's analysis. Conscience is the phenomenon which draws me out of my state of inauthenticity and provides me with the necessary space for understanding the truth of existence. It creates the *gap (Kluft)* between me, as a they-self, and myself as an authentic individual (Heidegger 1962, 168/130). Now, insofar as conscience comes *from me* it is an *auto-affection*; however, it is also described as an *alien* power and, so, is something other (*hetero*) than me. Is Wolin correct, then, in his assessment of a *duality* of people for Heidegger? Are some people simply attuned to *hear* the true significance of conscience/anxiety and others not? Heidegger never answers these questions. There is a further problem.

---

20 I acknowledge the fact that Heidegger says Dasein *can* and not *should* become the conscience of others. Wolin interprets this statement as evidence of Heidegger's elitist political philosophy (Wolin 1990, 56).

21 The similarity between the German terms *certainty (Gewissheit)* and *conscience (Gewissen)* should be pointed out.

Since conscience comes *from me*, we have to wonder how Dasein can become the conscience of others. Heidegger describes the difficulty: "(T)he call undoubtedly does not come from someone else who is with me in the world" (Heidegger 1962, 320/275). "The call... calls without uttering anything. The call discourses in the uncanny mode of *keeping silent*. And it does this only because, in calling the one to whom the appeal is made, it does not call him into the public idle talk of the 'they', but *calls* him *back* from this *into the reticence of his existent* potentiality-for-Being" (Heidegger 1962, 322/277). If conscience is a *silent appeal*, and the public idle talk of the they is ineffective, what means are at the liberator's disposal to open the other to the call of conscience? Heidegger does not explain how this productive interaction between people takes place and, so, leaves us wondering to what extent conscience is a power some people have over others.

Despite these limits, Heidegger does tell us that Dasein can be authentically *solicitous* or *caring (Fürsorge)* toward others by *leaping forth* to help liberate them (Heidegger 1962, 344/298).[22] Here, Dasein is not taking over some project for someone else; rather, Dasein assists in opening the other to the existential-ontological structures that indicate the essence of being human. Heidegger says, "This kind of solicitude pertains essentially to authentic care—that is, to the existence of the Other, not to a 'what' with which he is concerned; it helps the Other to become transparent to himself *in* his care and to become *free* for it" (Heidegger 1962, 159/122).

Heidegger clearly supports the evaluative position that some ways of life are *impoverished* (Heidegger 1962, 68/43; 220-1/176). More importantly, when he puts forth the idea that Dasein can help others out of their lostness in *the they*, it appears that authenticity does *prescribe* a path for us to follow, namely, a concernful interaction with others about the reality of Dasein and the world.[23] This is *what* an authentic person should do with the insights gained from fundamental ontology.

----

22 Heidegger distinguishes between two ways of dealing with the Other: *leaping in (einspringen)* and *leaping forth (vorspringen)*. The former is unproductive insofar as the goal is to open the other to the Existential-Analytic of Dasein (Heidegger 1962, 158/122). That is, *leaping in* keeps the other person alienated from the reality of Dasein by dominating and making the other dependent on me for help.

23 Vogel provides an insightful discussion on the limits of the ethical relation between people suggested in Heidegger's notion of *leaping forth*. The obliga-

I extend this insight beyond the interpersonal level. The fundamental goal of being authentically engaged with the other is to *bring about* an authentic community. From this perspective, consider what Heidegger means when he says that "(i)n communication (*Mitteilung*) and in battle (*Kampf*) the power of destiny *first* becomes free. The fateful destiny of Dasein in and with its 'generation' constitutes the complete, *authentic occurrence* (*das eigentliche Geschehen*) of Dasein" (Heidegger 1996, 352/384; emphasis added). The claim that "the power of destiny *first* becomes free" indicates a sense of a community which will be brought about through authentic action. An authentic individual's *leap* to help an other opens itself toward social solidarity.

The Disclosure of the Historical World

What is missing from Heidegger's account is exactly how we can be authentically solicitous with and for others. *What* it is we are trying to do is fairly clear. As authentic, I recognize my responsibility within a community. I sense my fate and our destiny. So, an aspect of being authentically solicitous with others is to have them recognize our common heritage and destiny. By doing so, the authentic individual helps to establish a communal bond in a renewed sense. But there is something missing in the analysis up to this point. What I want to expose is the need for an appropriate *hermeneutic axis point* for the awareness of our common history to be disclosed to co-historizing Daseins. Heidegger seems to assume this level of understanding but does not develop how this level of insight is achieved. Once this is explained, the authentic community suggested by fundamental ontology will have a guiding principle: tolerance.

Along with Wolin, I continually wonder how any particular individual has become open to the possibility of authentic resoluteness. We certainly see that other people can be so lost in their circumspective concerns that they need the assistance of an authentic Dasein to draw them toward their own conscience. What has given the Heideggerian exemplar so powerful an insight into the reality of human being? Heidegger, at times, seems to be aware of the issue: "(I)t is indisputable that a lively mutual acquaintanceship on the basis of Being-with often depends upon how

tion to assist others is not a principle which must be enacted in each and every case. The obligation is "to act toward him in ways *consistent with the possibility of being his conscience*" (Vogel 1994, 91).

far *one's own Dasein has understood itself at the time*" (Heidegger 1962, 162/125; emphasis added).[24]

The odd thing about Heidegger's analysis is that, in the end, it is conscience and *not someone else* who shows the truth of existence to the individual. It is conscience, as our anxious attunement to finitude, that provides the second-level awareness into the structure of self-world. Although anxiety and conscience may be suitable notions to account for our awareness of death, I do not think they are sufficient to bring about our historical awareness, especially our sense of destiny. I suggest that a confrontation with foreign ways of being-in-the-world is a *necessary* axis point for disclosing one's world in an existential-ontological sense. Furthermore, an attempt *to comprehend* a foreign world is the *necessary* axis point for disclosing one's own historical fate and destiny. Heidegger never develops these points given his perspective on the *Other* in *Being and Time*.

Heidegger's treatment of the Other is dominated by the idea of Being-with (*Mitsein*). The emphasis is placed on the *sameness* of others within Dasein's ontic world. Dasein is always already *with* others in terms of a practical, work-oriented view. We already share the *same world* (*derselben Welt*). Thus, Heidegger says, "By 'Others' we do not mean everyone else but me. They are rather those from whom... one does *not* distinguish oneself—those among whom one is too" (Heidegger 1962, 154/118).

Given this level of correlation between me and everyone else, Heidegger makes an important point regarding the meaning of being. Because we already belong to the same world, we already share an understanding of the things which surround us. Thus, verbal communication (*Mitteilung*), as a place where meaning is shared between people, is given a *derivative* status in Heidegger's analysis.[25] Meaning primordially occurs in the active engagement with practices, whereas the sphere of face-to-face dialogue

---

24 The liberator had to be shown the way, it seems, since hiding from, avoiding, even fighting against the truth is an individual's most normal, everyday way of dealing with reality (cf. Heidegger 1962, 234-5/190). Indeed, we could probably uncover a whole series of repressive attitudes when it comes to owning up to our hermeneutic nature, e.g., self-assurance, distraction, tranquilization (Heidegger 1962, 214-22/170–8).

25 However, if we consider the passage above, where communication is given a privileged role in establishing destiny, then we must be attentive to the context in which Heidegger discusses the derivative status of communication.

is a place of disengagement, i.e., a loss of the world's full existential significance. Linguistic assertions or propositional judgments about the world *derive* their significance from the pre-given realm of *discourse* (*Rede*), that is, the *referential nexus* of entities and purposes that makes up a coherent practice (Heidegger 1962, 203/160). We understand such a referential nexus by being able to work—which includes speaking and gesturing—competently within it. From out of that familiarity, discrete propositional judgments about the things within the nexus make sense. This is what Heidegger means when he says that the "primordial 'as' of an interpretation which understands circumspectively we call the 'existential-*hermeneutical* 'as' in distinction from the '*apophantical* 'as' of the assertion" (Heidegger 1962, 201/158).

By exclusively focusing on people with whom I already share a common world, Heidegger misses important *disclosing* events. I would like to suggest two additional triggering events that relate to the phenomenon of world-disclosure. The first can take place within an established tradition. The second takes place between traditions. Regarding the former, consider the master/apprentice relationship as an example.

Any master within a particular field will most likely be saddled with the responsibility for training someone new to the practice. Since the novice knows nothing of the tools, parts, physical demands, etc. involved with this world, the master must show a level of tolerance toward the apprentice's ignorance. The master must recognize that the novice does not come equipped with the fore-knowledge of the region in question and, so, a degree of clumsiness is going to occur during the training process. Without going into an elaborate account of how an apprentice becomes a master, I simply want to highlight the fact that the master's confrontation with a person unfamiliar with a world, as well as the novice's recognition of being an alien to this world, is the kind of axis point necessary (even if not sufficient) for the disclosure of the world *as world* to an individual. This follows because the master and apprentice can both reflect about *who* they are in terms of *a world*. The level of frustration involved with trying to help (and wanting to be helped by) someone enter a world can give way to a comprehension of how much one is tied (or not tied) to such a world. Certainly, such a level of reflection is not achieved in Heidegger's accounts of the breakdown of harmony through conspicuousness, obtrusiveness, and obstinacy. Heidegger admits that these phenomena remain *circumspectively* focused on the task at hand. But to understand the significance of the existential-ontological meaning of *world*, the individual must understand the correlation between Dasein and world. In authenticity, the individual recognizes how the referential totality of the world *refers back to* Dasein, having no significance without Dasein, just as Dasein is nothing without the world (Heidegger 1962, 417/365). This level of awareness can be gained through an encounter with someone who is a stranger (*ein Fremder*) to my world. The stranger draws out of me an awareness of my own intimate relationship to the world because the other presents a world different from my own. The other presents to me the reality of other worlds and, thereby, creates the space or gap (*Kluft*) necessary for reflection about my own being-in-the-world. There is a second point to make regarding the power of the other.

In this master/apprentice relationship, we can assume a level of *belonging to* the same culture. How do they—master and apprentice—become aware of this deeper *background* of co-commitment? A second kind of triggering event is necessary for disclosing the deeper, historical dimension of fate and destiny.

When we recognize our fate and destiny, we are critically aware of an *extreme limit* to the possibilities available to us when choosing a world. The experience of fate is the experience of a *limit situation* (*Grenzsituationen*).[26] How does this occur? I suggest that we become aware of our historical limits through a confrontation with a kind of otherness which *cannot be appropriated* into our being-in-the-world.

In *Being and Time*, Heidegger only briefly mentions an encounter with foreign ways of life. What he has to say about such confrontations seems to suggest the opposite of what I am arguing. He states that interest in other ways of life or cultures will foreclose a truly disclosive experience:

> With special regard to the interpretation of Dasein, the opinion may now arise that understanding the most alien cultures (*fremdesten Kulturen*) and "synthesizing" them with one's own may lead to Dasein's becoming for the first time thoroughly and genuinely enlightened about itself. Versatile curiosity and restlessly "knowing it all" masquerade as a universal understanding of Dasein (Heidegger 1962, 222/178).

---

26 Heidegger derives the notion of the *limit situation* from Karl Jaspers' *Psychology of Worldviews* (Heidegger 1962, 356/308; 496, note xv/301 fn. 7).

I maintain that Heidegger is not dismissing my proposal out of hand. To see why, we must take note of Heidegger's reference to *curiosity* (*Neugier*) in this quotation. Curiosity is, within the analytic of Dasein, a way of being absorbed in the world, i.e., a mode of fallenness or inauthenticity. One's curiosity is directed toward alien phenomena with the goal of *knowing* the phenomena in question.

Individuals can, of course, gain a genuine understanding of things which at first fascinate their curiosity. The apprentice can become the master. Heidegger is not suggesting otherwise. What Heidegger identifies as *versatile* curiosity is different from, what we can call, *productive* curiosity. Versatile curiosity takes an interest in a whole multitude of things; and this restless desire to *know it all* is an impossible task given the finite reality of being human. Versatile curiosity is an *impoverished* way of life insofar as the person is not attuned to the impossibility of maintaining too many worlds and, so, wastes time on too many pursuits.

Heidegger certainly put his finger on a rather common, restless attitude of *modern day* life. It is one of the reasons why communication (*Mitteilung*) is not treated with much significance within his analysis. Following on the heels of versatile curiosity, there is a tendency to be overly sure about matters we do not genuinely understand. Heidegger captures this way of inauthentic communication in what he calls *idle conversation* (*Gerede*). When we see and hear things on the television or read things in the newspaper, we often discuss the issues with a false sense of assurance. So, curiosity, in a pejorative sense, is a kind of busying oneself with all sorts of issues without really gaining an understanding of any. And idle conversation is the way we go about communicating with each other about things we do not really understand.

I am interested, therefore, in uncovering a confrontation with an alien culture which is not like Heidegger's notion of curiosity. At the point when the alien other appears to be *beyond my powers of synthesis*, then the most profound hermeneutic disclosure about myself can occur. When I am confronted with someone who cannot be understood, then a mode of historical disclosure becomes available to me.

A particularly pertinent example of this level of disclosure is the unifying mood which came about, in the United States and elsewhere, after the September 11, 2001, attacks on the World Trade Center and Pentagon Building. Part of our shock on this *fateful* day was caused by our understanding that these were deliberate acts. The recognition that people chose to fly airplanes into buildings was a source of stupefaction. What we would call acts of suicide and murder were *taken as* heroic and moral actions by another group of people. Although shocking, these events did trigger a sense of a communal bond between us. In relation to Heidegger's analysis, two particularly important points must be noted.

First, the others' actions brought a sense of *unheimlichkeit* to us. We were presented with a home-world (*Heimwelt*) that we could not comprehend. Now, this is vastly different from Heidegger's account of this rupturing mood. For Heidegger, it is precisely the *nothingness* or *alterity* of death, conscience, and one's own self without a world which triggers our concern for the meaning of being. Yet, with the alien other, we have a triggering event for this mood which is a *material* presence.

The second important point to note is that this mode of uncanniness (*Unheimlichkeit*) has a way of bringing out our background solidarity immediately. Our solidarity is not brought to us through the actions of an authentic comrade; rather, it is an affective disposition disclosed to us through our reaction to the alien homeworld. Regardless of our regionally distinct concerns, our deep bond to basic principles, norms or values can be revealed to us through the (shocking) actions of others.

When we confront an alien homeworld such a confrontation can force us to recognize the limited possibilities which have been handed down to us from the past as guiding our resolute actions toward the future. I recognize who I am when the alien other brings to me an awareness of my deep belonging to a community. Although I can try to *get into* the other's world, imagining how such actions could be taken as moral and heroic, I simply have no existential comprehension of this reality. Indeed, I discover that I just do not have the stomach for this kind of behavior. Recognizing this limit situation allows me to acknowledge my belonging to a heritage. The incomprehensibility of the other gives me an insight into myself as committed to a certain set of values. My (our) deep background is revealed through an alien homeworld.

If I am correct that other practical worlds are a necessary axis point for one's own historical world-disclosure to occur, thereby making authentic choice possible, we have to reformulate Heidegger's negative account of having a versatile curiosity with other cultures. Although it is possible to take an unproductive interest in what other people are do-ing, it remains the case that an awareness of other worlds is a necessary condition for an awareness of the contingency *of my heritage*. Only if I am confronted with that which seems to be totally beyond me can I ever recognize the contingency of a history as well as my deep belonging to a heritage. Heidegger, unfortunately, only speaks of the *voice of conscience* as this moment of radical disclosure. Thus, the key triggering event, for Heidegger, is the individual's sense of responsibility in the face of his or her own contingency. I do not deny that humans, at a certain age anyway, have a natural apprehension of their *non-relational possibility*, i.e., death. And I grant the significance this can have on caring for the meaningfulness of life. But being-authentic includes a historical comprehension as well. I do not see how conscience, as Heidegger explains this phenomenon, has the power to disclose this level of awareness to the individual. Again, it is the presence of another person's difference from me which can bring about this level of disclosure. Conscience, as Heidegger understands this phenomenon, seems to be built upon a prior experience with the material presence of an alien homeworld.

(In)Tolerance

Earlier, I claimed that fundamental ontology might suggest a more principled kind of action. The *truth* of pluralism is the ground for just such a principle. On the one hand, the truth of pluralism includes an acceptance of the fact that my world is not the only possible way of being in the world (cf. Vogel 1994, 101). On the other hand, given the problem of violence in some world-views, such an acceptance is troubling *without* a normative principle as a guide. Tolerance is the principle which can limit what kind of world-views are taken as legitimate insofar as tolerance is grounded in Heidegger's primordial truth of existence.[27]

In *Being and Time*, the word *Nachsicht* occurs at a particularly important point in the discussion of being-with-others. John Macquarrie and Edward Robinson translate *Nachsicht* as *forbearance*. Joan Stambaugh forces the issue by using the word *tolerance* in this context. The passage is as follows:

> Just as *circumspection* (*Umsicht*) belongs to taking care of things as a way of discovering things at hand, concern (*Füsorge*) is guided by considerateness (*Rücksicht*) and tolerance (*Nachtsicht*). With concern, both can go through the deficient and indifferent (*indifferenten*) modes

---

27 On the cosmopolitan ideal in Heidegger, see Vogel 1994, 69-102.

up to the point of *inconsiderateness* and the tolerance which is guided
by indifference (*Gleichgültigkeit*) (Heidegger 1996, 115/123).

Heidegger is clearly identifying kinds of tolerance, or ways to forbear,
the other. By mentioning degrees of tolerance, we see Heidegger's affinity to a kind of virtue ethics (Hatab 2000, 138-9). As with any virtue,
the goal is to find the mean between the extremes of deficient ways of
acting. In this case, tolerance toward others is the virtue in question.
How and *why* are we to be tolerant of others?

In general, to be tolerant means to be accepting of something that is
not normal, usual, or comfortable. There are at least two ways of being
tolerant toward such a difference. First, tolerance can be the means for
assimilating something different into one's own way of life. Just as it is
in the master/apprentice relationship, when the goal is to break down
the barriers between what is normal versus what is abnormal, tolerance
is a necessary means for a productive synthesis of otherness. Tolerance
is a behavioral attitude we must *develop* as a way of coping with the
frustration which comes along with the process of transformation.

Second, tolerance can be the means for dealing with the *inaccessibility*
of the other's world. Regarding this possibility, there are two attitudes
toward such a difference. First, analogous to *putting up with* the street
noise when living in a New York City apartment, we can forbear another
world simply because we cannot extinguish it. This kind of tolerance
would display a *Gleichgültigkeit* or *perfunctoriness* (as Macquarrie and
Robinson translate the term) toward the other's difference. Even though
I tolerate the other's world, I am put off by that difference. I do not
care for the other and my tolerance is an attempt to forget the other's
presence in my horizon of understanding.

Second, we have the kind of tolerance which is the appropriate, i.e.,
virtuous, response to an alien otherness. In this case, although there is
a heightened sense of alterity, my tolerance toward the other's world is
based upon the insights gained from fundamental ontology. I recognize
the other's commitment to a world simply because I understand the
reality of pluralism. Even though I do not *understand* the other's world,
there is a bond between us as humans with a history. Even if we are not
attuned to the things in the world in the same way, my understanding
of historical destiny allows me to 1) respect the other's difference and
2) let the other be as she is.

Tolerance is a virtue because, following Heidegger's lead, coming to an awareness of the contingency of a world is not easy to bear. Our initial reaction is to push what is other-than-me away given the power of the inauthentic tendency to take one's world as a permanent reality. We forget that normalcy or the *situation* is a fluid notion. Intolerance would be akin to being-inauthentic, i.e., indifferent, toward the disclosive power of the Other. Such intolerance can lead to the violent refusal to let the other act differently in the world. If we are to be freed from self-alienation (*Selbst-Entfremdung*), however, we must be prepared to recognize the significance of a foreign way of being in the world. The incomprehensibility of an other's world is an axis point around which my own understanding of human nature, i.e., the ontological-existential reality of myself, arises.

At this point, we are confronted with a difficult problem. How do we gain an *understanding* of the otherness of the other. The dilemma is as follows: my attempt to understand the other risks reducing the otherness of the other into my own way of understanding; however, if I do not try to comprehend the other, I may only be *assuming* a radical difference which does not exist between us. I suggest that the attempt at assimilation (real or imaginary) is a necessary condition for truly recognizing the otherness of the other.

Again, following Heidegger's analysis, we are not originally attuned to what is *alien*.[28] How, then, do we *become attuned to* the reality which is disclosed by the presence of the alien other? We must practice tolerance. I stress the importance of the *active* (not silent and passive) dimension of *becoming* tolerant.[29]

Becoming attuned to the genuine difference between my world and an other's world remains an assumption without an actual attempt to assimilate the alien way of existing. Unless I actually fail at *trying to work with* what is different from me, my claim regarding the incommensurable nature of the other's world is just another type of *rigid thinking* which is to be overcome by an authentic person. I may witness someone's *odd* actions, and have an aesthetic reaction to this difference, but without trying to join this world, I cannot actually claim that it is beyond me and,

---

28 Of course, Heidegger means the *alien voice of conscience*.

29 Heidegger's account of authentic discourse stresses the importance of *hearing, listening, and silence* in relation to others and conscience (Heidegger 1962, 204–10/161–6). These passive moods assume that one is already attuned to the essence of human reality. The question is how does one become so attuned?

thereby, truly understand my own limits. To have an actual, existential understanding of my own limit situation requires me to *radically fail* at trying to adopt another homeworld. There is no finer attunement to one's own limits than in such a failure.

If an attempt at assimilation is necessary for genuinely understanding one's own limits, then we run headlong into the problem Heidegger identifies as versatile curiosity. He is correct in stating that, given our limited time, we cannot just jump from one world view to the next. I cannot stop and try to assimilate every difference on the road of life. Authenticity requires me to remain committed to some way of being-in-the-world or else risk not knowing any. *This is precisely the point*: Heidegger's sense of resolute commitment includes a realization that, had I the time, the other's world may not be as different as it seems. An alien homeworld loses its status as a *radical alterity* and is understood as a world I could possibly adopt. Tolerance arises from out of this either active or imaginatively active engagement with the other's world.

Working this issue of tolerance into Heidegger's philosophy is one way of seeing his affinity to virtue ethics.[30] According to virtue theory, the goal of life is to master all the possible virtues since virtues are those behavioral characteristics which bring about human flourishing. Although Heidegger is vastly different from someone like Aristotle regarding the issue of human flourishing (Hatab 2000, 99-115), there is no doubt that Heidegger's account of human action is teleological. To be authentically resolute is the goal of life; and this way of *being* follows upon a disclosure of the truth of human existence. Tolerance helps to disclose the truth of human existence. The injunction to be tolerant stems from its function in drawing us to an awareness of who we are: historically finite beings. The obligation is grounded in its practical value.

Within the injunction to be tolerant, however, lies a correlational injunction to be intolerant of intolerance. Tolerance ends, then, where the attitude of intolerance begins. Both Plato and Heidegger appear to be using this line of reasoning when they highlight the liberator's use of violence in caring for the well-being of the cave-dwellers. We can cautiously identify with the need for violence in this situation because the liberator is now a foreigner whose assertions are taken as

---

30 Insofar as virtue ethics recognizes the role of proper social conditioning in the health of a person, there is a way beyond Wolin's concern with a *natural duality* of people in Heidegger's philosophy.

nonsense. The ignorance within the cave is so all consuming that verbal communication has little chance of revealing the limited perspective of the cave-dwellers to the cave-dwellers. The cave-dwellers cannot hear the truth. So, the only recourse left for the liberator is a direct kind of manipulation—a kind of *shock-therapy* approach to opening the other to the truth.[31] Although Heidegger's appeal to *physical* violence is extremely unsettling,[32] we see that no society can be authentic without the principle of tolerance already established within the *ethos* of a people. How to establish such an ethos within a world that does not respect the principle of tolerance is a problem well beyond the scope of our present inquiry.

Bibliography

Carman, Taylor. 2003. *Interpretation, Discourse, and Authenticity in* Being and Time. Cambridge: Cambridge University Press.

Dreyfus, Hubert. 1994. *Being-in-the-World: A Commentary on Heidegger's* Being and Time, *Division I.* Cambridge: Massachusetts Institute of Technology Press.

Hatab, Lawrence. 2000. *Ethics and Finitude: Heideggerian Contributions to Moral Philosophy.* Lanham: Rowman & Littlefield Publishers.

Heidegger, Martin. 1953. *Sein und Zeit.* Tübingen: Max Niemeyer Verlag,. Tr. *Being and Time* by John Macquarrie and Edward Robinson. San Francisco: Harper & Row, 1962. Tr. *Being and Time* by Joan Stambaugh. Albany: State University of New York Press, 1996.

———. 1961. *An Introduction to Metaphysics.* Tr. Ralph Manheim. New York: Doubleday & Company, Inc.

---

31 See Heidegger on the *Acts of Power* or *Gewalt-tätig* (Heidegger 1961, 129). Wolin, in his typical fascist reading of Heidegger, renders this term as the "Shock-troops of Being" (Wolin 1990, 126).

32 Heidegger suggests various kinds of violence: "The violence of poetic speech, of thinking projection, of building configuration, of the action that creates states" (Heidegger 1961, 132; see also Heidegger 1962, 359-60/311-12). Heidegger, unfortunately, never explains the limits to the kinds of violence he envisions.

   For Plato, the physical violence referred to in the story is an allegorical reference to *Socratic method* or *productive dialogue*. If this is the case, perhaps Heidegger dismisses too quickly the possibilities of authentic communication between liberator and cave-dweller in his *literal* rendition of the events in the cave.

————. 1977. "The Question Concerning Technology." In *Martin Heidegger: Basic Writings*. Ed. David Farrell Krell. New York: Harper & Row.

————. 2002. *The Essence of Human Freedom: An Introduction to Philosophy*. Tr. Ted Sadler. New York: Continuum.

Vogel, Lawrence. 1994. *The Fragile "We": Ethical Implications of Heidegger's Being and Time*. Evanston: Northwestern University Press.

Wolin, Richard. 1990. *The Politics of Being: The Political Thought of Martin Heidegger*. New York: Columbia University Press.

8

VICO & THE NEW SCIENCE OF INTERPRETATION
BEYOND PHILOSOPHICAL HERMENEUTICS & THE
HERMENEUTICS OF SUSPICION

DAVID INGRAM

The tendency among contemporary intellectual historians to project the prejudices of their own society onto their subjects is not always a reflection of unconscious conceit. A case in point is the problem one encounters when trying to fathom what Jules Michelet once famously referred to as the "petit pandemonium" of Giambattista Vico's *Scienza Nuova* (Michelet 1843, 4-5).[1] Finding meaningful coherence in the often confusing architectonic of this *baroque* masterpiece has perforce compelled commentators to read into it the ideas of their own age. As Vico himself observed, "whenever men can form no idea of distant and unknown things, they judge them by what is familiar and at hand" (Vico 1968, par. 122-23). This "axiom" of interpretation, he believed, "points to the inexhaustible source of all the errors about the principles of humanity" evinced by the enlightened natural law theorists of his day, who sought to interpret the barbarian peoples of antiquity as if they were civilized philosophers (122-23).

Yet if we accept the argument advanced by Hans-Georg Gadamer (Gadamer 1993), the mediation of past and present that occurs whenever commentators judge the past from what is familiar at hand need not obstruct understanding and in fact may be necessary for it. The legitimate demand to understand an original thinker of Vico's stature *exactly* as his contemporaries understood him—or as he understood himself—can at best be partially realized. For a literal replication of Vico's understanding—replete with all its parochial anachronisms—would simply render him meaningless to contemporary readers. What Vico means by *scienza* and *coscienza*, to take one obvious example, does not

---

1 All references to Vico's *Scienza Nuova* will be taken from the numbered paragraphs of *The New Science of Giambattista Vico* (Vico 1968).

exactly correspond to the English expressions "science" and "knowledge." The Italian words with their Latin roots imply a kind of familiarity that seems far removed from our more modern concept of a technical expertise. And then there is Vico's own peculiar usage of these words, which recall Scholastic and Cartesian philosophical antecedents.

Given the futility of trying to understand him exactly as his contemporaries understood him, it is hardly surprising that contemporary commentators have interpreted Vico in light of the pressing issues confronting today's philosophers and historians. Thus, in what has now become a standard tribute paid to Vico, Ernst Cassirer and, more recently, Isaiah Berlin have argued that Vico's single greatest accomplishment was to have seen (however dimly) what later philosophers and historians writing over a century later would fully comprehend: that historical knowledge possesses an interpretative logic that is radically different from the causal-explanatory logic definitive of natural scientific knowledge.[2]

Assuming that Cassirer and Berlin are right, it is imperative that hermeneuticists who follow in the steps of Vico understand what kind of interpretative logic he may have had in mind. Vico refers to a kind of self-knowledge (*reflessione*) that is very different from the Cartesian inspection of the mind, conceived as a method for knowing *physical nature* (Vico 1968, par. 236). In his opinion, the only true knowledge we can obtain while "reflecting within the modifications of our very own mind" (*dentro le modificazione della medisima nostra mente umana*—par. 331) is knowledge of the modifications of *human* nature, conceived as a relatively invariant process of historical evolution and devolution.

Why does he say this? What is special about reflecting on the past that sets it apart from mathematical and conceptual reflection? Vico provides us with many clues about what he means by 'mind' (*mente*), 'reflection' (*reflessione*), 'common sense' (*sensus communis*), 'imagination' (*fantasia*), and other terms he uses that have a bearing on our query. For his own part, Berlin thinks that the kind of 'understanding' (*verstehen*) we find in Vico is broadly equivalent to the kind of *Empfindung* and *Nacherleben* (sympathetic and imaginative identification with and

---

2 Ernst Cassirer, e.g., argued that "the real value in Vico's 'philosophy of history' … and what he did see clearly, and what he defended against Descartes, was the methodological uniqueness and distinctive value of historical knowledge" (Cassirer 1960, 52). Cf. also Berlin 1976.

experiential reconstruction of) cultural worldviews of the sort later expounded by Wilhelm Dilthey and other historicists.[3]

However promising this conjecture might be for answering our question, Gadamer's criticism of Berlin's type of historicism suggests that Berlin might be mistaken. For if Gadamer is right, historicism tacitly invokes precisely the kind of Cartesian reflection that Vico himself repudiates (Gadamer 1993, 187-91, 220-37). How then, can we reconcile Berlin's interpretation of Vico—with its implication that Vico was an historicist *avant la lettre* and (accepting Gadamer's view of historicism) a "closet" Cartesian—with the near universal opinion that Vico's notion of historical understanding is *un*-Cartesian?

I argue that we cannot accept Berlin's interpretation, and furthermore that Vico must have had in mind a different notion of *verstehen* possessing a different logic of reflection. The most obvious candidate for such an alternative notion of historical understanding is the dialectical (or rather, dialogical) one proposed by none other than Gadamer himself. Indeed, it is Gadamer who draws our attention to aspects of Vico's account of *verstehen* that anticipate such a notion of historical understanding. These aspects chiefly revolve around the importance of common sense and rhetoric in providing (in the precise sense intended by Martin Heidegger) an *ontological*; viz., *pre-methodological*, grounding for mutual understanding (Gadamer 1993, 19-24). In Gadamer's opinion, Vico's awareness of this ontological grounding is manifested in his belief that practical judgment (Aristotelian *phronesis*) is rooted in a *pre-rational* common sense, or intuitive certainty of what is just and good, that is conditioned by both acculturation in shared tradition and the unique circumstances of the agent's situation; and it is precisely this mode of historical being that calls forth a dialogical interplay between tradition and the agent's situation.

Yet, despite anticipating a dialogical model of *verstehen* in his discussion of common sense and rhetoric, Vico did end up embracing a more historicist interpretation one. As Gadamer notes, in explaining

---

3 Although Berlin notes that Vico "does not account for our knowledge of other selves—individual or collective, living or dead—by invoking the language of empathy, or analogical reasoning, or intuition or participation in the unity of the World Spirit" (Berlin 1976, 27), he elsewhere notes that Johann Gottfried Herder's description of the historical sense with "sympathetic insight – one's capacity for *einfühlen* ('empathy') ... bears an uncanny resemblance to that of Vico" (187).

how historical understanding is possible, Vico conceives the relationship between agent and history along the model of technical making
(Aristotelian *techne*). In Gadamer's opinion, this mistaken view about
the relationship between the agent and his historical "substance" commits Vico to a kind of subjective idealism; the historian is understood
as methodically re-creating a past she has already created, simply in
virtue of participating in one and the same universal history-creating
humanity. Thus, for Vico as for Dilthey, *verstehen* designates not an
ontological mode of human existing underlying all knowledge and
action whatsoever, but a distinct type of historical knowing that still
retains a vestigial link to rational, Cartesian methodology (Gadamer
1993, 230, 276, 373, 572).[4]

Can we then not say that Vico is proposing an anti-Cartesian account of historical knowledge? Yes and no. Berlin's view that Vico's
account implies empathetic identification correctly identifies one aspect
of a *complex* ontological (dialectical) and methodological account of
verstehen, namely the importance of fantasy (imagination) in creating
analogies ("correspondences") between what are otherwise dissimilar
worldviews and, more important, between human history and natural
process (Berlin 1976, 73).[5] He is also right in noting that one such
analogy links the "modifications" of our own minds as we grow from
childhood to maturity to the "modifications" of the human spirit as it
grows from childlike barbarity to rational civility (45). Following Max
Fisch (Vico 1968, A4, xxiii), I would go even further in arguing that
Vico's historical hermeneutics appeals to a structural analogy between
phylogenetic and ontogenetic development that anticipates the "hermeneutics of suspicion" advocated by Jürgen Habermas.

This evolutionary scheme is clearly beholden to rational insight and
generalizing method, and indeed supports the view that reason is the
crowning achievement of human evolution. At the same time, there are
ontological aspects of Vico's critical hermeneutics that qualify his belief

4   The view I am defending here—that Vico's rejection of Cartesian (or analytic)
rationality does not entail a rejection of rational methodology as such—has
recently been defended by Leon Pompa. I differ from Pompa, however, in
arguing that, for Vico, the kind of rational methodology intrinsic to historical
knowledge is continuous with the non-analytic (or synthetic) logic of poetic
imagination, which is pre-rational in its origins. Cf. Pompa 1990.

5   For a good discussion of the importance of rhetoric, judgment, imagination,
and analogical reasoning in Vico's new science, see Schaeffer 1990.

in the progressive nature of this development. Although Vico intends to unmask the ideological misapprehension that worships the past and extols the timeless authority of tradition—a conservative bias that Habermas and other critical theorists ascribe to Gadamer's philosophical hermeneutics—he also intends to unmask the unreasonable pretensions of any critical reason that aspires to replace traditional authority.

On one hand, he clearly believes that particular religions, institutions, and traditions are not timeless instantiations of eternal verities, but are human fictions that reflect the historically conditioned biases of particular types of human beings and of the particular political and economic classes to which they belong. Only in the last stage of social evolution, what Vico calls the Age of Men, can it be said that such religions, institutions, and traditions take on a rational form that favors everyone's universal interests equally and impartially. On the other hand—anticipating Rousseau, Nietzsche, and Weber—Vico holds that too much civilization produces moral decay. By demanding that every belief be analyzable into clear and distinct ideas possessing demonstrable certainty, hyperbolic reason undermines faith in traditional authority. Subsequent skepticism regarding the intrinsic worth of moral values encourages an instrumental rationalism oriented exclusively toward the efficient pursuit of individual self-interest, the egoism of which dissolves society into that "war of all against all" so famously depicted by Hobbes. As noted above, Vico's own construal of history as a Promethean act of instrumental self-creation does not entirely escape this "dialectic of enlightenment," as Adorno and Horkheimer famously dubbed it. To the extent that it does, however, Vichean hermeneutics endeavors to show how even rational criticism must accept certain traditional authorities unquestioningly, on faith.

Vico principally has in mind faith in divine providence (that everything historical can be seen as fulfilling a higher meaning and purpose). Of course, for modern-day secular thinkers like myself, one might plausibly interpret Vico's appeal to providence as an appeal to a logic of development imminent within all incipient languages and cultures whose beneficent effects become apparent to us from the vantage point of enlightened hindsight. Yet, regardless of how we understand Vichean providence, it is clear from Vico's text that critical reason cannot be the highest or final epistemic authority (as Descartes would have it) but must itself rest on the timeless and eternal (and hence quasi-divine) authority of language and tradition (as Gadamer's philosophical hermeneutics would have it).

For it is this background of potential meaningfulness that guides all forms of understanding, historical or natural scientific.

1. Vico and Cartesianism

A convenient way to begin our examination of Vico's new science of historical understanding is by recalling his famous criticism of Descartes' criterion of truth and its elevation of the causal-explanatory methodology of the physical sciences as the *via regia* to knowledge. In his Seventh Inaugural Address (1708) entitled *De Nostri Temporis Studiorum Ratione* ('Of The Study Methods of Our Time'), Vico had argued that physical science is not the demonstrable science that Descartes thought it was, because if it were, then we – not God - would have made the laws of physics. By contrast, geometry is demonstrable precisely because it is we who have stipulated its definitions and axioms (Vico 1965, 23).

Vico's astonishing claim owes much to the venerable medieval doctrine that knowledge is "per caussas." . For Augustine and Aquinas, God's knowledge is of this sort: because He created the world, He knows its intrinsic purposes. Invoking the Renaissance analogy between God and Man, Vico attributes a similar knowledge to human beings, but only with regard to what *they* create. God—not man—is the creator of physical nature. Human beings, therefore, can only demonstrate *how* – not *why* - the laws of physics function the way they do. Experimental physics thus yields at best probabilistic knowledge. It is entirely different with geometry, since we have stipulated the conventions which define the operations and meanings of mathematical entities.

Two years later (1710), in *De Antequissima*, Vico announced his famous doctrine that "the true and the made are convertible" (*verum et factum convertuntur*). However, he had not yet established—as Hobbes in fact had already done—that demonstrable knowledge can be applied to the real (human) world. Geometry did not apply to this world, in his opinion, since it only articulated distinctions fabricated by the human mind that are valid, *stricto sensu*, only in the inner world of ideas. Physics remained the most reliable "knowledge" of the real world, which in his opinion was highly fallible, albeit not as fallible as history. Having not attained the level of nomothetic explanation, history amounted to little more than what (as he put it in his Third Inaugural Lecture of 1702) "a potter, a cook, a cobbler, a summoner, an auctioneer in Rome" might provide a philologist studying Roman artifacts (Vico 1911, 35 ff.). This dismissive attitude toward history as an arbitrary collection of particular facts—so reminiscent of Descartes' remark that historians of Rome know little more than Cicero's servant girl—would later be abandoned by Vico in 1712. However, by now he had already jettisoned the Cartesian criterion of truth, based on the perception of clear and distinct ideas, as being too subjective and prone to error. More important, he had begun to elevate common sense certainty *(il certo)* of the world as directly lived and experienced by people in their everyday practical lives to a level of knowledge beyond the mere subjective opinion to which Descartes had apparently consigned it.

Elaborating the radical change in Vico's thinking announced in the *Diritto Universale* (1720), the first edition of Vico's *Scienza Nuova* (1725) recombines these ideas in startling fashion. Historical science is now elevated above deductive knowledge of the mathematical type and inductive knowledge of the natural scientific type. In essence, historical knowledge combines the virtues of these separate modes of knowledge without their attendant defects. Like mathematical knowledge, historical knowledge is about something human beings have made – the languages, institutions, and actions that make up social reality – and hence can be known *per caussas* and with a degree of certainty aspiring to demonstrable truth. Like natural scientific knowledge, it is about a factual reality that transcends subjective experience and mere conceptual analysis. To cite Vico:

> As geometry, when it constructs the world of quantity out of its elements, or contemplates that world, is creating it for itself, just so does our Science [create for itself the world of nations], but with a reality greater by so much as the institutions having to do with human affairs are more real than points, lines surfaces, and figures are (Vico 1968, par. 349).

In short, because we ourselves have injected our own purposes into the stuff of history, and because even what we have unintentionally created in history—languages, customs, traditions, etc.—is meaningful to us from within our own mental and spiritual life—we can understand history as something intrinsically intelligible in a way that we cannot understand physical nature. To paraphrase Berlin, I may have some knowledge of how trees and ants look and behave based upon external observation, but I cannot know what it means to *be* them in the same way I know—from the inside, as it were—what it means to *be* a human being (Berlin 1976, 23).

2. The Possibility of Historical Understanding: Combining Philosophical Reason and Aesthetic Imagination in the New Science

What is this new kind of historical self-knowledge that Vico is supposedly proposing? Berlin thinks he has an answer. Referring Vichean *reflissione* (self-knowledge) to the operations of *fantasia* (imagination), he submits that the kind of "imaginative reconstruction" characteristic of Vico's conception of historical understanding amounts to a kind of mental transposition into and identification with the otherwise alien worldviews of past epochs. In short, like later historicists in the German Romantic school, Vico is said to believe that present and past epochs are radically incommensurable, incomparable, and even untranslatable—so much so that Vico would vehemently deny Leonardo Bruni's claim, so typical of Renaissance humanism, that "Nothing is said in Greek that cannot be said in Latin" (Berlin 1976, 139).

Why attribute to Vico such an extreme—and implausible—view of incommensurability? The view is patently self-defeating, since one would have had to translate Greek and Latin into one's own language in order to know that they *were* incommensurable (untranslatable), thereby rendering them commensurable (Davidson 1984). Berlin himself offers scant evidence to show that Vico actually believed that cultural worldviews were this incommensurable. Vico's adamant refusal to accept the notion of a timeless human nature replete with a timeless natural law to govern it is not evidence that he held this radical view. For the *New Science* is very much written from the standpoint of a jurist who *did* believe in a natural law common to all peoples—albeit a law of historical evolution. To understand the present as an outgrowth of the past amounts to understanding the past as an anticipation of the present. This way of translating the *mente* of the past into the *mente* of the present preserves rather than obliterates the difference between past and present. The natural law theorists of Vico's day, however, did not translate the past into the present: rather, they simply projected the present onto the past. To cite Vico:

> The three princes of this doctrine [of natural law—D.I.], Hugo Grotius, John Selden, and Samuel Pufendorf, should have taken their start from the beginnings of the *gentes*, where their subject matter begins. But all three of them err together in this respect, by beginning in the middle; that is, with the latest times of the civilized nations (and thus with men enlightened by fully natural reason), from which the philosophers emerged and rose to meditation of a perfect idea of justice (Vico 1968, par. 394).

In contrast to the static notion of human nature appealed to by the natural law doctrines of his time, Vico's "natural law of gentes" rests upon a dynamic conception of human nature and of human nations (*gentes*). Both terms—*natura* and *genti* (the Italian plural of *gente*, whose Latin roots are *gens* and the plural nominative *gentes*)—refer to birth (*natio/(nascimento)*) and genesis, or growth and development (Vico 1968, par. 147).

By 'nation' Vico means a distinctive group of people who descend from common institutional origins peculiar to themselves, viz., institutions that are not shared by others and which develop according to an internal logic impelled mainly by internal class struggles. Vico himself restricts his study to the "gentile" nations for whom, unlike the Jews, the truth of God's providence was not revealed once and for all and who must therefore historically evolve toward this ideal state without ever completely attaining it (Vico 1968, par. 167, 365). The descendants of Ham and Japheth and the non-Hebraic descendants of Shem are described by Vico as having lost all language and civil institution and being reduced to utter bestiality (par. 369). The rebirth of these giant *bestioni* and *ferini* into a nation—or rather, "*un mondo delle nazioni*"—begins with their providential discovery of matrimonial and religious institutions. From that point on, each nation runs though three successive ages, or stages of natural genesis: that of Gods, that of heroes, and that of men. Only in the last age do human beings *approximately* achieve (for however fleeting a moment) the "rational humanity" that is "the true and proper nature of man" (par. 973), namely of "human reason fully developed" *and* reconciled to faith (par. 326, 924). Because this end is an ideal that is never completely achieved, the natural (although perhaps not inevitable) fate of most nations is dissolution and return to state of barbarism, whence the cycle of ages begins anew, albeit at a higher level.[6]

---

6 Vico believes that, following the flourishing of enlightenment during late antiquity and continuing through the fall of the Roman Empire, a new

Vico's pointed reference to a "natural law of gentes" common to all gentile peoples thus refers primarily to the fact that all peoples run through one and the same universal course of historical evolution and that all peoples, regardless of their peculiar differences, preserve and maintain themselves through institutions of marriage, burial, and religion (Vico 1968, par. 332-33). The important point to note in this adumbration is that, according to Vico, these universals of human society did not emerge through cultural diffusion or communication between different peoples, since the latter are "separately founded because remote from each other in time and space" (par. 332-33). Therefore, "the common ground of truth" underlying "uniform ideas originating among entire peoples unknown to each other" (par. 144) must be divine providence.

I will have more to say below about the importance of providence in Vico's new science. Presently it suffices to note the severity of the problem Vico has set for himself. Different nations may share a common natural law of development, but such a common ground of understanding will not aid in understanding earlier stages of human understanding that are so radically different from our enlightened nature. As Vico himself puts it:

> To discover the way in which this first human thinking arose in the gentile world, we encountered exasperating difficulties which have cost us the research of a good twenty years. [We had] to descend from these human and refined natures of ours to those quite wild and savage natures, which we cannot at all imagine and can comprehend with only great effort (par. 338).

In the passage cited above, Vico affirms that pre-civilized ways of understanding can be understood—the new science is proof of this—albeit with great difficulty. This affirmation alone suffices to rebut the incommensurability thesis attributed to him by Berlin. Still, the problem remains how radically different ways of understanding can be made commensurable from the vantage point of the historian. The key to bridging this gap—and the key to understanding what kind of historical understanding Vico may have had in mind—resides in his belief that

---

Christian era inaugurates the cycle of ages once more. Unlike its Egyptian and Greco-Roman precursors, this *ricorso* of historical development begins with a barbarism (the Dark Ages) that inherits a superior poetic wisdom, in that the God it worships is more human and morally superior than the pagan Gods of antiquity.

all modern languages (viz., rationalized prose languages whose clear and distinct conceptual distinctions between words facilitate useful communication) contain residues of their poetic past: "We find that the principles of these origins both of languages and of letters lie in the fact that the early gentile peoples, by a demonstrated necessity of nature, were poets who spoke in poetic characters" (par. 34).

The poetic wisdom of the divine and heroic ages of humanity consisted of creating the symbols (at first hieroglyphics) and metaphors out of which human institutions and social relationships are created. In Vico's opinion, these symbols and images worked through a logic that bore some resemblance to what Aristotle called the *ars topica*, the art of hitting upon common places (*topoi*), or analogies for fashioning the most rhetorically convincing (i.e., probable) explanation for some fact. Rather than using cause and effect to explain things, primitive human beings used resemblance. Things that belonged together by resemblance also had magical affinities with respect to their properties that could be used to explain their behavior.

For Vico, primitive humans rely upon a kind of "corporeal imagination" to invent "sensory topics," or "imaginative universals." Such humans naturally take what is most familiar to themselves—their own bodies and its feelings—as a reference point for inventing fables about nature, whose properties seem to resemble the properties of human action. To illustrate such anthropomorphizing: Vico notes how startling sounds such as thunder would be construed "in the first place" as a human-like grumble or shout—the voice of the sky but also of God, or Jove (Vico 1968, par. 377). The fright and subsequent flight to cave shelters—the origination of all settled, civilized life, according to Vico—was the first instinctual reflex of a mortal fear of God. Thus was born religion. By further analogical reasoning these early cave dwellers later interpreted the fact of settled life as something divinely sanctioned. Here begins the genesis of an heroic ethos that would explicitly link settled property with noble, divine-like authority and power. Presuming themselves to be descended from the Gods and the first race of mortal heroes, these nobles imagined themselves to be—their mortality in this world notwithstanding—as divine-like and immortal as the eternal and unchanging natural deities governing them. Hence they would naturally seek to guarantee their eternal patrimony through marriage laws establishing patrilineal descent. Likewise, they would establish burial laws and rites as further proof of their immortality.

Thus, Vico concludes that it is through a poetic logic of metaphorical association—not through an analytic logic of abstract reasoning—that the three fundamental institutions of religion, marriage, and burial that ground the possibility of law, morality, and society are instituted. As he notes, heroic emblems attest to this primitive amalgamation by analogically condensing religion, property, and legal authority into a single symbol or metaphor. The heraldic device of an oak tree, for instance, refers to noble descent (symbolized by fixed roots), settled property (symbolized by the shelter of a forest canopy), religion (symbolized by the binding together, or *religio*, of branches around a single trunk), and law (symbolized by an acorn, whose archaic Latin root is related to both God and law, or *ius*).

To return to our original query, the problem of historical understanding amounts to bridging the gap separating the modern historian's rational understanding, which is informed by the clear conceptual distinctions operant within ordinary speech, from the primitive agent's poetic understanding, which is informed by the collapsing of such distinctions necessary for creating original classifications and linkages based on superficial resemblances. In the *New Science*, philology provides one condition for bridging this gap, philosophy the other.

> Philosophy contemplates reason, whence comes knowledge of the true; philology observes that of which human choice is the author, whence comes consciousness of the certain. This axiom by its second part includes among the philologians all the grammarians, historians, critics, who have occupied themselves with the study of the languages and the deeds of peoples: deeds at home, as in their customs and laws, and deeds abroad, as in their wars, peaces, alliances, travels, commerce. This same axiom shows how the philosophers failed by half in not giving certainty to their reasonings by appeal to the authority of the philologians, and likewise how the latter failed by half by not taking care to give their authority the sanction of truth by appeal to the reasonings of the philosophers (Vico 1968, par. 138-40).

According to Vico, philology is a branch of *coscienza*, conscious experience and understanding of particular facts, including facts about particular historical human beings and their particular societies. *Coscienza* is capable of achieving certainty (*il certo*), either by the direct and unquestioned sensory experience of physical nature or by the direct and unquestioned understanding of language and other institutions. This is what Vico means by common sense (*sensus communis*) or "judgment without reflection." Here is where Vico draws his important distinction between two types of common sense: inner and outer. Again, although we can be said to have direct and indubitable sensory experience of physical nature—however rationally fallible it might be—it is, for Vico, of a different kind than the direct and indubitable understanding we have of the language and institutions that constitute our lives "from the inside." Indeed, if our common sense understanding of language and life can never aspire to the kind of rationally demonstrable certainty and universal truth that Vico associates with that other human science—geometry—it is nonetheless capable of achieving a certainty and demonstrability greater than that of physics.

Although Vico speaks of common sense as providing the kind of pre-reflective certitude philologists can claim for their findings, he elsewhere (as noted above) asserts that common sense qua common designates a kind of universal understanding that lies at the origin of all languages, no matter how different they are from one another. In this respect, philology can aid philosophy in its search for universal truths and, more important, can aid historical understanding by revealing a "common language" bridging what are otherwise radically distinct nations and epics.

> There must in the nature of human institutions be a mental language common to all nations, which uniformly grasps the substance of things feasible in human social life, and expresses it with as many diverse modifications as these same things have diverse aspects. A proof of this is afforded by proverbs or maxims of vulgar wisdom, in which substantially the same meanings find as many diverse expressions as there are nations ancient and modern. This common mental language is proper to our Science, by whose light linguistic scholars will be enabled to construct a mental vocabulary common to all the various articulate languages living and dead (par.161).

Clearly, philology is able to construct a common language bridging modern (conceptual) and ancient (poetic) languages because the former contains traces of the latter in its own etymology. Today's dead metaphors were yesterday's living metaphors and as such reveal something about the lives and institutions of earlier humans (par. 152). Indeed, according to Vico, today's clear and distinct ideas merely condense yesterday's metaphors:

> Take for example, "the blood boils in my heart," based on a property natural, eternal, and common to all mankind. They took the blood, the boiling, and the heart, and then made of them a single word, as it were, a genus, called in Greek *stomachos*, in Latin *ira*, and in Italian *collera* (par. 460).

Although philology goes far toward bridging the gap between present and past, it cannot succeed alone in this endeavor. Philosophy is needed to provide direct and rational insight into the universal laws governing the evolution from past to present implicit in the *corsi* run by all nations. How it accomplishes this is far from clear. Vico mentions that philosophers sometimes cognize universals by means of abstracting common properties from a comparison of particulars. Thus, he notes that before the Athenians enacted their laws they came to agreement independently about their utility, which agreement was then adumbrated by Socrates "by induction" in the form of "collecting uniform particulars which go to make up""intelligible genera or abstract universals" (Vico 1968, par., 1040). In his introductory commentary to the third edition of the *New Science*, Max Fisch also seems to imply that this is how philosophical reason supplements philology (Fisch, 1744, xxx). However, as Berlin rightly notes, that couldn't be the whole story, since induction based on observed similarities yields at best probabilistic "knowledge" of *how* things happen and not the demonstrable understanding of *why* things must happen that Vico claims for his historical science (Berlin 1976, 83).

Vico must therefore be understood as saying that philosophical reason takes up the "certain" findings of philological understanding and the less certain probabilistic findings of comparative history in rationally intuiting the universal stages of historical development. Just how this is possible—if God and not humanity is the creator of these natural laws—is unclear. As Habermas notes, Vico denies that historical agents make history with the same degree of transparent consciousness that God (for whom conceiving is creating) makes nature, here understood to include human nature and its historical laws. Like Hegel's cunning of reason (*List der Vernunft*), Vico's God makes historical agents accomplish higher ends without their conscious consent and participation. Furthermore, Vico's cyclical understanding of historical laws conforms more closely to the pagan view of "naturalized" history than to the Christian (or salvationist) view traditionally associated with the idea of providence. Since history does not progress in any straightforward linear manner, it is difficult for Vico to sustain that history as such reveals a clear and certain, rational pattern (or logic) of providential lawfulness (Habermas 1973, 244-247).

The last problem may indeed be insuperable. However, if we leave aside the problem of cyclical *ricorsi* and focus exclusively on the laws governing historical *corsi*, which do reveal a progressive development, a solution to the first problem may be at hand. Anticipating the absolute idealism of Hegel, Vico may have believed that human beings could participate directly in the divine mind. This idea seems less far-fetched when we recall that, for Vico, humans create religion—and God—in their own image (Vico 1968, par. 367). Like Hegel, Vico might then be understood as equating God with the human spirit, so that the providential *corsi* run by all nations would be a human creation fully knowable by them. Knowing themselves as historical beings would then be tantamount to knowing the self-actualization of God in history.

Such an intriguing solution to the problem of universal historical knowledge transcends the scope of our epistemological inquiry, which is focused on the possibility of a more mundane solution. One solution, alluded to earlier, appeals to the fact that analytical reason builds upon and incorporates the accomplishments of poetic wisdom. Just as Immanuel Kant would later argue that analytic reason (abstraction and induction) already presupposes synthetic (transcendental) reason, which deploys the schematism of the imagination to unify discrete sensory qualia into image-types (or schemas), so Vico argues that abstracting universal laws presupposes analogical reasoning, which creates imaginative universals. Following yet another clue suggested by Kant, such analogical reasoning can be compared to a kind of *reflective* judgment, which discovers universals (or types, such as "the beautiful") based upon feelings and intuitions associated with particulars.[7]

Drawing from an example that is closer to Vico's own experience as a jurist, judges defer to reflective judgment whenever they seek to discover the proper rule under which to subsume cases that are susceptible to conflicting interpretations. Cases that are especially recalcitrant to subsumption under given laws may call forth an additional act of reflective judgment in which the laws themselves are reinterpreted. A case in point is the right to privacy in American jurisprudence. This

---

7 Kant's examination of the amphibolies of reflection in the First Critique and his account of reflective judgment in the Third Critique further extend his treatment of synthetic reason. For discussion of this aspect of Kant's thought see Ingram 1985 and 1988.

right was created (or "discovered") in the landmark case *Griswold v. Connecticut* (1965) by a process of analogical reasoning, in which the freedom of couples to engage in family planning (including gaining access to birth control) was compared to earlier constitutional rulings regarding freedom from invasive search and seizure, freedom of speech, and other "similar" cases.

The important point to bear in mind is that the analogical reasoning deployed by jurists implicates a kind of non-analytical reflection. When Vico says that historical knowledge presupposes philosophical reason, it might very well be this kind of *aesthetic and inventive* reflection he has in mind. Indeed, in the next section we shall see that it must be this kind of reflection. But in that case, at least one form of enlightened reason *does* possess an elective affinity with pre-enlightened poetic wisdom. Such an affinity would bridge the gap between enlightened philosophical understanding and poetic wisdom. And it would also confirm one of the central tenets of philosophical hermeneutics as Gadamer understands it. For Gadamer, Vico's major contribution resides less in espousing a method of historical understanding than in preserving an ontological truth about human being in general: that the basis of practical reason (what Aristotle calls *phronesis*) is none other than the art of sound judgment cultivated on the basis of common sense (Gadamer 1993, 19-24). In other words, to the extent that any act of understanding involves the judicious art of asking just the right questions (i.e., of applying what one already knows to discover what one does not already know), any knowledge whatsoever can be said to rest upon the re-appropriation of an effective history, sedimented in tradition and language. Sound judgment of this kind cannot be exercised through methodical analysis, but must be acquired through experience.

But that cannot be all there is to historical understanding. Vico insists that such historical understanding also presupposes a method – or more precisely, knowledge of a sequential, law-like progression – that enables the historian to understand earlier forms of society as in some sense analogous to his or her own childhood. So construed, the new science deploys a pre-methodological form of analogical reasoning to discover a methodical form of explanation and understanding. For Vico this methodical form of understanding presupposes that social evolution (phylogenesis) replicates the stages of maturation from childhood (ontogenesis). Perhaps Vico believed that our lived participation in the natural cycle of birth, maturation, and death provided an analogue to understanding the necessity of a similar cycle in the birth, maturation and decline of nations (Vico 1968, par. 349). He himself draws the analogy between childhood and poetic wisdom, on one hand, and maturity and philosophical wisdom, on the other, as partial confirmation of his thesis (par. 186, 213, 408, 412-13, 447, 454, 498, 1032). The language, logic, and thought-processes of the earliest peoples—the "children of the human race" (par. 498)—replicate the language, logic, and thought-processes of childhood. Because we modern rationalists also passed through this stage, we can be said to have run through the *corso* that all nations run through in our own lifetime, and so can be said to be co-author of it to a degree that provides a modicum of historical knowledge *per caussas*.

Establishing an analogy between phylogenesis and ontogenesis might indeed be necessary for a speculative philosopher seeking to articulate a universal history of humanity. Whether such an analogy can be sustained is, of course, a matter of considerable contention on which Vico himself sheds very little light. Be that as it may, for our purposes the question about social evolution revolves around the problem of historical understanding simpliciter and not merely around the problem of establishing a universal course through which all nations traverse.

3. The Contemporary Relevance of Vico's
Science of Historical Understanding

Before we examine the hypothesis that Vico's historical hermeneutics rests upon a theory of social evolution, let us re-examine more closely why it cannot rest upon the historicist methodology attributed to it by Berlin. It is true that Vico sometimes sounds like an historicist when he talks about the radical gulf separating poetic from rational modes of understanding. The impression he gives that worldviews and modes of understanding are self-contained is further reinforced by his belief that the gentile nations developed their own peculiar common sense without communicating with one another (Vico 1968, par. 145).

Historicism is Cartesian in its view that the subject and object of knowledge are separated by such an immense gulf that knowledge can only be achieved by the knower "methodically" bracketing out her subjectivity in an effort to conform to the object. More precisely, historicists endeavor to bring about a true correspondence with their object by critically checking the effects of their own worldview, as these are shaped by language and culture. In their opinion, once the historian has cleared her head of all contemporary prejudices, she will be in a position to sympathetically enter into the mind of her subject. If this seems impossible, she can by-pass the deep, substantive differences she finds incomprehensible in her subject and, like a natural scientist using the inductive method, focus on the superficial formal resemblances between it and her own worldview.

In that case, historical science would be imitating natural science. This model of historical science, famously defended in the last century by Karl Popper and Carl Hempel, is deeply problematic for reasons we have already adduced. The universal laws that a naturalized historical science discovers through a comparative analysis of particular historical events will be useless in understanding why particular events had to happen the way they did. Explanations of particular historical events by appeal to general laws will never succeed because it is precisely the particular circumstances surrounding them—and above all, the particular purposes of the agents who made them—that enable us to understand why they had to happen the way they did. Stated differently, subsuming a particular event under a general covering law provides something less than a genuine causal explanation of the event, and really amounts to showing nothing more than how it resembles other events. In his own way, Vico seems to have already anticipated this objection to the covering-law method of historical explanation in his insistence that a true historical cause must refer to a meaningful purpose of an agent, be it human or superhuman.

In sum, although Vico often appeals to the comparative method in defending the universal patterns common to all nations at a certain stage of development (Vico 1968, par. 344-45), he cannot consistently hold that this "abstract" knowledge is the true knowledge afforded by his new science. Doing so would contradict his epistemological axiom that true knowledge explains why things happen *per caussas*, which is possible only because the knower has in some sense meaningfully and intentionally participated in the creation of what she knows. The use of observable associations between discrete types of events manifesting a certain stochastic frequency, as David Hume rightly noted, cannot explain, with the kind of "demonstrable necessity" Vico demands of his science, why one nation passes from one stage of social evolution to another. Such historical necessity, Vico says, must rather be understood in the first place as internally caused by the freely willed intentions of human beings and, in the second place, by the unintended consequences of such intentional acts. Such consequences must in turn be understood as serving higher ends vis-à-vis the meaningful realization of institutions that are in turn logically necessary for the meaningful realization of a fully human—and rational—way of life. In the last instance, this amounts to showing how one stage of understanding logically implies and irreversibly builds upon its predecessor—a kind of teleology that Vico attributes to "divine providence."

If the model of understanding appealed to by Vico is not the methodical suspension of subjective biases and imaginative identification described by historicists, then what is it? As we have seen, Vico's treatment of the connection between common sense, rhetoric, and judgment suggests that the kind of historical understanding he has in mind is closer to the *pre-methodological*, ontological understanding articulated by Heideggerians like Gadamer. According to Gadamer, we can never methodically rise above the parochial languages and traditions that have shaped our understanding because, as Vico well understood, they form the certain (if *conceptually* pre-reflective) common sense background to all understanding. However, saying that understanding is conditioned by the present does not prevent us from understanding the archaic past (or for that matter, other cultures). For the present and past are held together by a common and continuous culture whose changes in the course of historical reinterpretation work to preserve its authority; and even widely diverse cultures share a potential for mutual understanding (what Gadamer calls the speculative dimension of language) based on something analogous to Vico's pre-reflective common sense (Vico 1968, par. 356).

Vico warns us that historians must be careful not to "project" uncritically their "modern" and "enlightened" assumptions onto their archaic subjects. But self-critical understanding need not—and as we have seen, cannot—involve the wholesale bracketing of cultural and linguistic prejudices. Rather, since we must engage our parochial prejudices in understanding—they are, after all, the only familiar reference points we have for interrogating the world around us—we must engage them with the subject matter of the archaic text itself, in the form of simulated dialogue involving mutual questioning. Here understanding will be oriented toward a kind of agreement or mutual understanding, in which the original meaning of the archaic text is nonetheless reinterpreted—or rephrased—within the familiar language of the historian. So construed, historical interpretation will not be merely reproductive—preserving the truth of tradition in some timeless and unchanging form—but will also be poetic and creative.

As noted above, there are many indications within Vico's text that suggest that he shares the basic tenets of this philosophical hermeneutics. To begin with, he embraces the fact that poetic language creates and constitutes all meaning and identity, and so provides the *Ursprung* from which reason itself springs (Vico 1968, par. 362). Too, he thinks we can communicate with the past from the standpoint of the present—and learn from it. This communication is implicitly dialogical, since Vico believes that enlightened historical understanding can learn to appreciate the basic truth embedded in cultural tradition, namely that reason itself rests upon a providential authority that transcends its powers of analysis and clarification.

However, it would seem that Vico's new science goes beyond philosophical hermeneutics in several important respects. First, it does not vest *particular* traditional *beliefs* with a timeless claim to authority and wisdom. On the contrary, it unmasks their ideological pretensions by showing that they originate in ignorance (Vico 1968, par. 375) and class domination. Such ideological justifications of domination may be necessary in early stages of human evolution, but they are deceptions nonetheless—falsehoods concealing the rational truth implicit in Christian humanism (par. 375). Second, the new science is able to do this partly because it appeals to a view of historical evolution that sees the rational age of men—the Cartesian age of clear and distinct ideas—as a secular instantiation of Christian humanism, which articulates the universal equality and freedom of all (reasonable) men as having been made in the image of God. Finally, because the new science is itself a product of this age, it must incorporate within its mode of historical understanding the critical methods of philosophical science that enable it to expose the deceptions of earlier ages.

4. Between Critical and Redemptive Hermeneutics: Vichean Science as Humanistic Praxis and Theological Consolation

What critical methods did Vico have in mind? They could not be the methods of conceptual analysis proposed by Descartes, since these require abstracting from historical understanding. Nonetheless, there is something vaguely Cartesian about Vico's description of historical methods. These methods involve rendering "clear and distinct" (par. 390) certain "modifications of the mind" (par. 349) that are objectified in the historical traces of our own language. Vichean science begins by analyzing the rich data of history (through "a severe analysis of human thoughts"[par. 347]), in order to uncover certain universal and unquestioned principles—principles, to be sure, whose certainty is guaranteed not by pure reason demanding indubitable certainty but rather by a kind of pre-reflective common sense establishing what is beyond question. With a kind of geometrical rigor, it deduces from these principles—of religion, marriage, and burial—something like a necessary and universal sequence of developmental stages, or what he elsewhere calls a "history of ideas" (par. 347). This history, in turn, enables the new science to prove the rational superiority of Christian humanism in comparison to pre-rational religion (early Christianity included), which justifies hierarchy and inequality.

Vico's "hermeneutics of suspicion"—the unmasking of ideology as subterfuge for class domination—proceeds by linking the understanding of meanings to the explanation of causes. The historical agent's purposes that lend action meaning produce both intended and unintended effects, and so are causes in this sense. However, such purposes have concealed within them ulterior meanings and aims that are not intended—indeed, are not even known—by the agent. The religious myths that validate the heroic natural law that "might makes right" are really an expression of a particular human caste system and not a true depiction of divinity. But this deeper meaning is concealed from both the powerful who invoke the law to advance their ends as well as from the weak who submit to it in violation of their ends. Likewise, the fact that such a caste system and its corresponding ideological form represent a necessary stage in human evolution is also concealed from them. These two sets of deeper meanings—the genesis of natural law out of contingent systems of human domination and the genesis of a stage of social evolution according to a necessary logic—act to compel human action in some causally necessary way.

Scholars such as Paul Ricoeur and Jürgen Habermas have convincingly argued that the kind of hermeneutics of suspicion that I have attributed to Vico's new science can be compared to psychoanalytic interpretation.[8]

8 See Ricoeur 1970 and Habermas 1971.

Like Freudian psychoanalysis, Vichean science approaches its subject matter with suspicion: the literal or surface meaning of a neurotic episode or social ideology is misunderstood or not understood at all by the agent, so that what she thinks she is doing does not correspond to what she is really doing. Her behavior therefore bears the trace of an unconscious motivation that "compels" her to behave in mysterious ways.

It bears repeating that this is precisely the kind of concealed purpose that, according to Vico, causally compels historical agents to bring about—against their own free will—the higher purposes ordained by Providence and the developmental logic implicit in the idea of humanity. In this sense, historical agents both are and are not the agents of history. They become fully agents only after they understand the deeper humanity animating their own behavior. The *New Science* aids in this endeavor in two ways. First, it vindicates religion, moral moderation, and faith in the immortality of the soul by showing that they are the certain and unquestionable presuppositions underlying any form of human life. Second, it shows how the achievement of rational humanism—indeed, the very science that criticizes unquestioned presuppositions—necessarily unfolds out of these very same taken-for-granted, commonsense institutions.

But of course the new science is more than just "rational theology." It is rational theology used to unmask ideology. Just as psychoanalysis depends upon a (mythic) theory of ontogenetic (psycho-sexual) development in order to explain how the agent's neurotic episodes can be understood in terms of a failed attempt at resolving crises that necessarily unfold within the hidden drama of sexual maturation, so too Vichean history depends upon a theory of social evolution to explain how society's ideological compulsions can be understood in terms of failed attempts at being fully human – or fully adult. Habermas (following Alfred Lorenzer) has shown how such compulsions can be understood in terms of a model of "distorted communication" (Habermas 1971, 256). Neurotic behavior is a "symbolic" re-enactment of a childhood trauma written in the paleo-symbolic code of the unconscious in which distinct persons, things, and events from childhood are "poetically" condensed or displaced through use of metonym, synecdoche, or metaphor. One must have an understanding of this language—and the various manifestations it assumes in the course of psycho-sexual development—to decipher the hidden meaning of the neurotic's behavior, which is both repetition of and fixation on an earlier infantile stage of development.

Once this meaning is revealed to the neurotic, her behavior ceases to be compelled by the logic of blind causality and can be rationally and freely controlled.

A similar kind of distorted communication seems to explain ideo-logically rigidified behavior. The mechanical enactment of destructive (masochistic and sadistic) behavior—for instance, the regression of supposedly enlightened individuals into a fascist movement—can be explained in terms of the hypnotic effect that pre-rational propaganda has on the average mind. Fascist propaganda is similar to those "mute" mytho-poetic (hieroglyphic) languages spoken by priests and children. These languages, too, condense feeling and thought; play upon sublimi-nal, unconscious associations between sexual desire and violence; and deliberately conflate fantasy with fact, fact with norm, and norm with personal charisma, in such a way as to resist rational questioning. As Vico notes, such languages are more like divine incantations—or ritu-als—than meaningful utterances containing clear referential (factual) meanings and interactive intentions.

Vico's intriguing idea that each stage of social evolution possesses its own distinctive level of linguistic, logical, and cognitive-moral develop-ment remarkably anticipates well-known theories of child development advanced by Jean Piaget and, more recently, Habermas. According to Habermas, the process of cultural and societal rationalization that ac-companies social evolution can be understood as a process of "linguis-tification" whereby primitive, mythopoetic modes of language use are gradually supplanted by more prosaic and utilitarian forms of rational communication (Habermas 1984, 67-69, 72 ff.; 1984, 3-111). This has important implications for Habermas's approach to ideology critique. Whereas early "poetic" modes of linguistic usage collapse distinctions between facts, values, and personal expressions/fantasies—a syndrome that still survives in early modern conceptions of natural, divine-com-mand theories of natural law—modern "prosaic" communication separates them out according to their own irreducibly distinct logics. Because scientific-descriptive, legal-moral, and aesthetic-expressive utterances are now treated as if they were logically distinct from one another, they are uniquely susceptible to criticism by appeal to "clear and distinct" standards of evidence (Habermas 1987, 188-97).

The centrality of clear and distinct standards of evidence to rational critique returns us to our original theme: the manner in which Vichean science both is and is not Cartesian. As we have seen, even the hermeneutics of suspicion must stop short of demanding absolute clarity and indubitable certainty with respect to its subject matter. Ideology critique can never aspire to complete transparent understanding of historical meaning because even it must take for granted some unquestioned presuppositions. Furthermore, when pure reason becomes uncritical of its own hyperbolic pretensions—demanding absolute justification for every conceivable authority—we descend into a kind of Jacobin Terror in which all culture becomes suspect. Such "barbarism of reflection," as Vico refers to it, is irrational because it is contrary to what any self-critical reason could reasonably demand.

In sum, critical reason becomes "redemptive" at the point in which it becomes self-evident that meaning arises out of a pre-rational act of poetic imagination.[9] For theologically inspired critical theorists like Vico and Walter Benjamin, language represents a sedimentation of anonymous, meaning-creating syntheses that can never be replicated by human beings acting rationally and deliberatively. The rhetorical power of modern language owes an infinite debt to a poetic past whose roots are essentially pre-rational. True understanding, therefore, will respect and preserve that past, even as it criticizes it.

Works Cited

Berlin, Isaiah. 1976. *Vico and Herder: Two Studies in the History of Ideas.* London: Hogarth Press.

Cassirer, Ernst. 1960. *The Logic of the Humanities,* trans. C.S. Howe. New Haven: Yale University Press.

Gadamer, Hans-Georg. 1993. *Truth and Method,* 2nd revised edition. New York: Continuum.

Habermas, J. 1971. *Knowledge and Human Interests.* Boston: Beacon Press.

———. 1973. *Theory and Practice.* Boston: Beacon Press.

———. 1979. "Consciousness-Raising or Redemptive Criticism: The Contemporaneity of Walter Benjamin." *New German Critique* 17, 30-59.

———. 1984. *The Theory of Communicative Action, Volume One: Reason and the Rationalization of Society.* Boston: Beacon Press.

———. 1987. *The Theory of Communicative Action, Volume Two: Lifeworld and System.* Boston: Beacon Press.

---

9   Habermas acknowledges this essential limit to ideology critique: in his essay, "Consciousness-Raising or Redemptive Criticism: The Contemporaneity of Walter Benjamin" (1979).

Ingram, David. 1985. "Hegel and Leibniz on Individuation." *Kant-Studien* 76/4, 420-435.

———. 1988. "The Post-Modern Kantianism of Arendt." *Review of Metaphysics* 41, 51-57.

Michelet, J. 1843. *Histoire romaine. République.* Tome I. 2e edition. Paris: Hachette.

Pompa, L. 1990. *Vico: A Study of the New Science*, 2nd edition. Cambridge: Cambridge University Press.

Ricoeur, Paul. 1970. *Freud and Philosophy: An Essay on Interpretation.* New Haven: Yale University Press.

Schaeffer, John D. 1990. *Sensus Communis: Vico, Rhetoric, and the Limits of Relativism.* Durham, NC.: Duke University Press.

Vico, Giambattista. 1911-41. *Oratio*, III, *Opere*, vol. 1, trans. Fausto Nicolini. Bari: Laterza.

———. 1965. *On the Study Methods of Our Time*, trans. Elio Gianturco. New York: Bobbs-Merrill.

———. 1968. *The New Science of Giambattista Vico*, trans. Bergin and Fisch. Ithaca, N.Y.: Cornell University Press.

9

SPEAKING TO THE WORLD
THROUGH HUSSERL & MERLEAU-PONTY

D. R. KOUKAL

Introduction: why must phenomenology speak to the world?

Some years ago, I was asked why phenomenology would want to speak to the rest of the world. In my view, the implications of the question were two-fold: why would people want to hear what phenomenologists have to say, and why would we phenomenologists want to talk to non-phenomenologists anyhow? I remember that my reply at the time was not especially articulate, because I had thought the answer self-evident.

Here is a more lucid response to this question. Husserl makes it clear that phenomenology seeks to constitute a more fundamental meaning of the world by temporarily "bracketing" the various presuppositions of the different realms of human activity for the purpose of intuiting the essential structures of experience that appear to a consciousness purified by the method of the *epoché*. Husserl also makes it clear that equally essential to phenomenology's task is the communication of phenomenology's insights to the various regions of human activity which it claims to ground through *its* activity. In doing so, phenomenology invites all of humanity to return to "the things themselves" that underlie all of our various preconceptions of these things, so that it may have a deeper understanding of the lived world common to all. *This* is why phenomenology must speak to the world—to live up to its own claim as being a first philosophy that contacts life and does so directly, thereby allowing us the possibility of seeing it again, as if for the first time. This is often forgotten about phenomenology: it is not only about *intuition*, but also about *expression*.

But—there is always the "but"— this means that phenomenology must employ a manner of expression that somehow transcends its own region of activity to speak in a multitude of *meaningful* ways to other, radically different regions of human activity. This goes to the question of *how* phenomenology must speak to the world, which in turn raises the problems involved in the *mobility of phenomenological meaning*. These are the chief problems to be investigated in this essay, which are three-fold. First, I will explore the problem of conveying phenomenological insights among practicing phenomenologists, which is parasitic on the formation of a phenomenological community. Secondly, there is the problem of setting down these insights in a way that will encourage their active appropriation by subsequent generations of phenomenological researchers. Finally, the most challenging problem is that of conveying phenomenological meaning to those *outside* the phenomenological community—particularly to those Husserl calls positive scientists—so that they may understand the insights of phenomenology as grounding the explanatory power of the theories they apply to various regions of experience.

This investigation will yield not only negative insights into what phenomenological expression can *not* be like; it will also yield a clear sense of the demands being made on phenomenological expression, and suggests a possible way (through the work of Maurice Merleau-Ponty) in which practicing phenomenologists can meet these demands. However, this prescribed manner of expression creates a new difficulty in that it flies in the face of Husserl's demand for rigor in the practice of phenomenology. The essay ends with a call to meet this difficulty by thematizing a notion of rigor particular to phenomenological practice. Only by meeting this difficulty can phenomenology ever finally return to "the things themselves" and speak of them to the larger world, as demanded by phenomenology itself.

1. The problem of the *epoché* as a potential barrier to the formation of phenomenological community

What must first be stressed is that Husserl considered the practice of phenomenology to be *collaborative* in nature, based on the model of scientific community. What makes this collaboration possible is the production of insightful statements which are to be taken up and utilized by subsequent generations of researchers. This is how scientific communities are founded and maintained, and how scientific meaning is constituted. Since Husserl considers phenomenology to be the founding science of all sciences and rational inquiries, this must hold for the practice of phenomenology as well. The generation and accumulation of insightful statements in principle allows a depth of investigation beyond the capabilities of any single subject, or any single generation of subjects. Like the meanings of the various positive sciences, phenomenological meaning is to be constituted intersubjectively, within a phenomenological community.[1]

However, because of the radical nature of phenomenology, a problem in the communication of phenomenological insight immediately arises. This is a problem with which Husserl struggled intermittently, commencing with the *Logical Investigations*,[2] and it is a problem with which he never fully came to terms. This problem, which only grew more apparent after Husserl's discovery of the *epoché*,[3] is stated most starkly by Husserl's last assistant Eugen Fink in his *Sixth Cartesian Meditation*. According to Fink, the language of the natural attitude must somehow be transformed by the phenomenologist, who must "judge the suitability of mundane concepts and representations for analogously indicating transcendental concepts" (Fink 1994, 96).[4] In the absence of such a transformation, the phenomenologist risks slipping out of the transcendental attitude with every word she speaks (Fink 1994, 86).[5] If individual phenomenologists are unable to affect such a

1   Edmund Husserl, "Philosophie als strenge Wissenschaft," *Logos* I (1910-11). Translated by Quentin Lauer and published as "Philosophy as a Rigorous Science" with another, late essay in Husserl 1965, 139. In the *Logical Investigations*, Husserl calls for "resolute cooperation among a generation of research-workers" to overcome the difficulties of phenomenology. See *Logical Investigations*, volume 1(Husserl 1970a), 250- 256. Also see *Ideas I* (Husserl 1982), § 66; and *Formal and Transcendental Logic* (Husserl 1969), § 5.

2   See, for instance Husserl 1970a, 256; 1964, 24; 1960, § 5; 1982, §§ 67, 73-74, 124-126; 1970b, § 55.

3   Though Husserl does not programmatically present the *epoché* until *Ideas I* in 1913, many scholars claim that Husserl discovered the phenomenological version of it much earlier, in 1905. See Mohanty 1995, 62; also see Bernet, Kern, and Marbach 1993, 59.

4   Fink makes almost exactly the same point in Fink 1970, 143-44. This article was originally published in *Kantstudien* in 1933, which was explicitly endorsed by Husserl in his preface to the article.

5   This reminds us of Husserl's statement in the *Crisis* about "new sorts of apperceptions which are exclusively tied to the phenomenological reduction,

transformation of language, they will be incapable of pointing beyond the mundane meanings of words to their transcendental significance. This would amount to phenomenologists being unable to cooperate as a community because of an inability to communicate. And if this is the case, then phenomenology cannot become the "founding" science of all sciences, as envisioned by Husserl. Indeed, it would be incapable of founding *itself* as a science.

In the end, Fink sees the danger of seduction by mundane meanings as being ineradicable. In his view, the divergence of signifying that is present in every transcendental sentence between the natural sense of words and that transcendental sense that is indicated in them can never be abolished. Husserl is clearly alive to this problem but declares it exaggerated. Typically, and reminiscent of the quasi-Cartesian strategy that he intermittently employs throughout his published work on this issue, Husserl counters Fink's assessment of the problem by appealing to "equivocation-free" and "unambiguous" expression.

2. The problem of the inscription of insights as a barrier to their active appropriation by subsequent generations of phenomenological researchers

Assuming for the moment that practicing phenomenologists are able to overcome the difficulties just described in *generating* phenomenological insights, there still remains the problem of being able to *communicate* these insights to future generations of phenomenologists. According to Husserl, this requires that these insights become "a documented, ever available treasure for knowledge and advancing research ..." (Husserl 1970a, 250). In short, these insights must be written down, archived, and stored up for future reference. In the "Origin of Geometry," Husserl argues that inscription allows the possibility of communication without personal address, which may awaken familiar significations within a future phenomenological community of empathy and language. With such active recollections comes the capacity for repetition at will of the appropriate mental activities that generated the insight underlying a given inscription. According to Husserl, such repetitions can result in

---

together with a *new sort of language* (new even if I use *ordinary language*) ..."
See 1970b, § 59.

"co-accomplishments" through which the "original production and the product of one subject can be *actively* understood by the others."[6]

However, in the same essay, Husserl warns that such inscriptions can be passively taken over and accepted as self-evident, but only at the level of understanding an expression, not the original self-evidence which inspired the expression. This passive "taking up" has no reference to this original activity, and as each "taking up" gives rise to further written expressions, a realm is created where things begin to "melt together associatively" into complex combinations (Husserl 1970b, 361). As such combinations multiply we fall victim, in Husserl's words, to "the seduction of language," whereby we lapse into "a kind of talking and reading dominated purely by association" (362). As phenomenology makes progress through these merely passive and associative modes of communication, the capacity for reactivating these originary phenomenological insights becomes diminished, thereby undermining the very essence of a phenomenological community (Husserl 1970b, 365).[7]

3. The problem of conveying phenomenological insights to those realms of human activity outside the realm of phenomenology

Each human activity manifests its own relationship to the world. For example, the positive sciences are all united by a general way of relating to the world. At the same time, each of the individual positive sciences relate to the world differently—physicists relate to the world one way, biologists another, etc. The same can be said of the formal sciences of logic and mathematics, and of all the "human sciences," such as sociology and political science. Philosophy too relates to the world in a certain way, and the same distinctions hold among philosophy's various species and sub-species: continental and analytical philosophies relate to the world differently, as do empiricists, idealists, structuralists, post-structuralists, etc.

Each of these human activities express their particular relationship to the world in different ways. Physicists employ the principles derived from

---

6 "The Origin of Geometry," pp. 353-361. The essay is collected as Appendix VI in Carr's translation of the *Crisis* (Husserl 1970b).

7 Jacques Derrida pursues the acute implications of these difficulties in Derrida 1978.

the work of Newton, Einstein, and quantum physicists, among others. Biologists draw on theories of evolution and the work of other biologists. Logicians and mathematicians apply the theorems and formulae drawn from their respective and mature disciplines, and the same holds true for political scientists, sociologists, and philosophers, all of whom make use of highly specialized lexicons, often derived from theoretical constructions, in the practice of their respective inquiries.

The Russian literary theorist Mikhail Bakhtin would refer to these various expressive spheres as speech genres. For Bakhtin, there are as many different speech genres as there are human activities (Bakhtin 1986, 60), and each speech genre is relatively stable, thereby "enabling a person to interpret and evaluate his own self and his surrounding reality" (1984, 47). On this view, language enjoys a kind of unity only in the pristine realm of abstraction (1981, 288). In actuality, language is an intersection of a multitude of "social-linguistic points of view,"[8] all of which compete with one another within a single linguistic community (1981, 273).[9]

Bakhtin's theory shows how speech genres allow those involved in a common human activity to practice that activity, and by extension establish this activity as a social institution: Science, Philosophy, Physics, Idealism, etc. At another level, his theory shows how speech genres may hinder communication between different spheres of activity. Failures of communication are commonplace between the practitioners of different kinds of inquiries; citing specific examples seems unnecessary.

These failures of communication are due to specialization, which in essence fragments the whole of the lifeworld. Husserl praises specialization on one level, and criticizes it on another. He praises it because of the success it brings in attaining valuable knowledge for humankind, within each given sphere of inquiry. Yet at the same time, he criticizes specialization because of what it forgets and leaves behind: the idea of a one or all-encompassing science, the science of the totality of what is, as founded on the unity of the lifeworld.[10] The fact that it is often difficult

---

8   See also 291, where Bakhtin refers to this as the "languages of heteroglossia."

9   According to Bakhtin, speech genres attach to a variety of social groupings: social classes, ideologies, geographic regions, professional and vocational circles, schools of thought, tendencies, etc.

10 Husserl 1970b, § 11, 62; § 3, 8.

to communicate across specialties is proof of the prevalent forgetfulness of this unity, this one field that all specialties have in common.

According to Husserl, this forgetfulness is due to the fact that these various human activities tend to relate to the world through "theoretical-logical substructions."

> The contrast between the subjectivity of the lifeworld and the "objective," the "true" world, lies in the fact that the latter is a theoretical-logical substruction, the substruction of something that is in principle not perceivable, in principle not experiencable in its proper being, whereas the subjective, in the lifeworld, is distinguished in all respects by its being actually experiencable (Husserl 1970b, §34d, 127).

For Husserl, these theoretical-logical substructions of the "objective" world are but shadows of the lifeworld; stated conversely, the subjective-relative realm of the lifeworld "ultimately grounds the theoretical-logical ontic validity for all objective verification" (1970b, §34b, 126). *All* human activities relate primordially to the lifeworld, and that which exists in the lifeworld has a certain objective validity, insofar as it is a premise for objective inquiry. However, it is a premise that is not only unacknowledged but often derisively dismissed by such "objective" inquiries as "*merely* subjective and relative" (§34b, 126; emphasis added). What sets the human activity of phenomenology apart from these "objective" inquiries is a steadfast refusal to dismiss the pretheoretical domain of experience which grounds them (§34d, 129). In fact, phenomenology claims to articulate this subjective-relative experience in order to show how the theoretical is founded on the lifeworld.

So, beneath each of Bakhtin's speech genres is a human activity, and beneath each human activity is the lifeworld. Phenomenology, in essence, claims to speak for this lifeworld, beneath and across speech genres and by extension across the various human activities grounded in the lifeworld. But what kind of language can phenomenology speak, that will be heard and heeded by all of these disparate activities? Because of its special place as the "grounding" science of all sciences, phenomenology as a human practice must resist the temptation to create its own specialized and insular lexicon. When this happens, phenomenologists forget about the lifeworld in its unity, and become mere practitioners of just one more school of thought debating the theoretical subtleties and adequacy of the scholarly apparatus within the sphere of "academic philosophy." This scholastic mode of expression does not follow the spirit of phenomenology which urges us to return to "the things themselves." This, by extension, retards the communication of phenomenological insights to the various realms of human activities founded on the life-world. Phenomenology cannot afford the luxury of creating a speech genre in this exclusive sense. Phenomenology's goal of speaking beyond its realm of human activity to other human activities derivative of the lifeworld demands an emphatically *inclusive* mode of discourse.

It is essential to remember at this point that communication across speech genres is possible in principle. In fact, experience tells us that instances of cross-communication do occur, and Bakhtin's theory implicitly offers an account of how this is possible. Because language is in actuality an interplay of different speech genres rather than a pristine unity, Bakhtin suggests that there is within every utterance a certain level of hybridization whereby one genre is rendered in light of another. This allows a kind of fluency that permits a tacit understanding of an utterance and the possibility of deeper communication across speech genres.[11]

This dynamic of "hybridization" (or "dialogized heteroglossia") seems to leave space for a phenomenological speech genre that would not only allow the practice of phenomenology, but also the possibility of communicating its insights to the other realms of human activity founded on the lifeworld. Yet it must be acknowledged that Bakhtin's theory of speech genres goes only so far in this regard. A phenomenological speech genre would have to be something much more: a genre that must intentionally engage with common language in such a way that it could express a primordial realm of experience common to *all* human activities, so as to make all of these activities more fully meaningful to those who practice them.[12] Indeed, it should be abundantly clear that the practice of phenomenology in its fullest sense rests on its ability to communicate its insights in just such a manner.

---

11 This reflects Fred Evans's reading of Bakhtin. See Evans 1998a and 1993, 189-93.

12 Erazim Kohák nicely illustrates the distinction between the languages of the various "special regional ontologies" and the language of "a philosophy which seeks to grasp and evoke the sense of being" in 1986, 53-4.

4. How phenomenologists can *not* speak to the world

In various places Husserl deems various modes of expression inappropriate for the practice of phenomenology. Perhaps most strongly in *Ideas I*, and then later in the *Crisis* texts, he claims that since phenomenology is an eidetic science concerned with generic (rather than ideal) essences as they appear morphologically in a pretheoretical lifeworld, the terms that express these essences must be non-mathematical in nature (Husserl 1982, §74).[13] This puts the use of technical-formal languages such as mathematics or logic out of play. When positive scientists use mathematics to express ideal essences in a univocal way, they are doing so appropriately. But employing the same expressive strategy in regard to the generic essences of phenomenology is to purchase "exactitude" at the expense of expressing such an essence appropriately, in its givenness. In other words, the use of a formal or technical symbolic system is too divorced from lived experience. Both mathematics and logic are exact or ideal sciences that are built *on* the lifeworld, but they do not speak *from* the lifeworld itself. Thus, as a potential means of communication, these modes of expression are inappropriate to the "subject matter" of phenomenology.

This would seem to force Husserl to draw on common or everyday language as the source of phenomenological expression, but Husserl is undeniably suspicious of the equivocations and ambiguities besetting our everyday language, and in places calls for a reform of the prevailing terminology used in talking about our relationship to the world. In this Husserl seems to be advocating the formation of a kind of analytic discourse akin to Thomas Hobbes's Euclidean attempt to reduce all words to names in an effort to eliminate the ambiguities of everyday language.[14] The problem with such analytic discourse is that it tends to serve a strict dualism between subject and object and seeks to break down the organic whole of experience into discrete elements, which are then exhaustively described in terms of their external relationships (e.g., spatial, temporal, causal) to one another. In analytic discourse, language is regarded as consisting of words whose meanings are not dependent on the context in which they were used; thus, the aim is to make words

---

13 Husserl makes a further distinction between material and singular essences in § 12.

14 See Hobbes 1994, chapter IV: "Of Speech."

univocal—"transparent"—so they can be employed as tools in the service of unambiguous concepts, which statically fixes each element in its field of reference in the achievement of a pre-established goal.[15] All of this is anathema to the spirit of phenomenology, and hard to reconcile with Husserl's claim in *Ideas I* that the terms used to express phenomeno-logical essences "are *essentially, rather than accidentally, inexact*" (1982, §74; emphasis in original). Given this claim and his explicit rejection of technical-formal languages, Husserl cannot be speaking of univoc-ity in the same way that a logician, a mathematician, or a Hobbesian materialist would speak of univocity.

Whatever Husserl means by this term, it seems clear that it can only be deployed in reference to common or everyday language. On one level this makes a great deal of sense. As was noted earlier, phenomenology, like all human activities, begins in the lifeworld. More specifically, phe-nomenological activity always starts from the objectified world of the natural attitude, which is then bracketed through the method of the *epoché*. This bracketing breaks our familiar acceptance of things and brings particular facts into a context where they can be understood in terms of the fundamental structures of experience.[16] However, as Fink points out, this change in attitude is not accompanied by a new language with which things are to be described. The phenomenologist, like any speaking subject, has no choice but to start with the language at hand. Out of this instituted language, different speech genres are formed. A phenomenological speech genre must also start here, but again, it must be careful not to become insular and exclusive if it is to attain its goal of communicating phenomenological meaning to other realms of human practice.

This would seem to affirm that the phenomenologist must stay "close" to the language of the lifeworld, so to speak, i.e., close to the language that is found in the lifeworld.[17] Phenomenological expressions drawn from the language of the lifeworld would not only be more likely to be adequate

15 The phrase "analytic discourse" belongs to Evans, who draws on Foucault and Reiss. See Evans 1993, 51. Hobbes is not a dualist, but it is clear that his re-conception of language is meant to serve a pre-established goal: science, or to use Hobbes's phrase, "the knowledge of causes."

16 See Merleau-Ponty 1962, xv-xvii.

17 J N. Mohanty makes this point in comparing Husserl's view of language to the positivistic views of language, particularly that of the formalist view that deeply distrusts ordinary language. This view, according to Mohanty, manifests

to the phenomena that appear to the practicing phenomenologist; such expressions would also allow the phenomenologist to communicate the essences of phenomena to those outside the phenomenological realm, because the language of the lifeworld is the source of all speech genres. Drawing on the language of the lifeworld would generate a more organic discourse, as opposed to the analytic kind of discourse just described. Organic discourse aims to treat a domain holistically by attempting to preserve and express the inseparability that typifies our relationship to our surroundings. It does so by first distinguishing but not separating the elements of its domain of inquiry. Secondly, organic discourse describes the relationship between these elements in terms of a totality that each element at least partially reflects or modulates. And third, it seeks to fulfill the self-world relationship by stressing the reciprocity between subject and object.[18]

Yet, invoking organic discourse does not by itself provide us with an antidote to analytic discourse, and by extension, a phenomenological speech genre. The language of the lifeworld on which organic discourse draws cannot be considered a kind of pure and homogeneous ur-language, for the very reason that language is a product of a *lived world*. As both Fink and Bakhtin point out, the notion of a "pristine" language is an abstraction. Language is instead shot through with a multitude of speech genres and is hence suffused with mundane as opposed to transcendental meanings. On this view, "the things themselves" are entangled in language, and must somehow be extricated by the phenomenologist in order to bring phenomenological insight into being. The tension between a word's mundane meaning and transcendental meaning is inevitable and cannot be overcome. It may be the case, however, that this tension can be exploited.

5. From Husserl to Merleau-Ponty?
Filling the silence with the expressive risk of originary speech

Because of his intense focus on the essence of meaning as it relates to a solitary ego, Husserl deals with the intersubjective constitution of

---

"a hidden metaphysical obsession" to reform language that obscures the essence of language as a *Lebensform*. See Mohanty 1969, 72-3.

18 Fred Evans actually refers to phenomenological discourse as a "variant" of organic discourse. See Evans 1993, 51, 172, 175.

meaning only implicitly, and leaves the social dimension of language undeveloped, or at least underemphasized.[19] Indeed, Husserl's analysis of language has been likened to an anatomical dissection of the living process of language which results in the unity of this organism being torn asunder by his analytical acumen.[20] In order to address this deficiency, I will turn to the work of Maurice Merleau-Ponty, who has attempted to preserve the living unity of language through his phenomenology of the speech act. Given Merleau-Ponty's radical reinterpretation of Husserl, this move will undoubtedly be viewed as controversial. But unlike Husserl, Merleau-Ponty provides us not only with a far more developed analysis of the intersubjective constitution of meaning through speech; he also preserves a place for ambiguity in his analysis, which Husserl sought to eliminate but which the phenomenon of speech demands. Though it is primarily on these grounds that I justify my move into Merleau-Ponty, I will also present textual evidence in the conclusion of this essay which suggests that Husserl and Merleau-Ponty share more affinities in connection with an appropriate language of phenomenology than is typically thought.

Merleau-Ponty conceives of instituted language (what I have been calling "the language of the lifeworld") as possessing silent or "unsaid" dimensions in situations that require originary expression. These silent parts of instituted language may be conceived of as referring to the "gaps" in our perceptual horizon that beckon and invite us to re-vitalize language and unify thought and perception, to "complete a picture" (so to speak) in the face of lived experience.[21] The trick is to somehow shake one's self loose from the "empirical sediment" of discourse in order to complete this picture, through what he calls authentic or originary speech. All of this is especially true for the phenomenologist, whose very vocation is comprised of trying to evoke a sense of the structures of experience that are there but not apparent. Phenomenological meaning is constituted through originary, or more precisely *evocative*, speech.

Once in the transcendental attitude, the practicing phenomenologist is confronted with two fundamental choices. She may choose to simply

---

19 See Luckmann 1972, 471-72. In contrast, Donn Welton cites passages from a variety of Husserl's later texts which suggest that Husserl was aware of this deficiency and was working to correct it. See Welton 1983, 313-17.

20 See Mohanty 1969, 74.

21 See Lanigan 1984, 6-16; 1975, 127-141; 1977, 78-83.

take up instituted or empirical speech, which amounts to the continued sedimentation of speech in an affirmation of the *Weltanschauung* as an uninterrupted meaning.[22] The phenomenologist who makes this choice makes use of merely empirical speech which is suffused with the mundane meanings of either the natural attitude or the speech genre of academic phenomenology. This manner of expression skims along the surface of language, among the empirical facts surrounding the "things themselves." In Merleau-Ponty's words, such speech "arouse in us only second-order thoughts... [that] are in turn translated into other words which demand from us no real effort of expression and will demand of our hearers no effort of comprehension" (Merleau-Ponty 1962, 184). In this mode of speech, the phenomenologist purchases empirical or scholarly "precision" at the heavy price of loosing her ties to the lifeworld. For Merleau-Ponty, this way of speaking is simply a way of remaining silent (Merleau-Ponty 1973, 20).[23]

In a second expressive option, the practicing phenomenologist can refuse to remain silent in this way by confronting a situation rife with ambiguity due to a tension between thought and perception, between facts and essences. These tensions, and the anxiety arising from them, are understood by the phenomenologist as a silence where there are no apparent answers or solutions—where there are no words, i.e., where there is silence. This lack of words heightens the ambiguities, the tensions and the anxiety to a point where the phenomenologist either shirks back to take refuge in the "silence" of a speech genre, or risks chaotic action by taking the anxiety of the ambiguity and breaking the silence, not with empirical meaning derived from past experience or the lexicon of a speech genre, but with authentic meaning *taken* from the ambiguous tension itself.[24] In this act of speaking, the phenomenologist

22 Lanigan 1984, 21.

23 This text was set aside by Merleau-Ponty and never finished. Also see Lanigan 1984, 27.

24 This sentence gives the impression that Merleau-Ponty views silence in both positive and negative terms. In many instances he views silence negatively, in terms of a "de-vitalized" part of instituted language that the speaking subject "steps into." See, for instance, Merleau-Ponty 1962, xv, 184, 389, 403; 1964, 44. Yet at another level in Merleau-Ponty's thought, silence is understood in a less negative way. Remember that for Merleau-Ponty the body itself is a power of expression, and as such it is always expressive. In this way, even a silent body, a body that does not speak, can express meaning—i.e., "a silence can speak

brings her "semiotic intentionality" into public being, where others may perceive in the structure of the intentionality a *thematic* answer to the ambiguity, whereby thought and perception become unified (Lanigan 1984, 26-7).

Thus, speaking as an effective (or, more precisely, *affective*) phenomenologist by its very nature requires an expressive risk, built on a confrontation with the ambiguous tension underlying a silence, a tension which the phenomenologist alleviates through a significative intention. This significative intention is animated by the particular expressive style of the phenomenologist, who must be more adventuresome in her engagement with language, up to and including the use of metaphor and other literary tropes. What all tropes have in common—so long as they are used skillfully—is an ability to "surprise" us, to "jolt" us, to "shake us up" in a way that allows a new meaning to tumble from language so that we see the world in a new or more primordial way.[25] Clearly this is what is required of phenomenological expression. Yet at the same time, it is important to stress that such expression would not be interested in engaging in expressive novelty for its own sake; rather, it would engage in such novelty for the sake of the thing itself. Phenomenological expression would have to be "lively" enough to evoke the dimensions of the lived world under investigation, but not so beyond the linguistic pale that it obscures these dimensions.

In other words, in order to say anything new, we must develop a "feel" for language in order to engage in an originary speech act. Merleau-Ponty's examples of such a speech act include a child's first contact with the world of language, the lover's poetic words to his beloved, the philosopher's attempt to bring a new thought into being, the novelist's endeavor to create a world—in short, any instance where the particularity of a lived world confronts the muteness of a spoken world.[26] Here the "second-order" expression of instituted language will not suffice, since the meaning to be established is new. It is here, in silence, that originary

volumes." In these instances, "silence" is pregnant, and Merleau-Ponty is using the term as an honorific. See Merleau-Ponty's discussion of the aphasia patient (1962, 164 ff.).

25 Eleanor Godway speaks of "a shift, a dislocation, a jump we are required to make, and we move from momentary puzzlement to 'Aha, I get it,' as the new image comes into focus" (1993, 392).

26 Merleau-Ponty 1962, 179, 184, 384, 389. Also see Ihde 1983, 170; Schmidt 1985, 114-15; Coyne 1980; Robert D. Walsh 1984; Godway 1993, 391.

speech may be realized. The speaking subject must shake "the linguistic or narrative apparatus in order to tear a new sound from it," thereby "transform[ing] a certain kind of silence into speech" (Merleau-Ponty 1964,46; 1962,184). Silence, then, is the essential condition for originary speech, which does not choose ready-made signification; it is instead a "lurking signification that has not yet found its voice" (Coyne 1980, 320). Originary speech gropes around a signifying intention within the space between words. It is with these "threads of silence," which wind their way between words, that originating speech is made. In language we find a tacit field of linguistic possibilities, which allows the creation of new and motivated meanings on the part of the speaking subject. There is a kind of dialectic[27] at work in Merleau-Ponty's phenomenology of the speech act; originary speech is in a sense a synthesis that emerges from the creative tension between the sedimented meaning existent in a linguistic community, and the desire of speaking subjects to express themselves to the linguistic community of which they are a part, and without which they could not speak at all.

On this line, Merleau-Ponty sees the task of the originary speaker as revealing the speaking speech that is already there in language, submerged within it. He speaks of words as having a silent life; they are "like animals at the bottom of the ocean ... that come together and separate according to the needs of their lateral or indirect signification" (1973, 87). Speakers all "swim" in the same "ocean,"; each *is a part* of the living organism of language, so any change comes from *within* language; indeed, from where else can such linguistic change begin? Merleau-Ponty's metaphor shows more vividly how there can be a relationship between the speaking subject and the institution of language: speaking subjects are like fish that can only live in the "ocean" of language; to this extent, we are all "creatures" of language.

Bearing this in mind, phenomenology must embrace a mode of expression capable of evoking life, or more precisely, the experiential structures of the lifeworld, to which it must remain faithful. Like the poetic lover's exaltation of his beloved or the novelist attempting to create a world, the phenomenologist is also confronted with the mute world of instituted language, one that has forgotten the primordiality of her insights into the essential structures of experience. Like the poet and the novelist, the phenomenologist must nevertheless confront this muteness by drawing on both her insights into the phenomenal world

27 See Edie 1984.

and the fact that she too lives in language. But unlike the enamored poet, who seeks to celebrate the particularites of his beloved, or the novelist, who is attempting to create a world, the phenomenologist is required to rise above the particularities of her mundane subjectivity and remind her audience of the essential structures of a world lived by all—and not just professional phenomenologists. In this connection it must be stressed that a practicing phenomenologist is not trying to say anything new; rather, she is attempting to evoke the sense of something that is there but which has been covered over by habitual attitudes and mundane modes of consciousness and expression—i.e., the fundamental structures of experience. To the extent that the phenomenologist wants to reveal, thematize and communicate the essential structures of this forgotten world to those beyond the phenomenological realm of investigation, she must choose her words carefully. And to the degree that "the things themselves" are bound up in language, these carefully chosen words may serve at once the evocation, the justification, and the establishment of phenomenological truth.

This may seem to be a delicate balance for the practicing phenomenologist to strike: to "disturb" the sedimented institution of language with originary speech so that the lived world may be evoked, but in a way that does not "betray" the lifeworld for the sake of an empty expressive innovation. However, for Merleau-Ponty, there is no hard and fast distinction between "originary" speech on the one side, and sedimented "empirical" language on the other. Merleau-Ponty sees empirical speech as derivative of originary speech, which means that empirical speech was once "alive" and originary. This in turn means that there is a certain dormant authenticity in all that has been spoken. For Merleau-Ponty, *all* of language is "alive" or authentic to one degree or another. To draw on one of Merleau-Ponty's own evocative metaphors, empirical speech still points to the "surface" of a world, which does not preclude the possibility of "submerged" meanings "com[ing] together and separat[ing] according to the needs of their lateral or indirect signification[s]" and then "breaking" the surface, disturbing it in a "breach" of expressive authenticity (1973, 87). Originary speech "swims" in the same "ocean" beneath empirical speech, and always in the same direction: toward the world and the things in it, making all language intentional and to that extent meaningful.

Following this line of thought, phenomena or the "things themselves" are already inescapably *immersed* in Merleau-Ponty's living ocean of language. Just as an ocean never ceases flowing, language never ceases being "on the way" to meaning, which by extension means that language has no place for "pure" meaning.[28] Originary speech flows into and is intermingled with empirical speech, which in turn flows into and mixes with originary speech. But to swim in just one part of this ocean would be to sink into a deep and impenetrable silence. Speaking in an excessively empirical style is to speak only on the banal surface of language; speaking in an excessively authentic style is to overreach and dive too deeply, where no one will follow. In order to genuinely live as speaking beings in this ocean of language, we must constantly explore its surface and plumb its depths, never confining ourselves to only one of its many dimensions.

6. Conclusion:
phenomenological expression and the question of rigor

It is important to note at this juncture that the poet and the novelist do not typically use a specialized language, as does, say, the professional philosopher. In most instances it seems necessary to first understand philosophy in order to understand what a contemporary professional philosopher has written. But one does not necessarily have to be a writer in order to be entertained, elevated or to attain an understanding of what a poet or novelist has written. Though professional philosophers, poets and novelists all draw their words from the language of the lifeworld, philosophers are drawing mostly from its empirical dimension, whereas successful poets and novelists have a surer "feel" for the possibilities of language. These possibilities inform the writerly "manner" of taking up language, yet this manner does not prevent the sounding of a multitude of "subjective" voices. James Joyce, Virginia Woolf, Ernest Hemingway, Toni Morrison, and Salman Rushdie manifest an astounding variety of style, but what holds these disparate styles together is the "feel" for a lived

---

28 In "Indirect Voices" Merleau-Ponty suggests in several places that "new" meaning is already hinted at in "established" meaning (1964, 39-47). Evans refers to a creative speech act as throwing "itself out of focus toward the new meaning that is already hinted at within the diacritical structure of language" (Evans 1998b, 179).

and living language.[29] In contrast, oftentimes professional philosophers are united by a sterile academic style that displays little feel for a lived language, and which tends to mute their own voices. Strictly academic phenomenologists remain mute in exactly this sense.

If it is the case that the "things themselves" are already immersed in the language we find ourselves in, then it would seem that in order to speak from the things themselves we must speak from the language of the lifeworld, which embraces both the authentic and the empirical dimensions. But in order to do this, and do the things themselves justice without obscuring them further, it would seem necessary for the phenomenologist to acquire a sense of the "rhythm" of language, as it constantly flows and finds its equilibrium between its empirical and authentic dimensions. To do this, Merleau-Ponty says, "we only have to lend ourselves to its life, its movement of differentiation and articulation, and to its eloquent gestures" (1964, 42).[30] Phenomenologists must "lend themselves" to the life of language, as do poets and novelists, because they explicitly claim to speak from the lifeworld. Because phenomenologists make this claim, they must attempt to develop the "feel" for language that is characteristic of the more literary pursuits. The speech genre of literature displays the most vitality, because it is here—in the language of the lifeworld—that all people live. Though most of these people live outside the phenomenological realm, it is in principle possible for phenomenologists to reach them where they live, because all share a lived—and spoken—world, provided that phenomenologists come to appreciate the living and literary texture of language. Thus we as phenomenologists must reconsider our commitment to the only apparent "transparency" of academic philosophical discourse and risk returning the concrete speech act to the milieu from which it arises, i.e., from the relationship that obtains between speaker and community.[31] This reevaluation of our expressive strategies is essential to the formation of a phenomenological community, the founding of phenomenology

29 Here is Merleau-Ponty quoting Claudel: "We mould and animate the reader, we cause him to participate in our creative or poetic action, putting into the hidden mouth of his mind the message of a certain object or of a certain feeling" (1962, 389).

30 As Dale E. Smith reminds us, for Merleau-Ponty the word is not appraised intellectually via a translation process; rather, "the word is lived" (Smith 1977, 48).

31 See Coyne 1980, 308.

as an enduring and mature science capable of reactivating its original insights, and which enhances the possibility that these insights can be effectively communicated to the multifarious human activities that phenomenology seeks to ground.

The idea that the practicing phenomenologist must employ the eloquent language of literature raises the admittedly difficult question of how this more ambiguous form of expression can conform to the standard of rigor demanded by Husserl. Yet, on the rare occasion when he could free himself from his Cartesian predilection for univocity on this matter, even Husserl claims that the suggestive power of poetry and the other literary arts is essential in the fostering of ideation (Husserl 1982, §70, 162); in another instance, he tells us that phenomenologists may well have to hark back to the language of the mystics in describing phenomena in their givenness (1964, 50). These passages suggest that we must give serious consideration to the idea that Husserl was possibly more open to the notion that equivocal forms of expression could serve the practice of phenomenology. If this is so, then we must follow Merleau-Ponty's eloquent elaboration of this notion, and entertain the ways in which the idea of "rigor" may not belong exclusively to the positive sciences. And this, I believe, must involve using all of the expressive means at our disposal in the attempt to articulate an idea of rigor peculiar to the practice of phenomenology, conceived as both a matter of intuition *and* expression.

Works cited

Bakhin, M.M. 1981. *The Dialogical Imagination,* trans. Caryl Emerson and Michael Holquist. Austin: University of Texas Press.

———. 1984. *Problems of Dostoyevsky's Poetics,* trans. Caryl Emerson and Michael Holquist. Austin: University of Texas Press.

———. 1986. *Speech Genres and Other Late Essays,* trans. Vern W. McGee, eds. Caryl Emerson and Michael Holquist. Austin: University of Texas Press.

Bernet, Rudolf, Iso Kern, and Eduard Marbach. 1993. *An Introduction to Husserlian Phenomenology.* Evanston, Ill.: Northwestern University Press.

Coyne, Margaret Urban. 1980. "Merleau-Ponty on Language: An Interrupted Journey toward a Phenomenology of Speaking." *International Philosophical Quarterly* 20 (September).

Derrida, Jacques. 1978. *Edmund Husserl's "Origin of Geometry": An Introduction,* trans. J.P. Leavey, Jr. Stony Brook, N.Y.: Nicolas Hays, Ltd. [originally published in 1962].

Edie, James M. 1984. "Merleau-Ponty: The Triumph of Dialectics Over Structuralism." *Man and World* 17, 299-312.

Evans, Fred. 1993. *Psychology and Nihilism: A Genealogical Critique of the Computational Model of Mind*. Albany: State University of New York Press.

————. 1998a. "Bakhtin, Communication, and the Politics of Multiculturalism" *Constellations: An International Journal of Critical and Democratic Theory* 3.

————. 1998b. "'Solar love': Nietzsche, Merleau-Ponty, and the fortunes of perception." *Continental Philosophy Review* 31.

Fink, Eugen. 1970. "The Phenomenological Philosophy of Edmund Husserl and Contemporary Criticism" in *The Phenomenology of Husserl: Selected Critical Readings*, ed. and trans. R.O. Elveton. Chicago: Quadrangle Books.

————. 1994. *Sixth Cartesian Meditation: The Idea of a Transcendental Theory of Method*, trans. Ronald Bruzina. Bloomington: Indiana University Press.

Godway, Eleanor. 1993. "Wild being, the prepredicative and expression: How Merleau-Ponty uses phenomenology to develop an ontology." *Man and World* 26.

Hobbes, Thomas. 1994. *Leviathan* ed. Edwin Curley. Indianapolis: Hackett.

Husserl, Edmund. 1960. *Cartesian Meditations: An Introduction to Phenomenology*, trans. Dorion Cairns. The Hague: Martinus Nijhoff.

————. 1964. *The Idea of Phenomenology*, trans. William P. Alston and George Nakhnikian. The Hague: Martinus Nijhoff.

————. 1965. *Phenomenology and the Crisis of Philosophy*, trans. Quentin Lauer. New York: Harper & Row.

————. 1969. *Formal and Transcendental Logic*, trans. Dorion Cairns. The Hague: Martinus Nijhoff.

————. 1970a. *Logical Investigations*, vol. 1, trans. J.N. Findlay. London: Routledge and Kegan Paul; New York: Humanities Press.

————. 1970b. *The Crisis of European Sciences and Transcendental Phenomenology*, trans. David Carr. Evanston, Ill.: Northwestern University Press.

————. 1982. *Ideas Pertaining to a Pure Phenomenology and to a Phenomenological Philosophy*, vol. 1, trans. F. Kersten. Dordrecht, The Netherlands: Martinus Nijhoff.

Ihde, Don. 1983. *Sense and Significance*. Atlantic Highlands, NJ: Humanities Press.

Kohák, Erazim. 1986. *The Embers and the Stars*. Chicago: University of Chicago Press.

Lanigan, Richard L. 1972. *Speaking and Semiology: Maurice Merleau-Ponty's Phenomenological Theory of Existential Communication*. The Hague: Mouton and Co. N.V., Publishers.

————. 1975. "Merleau-Ponty, Semiology, and the New Rhetoric." *The Southern Speech Communication Journal* 40 (Winter).

————. 1977. *Speech Act Phenomenology*. The Hague: Martinus Nijhoff.

————. 1984. *Semiotic Phenomenology of Rhetoric: Eidetic Practice in Henry Grattan's Discourse on Tolerance*. Latham, Md.: The Center for Advanced Research in Phenomenology and University Press of America.

Luckmann, Thomas. 1972. "The Constitution of Language in the World of Everyday Life," in *Life-World and Consciousness: Essays for Aron Gurwitsch*, ed. Lester E. Embree. Evanston, Ill.: Northwestern University Press.

Merleau-Ponty, Maurice. 1962. *Phenomenology of Perception*, trans. Colin Smith. London: Routledge & Kegan Paul, Ltd. [Originally published as *Phénoménologie de la perception*. Paris: Gallimard, 1945.]

————. 1964. *Signs*, trans. Richard C. McCleary. Evanston, Ill.: Northwestern University Press. [Originally published as *Signes*. Paris: Gallimard, 1960.]

————. 1973. *The Prose of the World*, trans. John O'Neill. Evanston, Ill.: Northwestern University Press. [Originally published as *La prose du monde*. Paris: Gallimard, 1969.]

Mohanty, J.N. 1969. *Edmund Husserl's Theory of Meaning*, 2nd ed. The Hague: Martinus Nijhoff.

————. 1995. "The Development of Husserl's Thought" in *The Cambridge Companion to Husserl*. New York: Cambridge University Press.

Schmidt, James. 1985. *Maurice Merleau-Ponty: Between Phenomenology and Structuralism*. New York: St. Martin's Press.

Smith, Dale E. 1977. "Language and the Genesis of Meaning in Merleau-Ponty." *Kinesis* 8 (Fall).

Walsh, Robert D. 1984. "An Organism of Words: Ruminations on the Philosophical-Poetics of Merleau-Ponty." *Kinesis* 14 (Fall), 13-41.

Welton, Donn. 1983. *The Origins of Meaning: A Critical Study of the Thresholds of Husserlian Phenomenology*. The Hague; Martinus Nijhoff.

10

EMERGENCE & INTERPRETATION

KENNETH MALY

I have opened in front of me three books: *Entanglement*, by Amir D. Aczel (2003); *Complexity*, by M. Mitchell Waldrop (1992); and *Emergence*, by Steven Johnson (2001). What joins all three of these books—and what enjoins the matters being discussed—is the notion of the nonlinear dynamic whereby thinking moves beyond principles of certainty, hierarchy, unified "reality"—to the dynamic of self-organizing, adapting, spontaneous and creating "systems" or happenings. Each in its own unique way, all three books take up the matter of the way gathering takes place, of how patterns of happening are unexpected and unpredictable, and of how things come forth in the world beyond the rules of "engagement" as defined by mathematical logic or scientific analysis. These latter rules of engagement belong to the dominant paradigm for at least 300 years.

Perhaps one can gather the matters discussed and opened up in the three books under the name: emergence. How could one say what "truly emergent happening" means? Things happen in the world (scientists are prone to say: universe). What is the dynamic that governs this emergent happening? What governs or guides the behavior of ants, sharks, quarks, and humans? And when the rules of "objective" rationalism no longer dominate, in the entangling, complex emergent world—then how do we proceed? These books take up the question of emergent behavior, nonlinear dynamic, and entanglement—but they do not leap directly into the domain of emergence as such. So what is emergence, anyway? The dynamic of emergences as such, not limited by the domain of things emerging?

It would seem that this realm of "emergence" and what is own to the dynamic of emergent unfolding is now available for our consideration—and that we might just be able to discover what it is *in its ownness, as it is in this ownness*. But then we realize that, no matter how careful we are as we bring our knowing awareness to this phenomenon—and as much as we try not to "intervene" or "interrupt," lest we not be "true" to what shows itself—it is still our thinking response that interprets what is manifest. It is impossible to separate out what thinking brings to the phenomenon. What we observe in the phenomenon and its self-showing is tied to how we observe—with what lenses, with what history of being that we bring with. Our joyful struggle is to think and respond within this con-tension, this πόλεμος.

Some today want to give up this struggle and to say simply: Everything is interpretation. There is nothing that is "as such." All is social construction. (Here we leave aside the fact that there are still those who would say that the world is objectively real, independent of thinking's participation: Something *is* the way it is, regardless of interpretation.) A world of "reality" independent of our perceiving or interpreting would actually be meaningless to us, since we would have no connecting access to it, either through perception or through our intellect. Descriptions or interpretations of what is, of the way things are, gather what shows itself and organize the phenomena. And in this interpretation they take for granted that there is no substantial, independent or separate "reality."

Another way to say the struggle, the πόλεμος, is to recognize that, whereas what we perceive in the world, as it manifests, is not something "created" in our minds, still whatever we grasp or the way in which we take in the world, follows from experiences we have gathered and paradigms that we have inherited, historically thrown to us.

The Buddhist teacher Khyentse Rinpoche put the matter this way: "When a reflection appears in a mirror, you cannot say that it is part of the mirror, nor that it lies elsewhere. In the same way, perceptions of exterior phenomena take place neither in the mind nor outside. Phenomena are not really existent or nonexistent. So the realization of the ultimate nature of things lies beyond the concepts of being and nonbeing."[1]

Thus the title of my essay: 'Emergence and Interpretation." How to think the convergence of these two contributing factors to the way things are? Shall we or dare we hold on to the notion of "material realism," "independent and objective reality," or even elementary particles? Or: Is it own to our minds and to the way things are simply to reduce

---

1   As quoted in Ricard and Thuan 2001, 123.

everything to a constructed world? How to participatorily think this conundrum?

One way to say what happens in Heidegger's work of thinking (and in his *opus*) is that his thinking continually, with undivided attention, passionately circles around the domain (called the "question of being") that:

+ does not reside *in* human beings, even as humans participate in its makeup

+ is not conceived, created, or controlled by human reason

+ is not a thing, an entity, or a being—is rather nothing, no-thing

+ cannot be gotten at within or via analytic thought or the language of definition, literalness, or denotation

+ is other than the being of metaphysics.[2]

Named unconcealment, the temporality of being, ἀλήθεια, λόγος, enowning, timespace, regioning of the region, fourfold—in all these names, Heidegger's thinking stays with this one matter: how to think/ say that which sustains things/beings without itself being *a* being, how to think/say the dynamic of emergence, ongoing unfolding, uncon-cealment itself, as what sustains thinking/saying—and thus sustains being-human.

Emergence and interpretation are the matter of hermeneutic phe-nomenology, as *Heidegger* uses the word. This means: phenomenol-ogy as a gathering-saying of what shows itself from within itself as it shows itself. This phenomenology enacts a thinking that tends to the *phenomenon*—what shows itself—with keen awareness. It interprets and says this self-showing, always sustained by what self-shows and the self-showing as such, always held to that "mark."

The "phenomena" that need to be observed include the "things" as they show themselves as well as the self-showing or emergent emerging as such, which always include the saying/showing as such—language as *it* says-shows.

Heidegger's phenomenology is in line with Husserl's phenomenol-ogy of reflexive intuition, eidetic evidence, and intentionality and with

---

2 Parts of what follows here appears in Maly, *n.d.*

Merleau-Ponty's perceptual consciousness. But it is vastly and essentially different from those phenomenologies. For both Husserl and much of Merleau-Ponty are within subjectivity, whereas Heidegger's phenomenology breaks out of that defining limit. For Heidegger, what self-shows and the self-showing as such (the emergent emerging) both include what humans bring to the phenomenon as well as take into account what humans "receive" in the phenomenon. Thus, at the core of Heidegger's phenomenology, from *Sein und Zeit* onward, the subject-object distinction collapses. This essay attempts to enact the thinking of that collapse and what emerges from within it. It tries to think "the way things are" in their interbeing and dynamic relatedness—and not in their distinctness and isolation. To think gathering and permeation as the heart of the matter that shows itself alongside things in their distinctness and separateness. And to think this in the non-dualistic manner to which subject-object thinking is not accustomed. And to let emerge the convergence of gathering/emergence and interpretation, i.e., hermeneutic phenomenology.

The convergence of emergence and interpretation. We humans always already participate in the unfolding of the way things are. If we are to do this in a way that is not subjectivity-oriented, not driven by human will or choice, not founded within any domain of ego-subjectivity—then how shall we enact it?

In hermeneutic phenomenology there are several names for the various imagings of the convergence: what is and our understanding of it; pre-theoretical experience and saying/showing that experience; the phenomenon (what self-shows) and hermeneutics (interpreting the phenomenon, to its "own"); the non-theoretical and en-owning it; emergence and interpretation; that which is not defined by us coming upon us and our necessary participation in "how it is."

It is incumbent on thinking not to reduce these many namings of this convergence. A first step/opening toward this convergence takes place when Heidegger thinks Da-sein in *Being and Time* as undoing the duality of subject-object (underneath objectifying subjectivity). A second step takes place when he thinks the ontological difference: being over against beings, the being of what is over against what is. The third step takes place in the thinking of the "essential turning" of en-owning in *Contributions to Philosophy (From Enowning)*,[3] where be-ing is no longer thought in terms of beings (that which is), but rather in its own full, deep sway–being. And this be-ing includes the participation of human being, of Da-sein.

Humans thus enter into a completely other domain of historical unfolding. Here the name for the convergence of emergence and inter-pretation (hermeneutic phenomenology) becomes the relationship of be-ing and humans. Two questions coalesce: How do humans participate in the emergence (how does the observer participate in the observed)? And then: How does be-ing "need" Da-sein, while Da-sein belongs to be-ing?

How can thinking think and say what is "own" to human Da-sein in today's world, which does not know where it fits, where it is "unto its own"? Where is the ground that is own to humans? This "ground" is other than the ground or foundation that metaphysical thinking has provided up to now. This metaphysical ground is formed under the domination of calculative and representational thinking, a ground that is taken to be "objective" and valid and absolute, whose names are: ἰδέα (Plato), ἐντελέχεια (Aristotle), *cogito* (Descartes), reason (Kant), ab-solute spirit (Hegel, Schelling), will to power (Nietzsche). The shared "quality" of each is such as to take away from what is own to Da-sein and to be-ing.

Heidegger's thinking intends to bring humans and beings ("back"?) to the place in which they originarily belong, to that way of being which is their own (*eigen*). Thus, the key word for thinking these matters is *en-owning* (*Er-eignis*). *Contributions* is Heidegger's attempt to enact the thinking that re-connects humans and be-ing, and this happens in the thinking of be-ing as en-owning, of the truth of being in the deep sway of en-owning.

Put in a languaging that images this complex and cutting-edge phenomenon, Heidegger says that be-ing enowns Da-sein, and Da-sein, enowned, throws this enowning open—and this convergence of the enowning throw of be-ing *to* Da-sein and the throwing open that enowned Da-sein does *is the originary turning of en-owning.* This opens up two core matters: One, whatever "be-ing" is or names, "it" is no-thing: The word *be-ing* does not name an entity, a being, highest being, or anything substantial. The very words "be-ing as enowning" (*Seyn*

---

3 Heidegger 1989. The first number refers to the English translation. The second number refers to the original German edition. All translations of this text are mine.

als Ereignis) undo this traditional metaphysical weave—unto perhaps another weaving? It is too early to know how this might unfold, historically. Two, there is an intertwining of levels and a circularity, which will unfold in the course of this work of thinking. Indeed, the intertwinings named here will emerge as *the* inseparable dynamic.

Our inherited language and conceptual formation is indebted to substance- and subjectivity-metaphysics. In this paradigm our traditional and inherited language has us take humans and being as two separate entities whose relation is in question. But the thinking of en-owning calls for thinking beyond this duality. This is what Heidegger is saying in section 115 of *Contributions*, when he says: "The leap, the most daring move in proceeding from inceptual thinking, abandons and throws aside everything familiar, expecting nothing from beings immediately [in their immediacy]. Rather, above all else it releases belongingness to be-ing in its full essential [deep] swaying as enowning." (161/227) This is the path that we must follow up on, hold ourselves to.

Ereignis usually means "event" in German. It is clear that this translation will not work for our thinking here. Heidegger makes clear that the *eigen* part of the word says "own" and the *er-* part of the words says something like "enabling," "bringing into the condition of," "welling up": bringing into its own, coming into one's own, the very action by which this own (to humans, to things, to be-ing) is enacted in thinking. *Ereignis* names the enabling and enacting character of this enowning.

This enacting character (the enaction of thinking) is *from* enowning in its full, deep sway (the enowning throw of be-ing and the throwing open that Da-sein, enowned, does—and this whole dynamic as the originary turning that is enowning). Thus "from enowning" says: from within the originary experience of being enowned by/to be-ing and of belonging to be-ing. The "call" or throw of be-ing is *Zuwurf* or *Zuruf*. In participating in response to this call, thinking says (brings to language) enowning in its full, deep sway (the enowning throw of be-ing and the throwing open that Da-sein, enowned, does = the originary turning that is enowning). I quite deliberately repeat that phrase here, for its crucial saying. The deep sway of enowning is the historical unfolding of the enowning call/throw of be-ing to Da-sein and Da-sein's enowned response as it throws-open this call/throw.

One of the matters before us is to think how this language of the inhering dynamic convergence of enowning throw of be-ing and Da-sein's enowned throwing-open what is thrown is mirrored in the language of emergence and interpretation (hermeneutics). Language/saying/word is part and parcel to the emergence of be-ing—be-ing as enowning, be-ing as emergent emerging.

The enactive stillness of withdrawal. If be-ing is not an entity—and not some "thing" at all–then the originarily historical thinking that "enjoins the deep sway of be-ing" (Heidegger 1989, 9/11) calls for heeding the self-sheltering (*Sichverbergen*) that is involved in the enowning throw of be-ing and must itself then work "in the style of reservedness [*Verhaltenheit*]." (9/12) Heidegger asks: "What saying accomplishes the utmost reticence [*Erschweigung*] in thinking?" (10/15)

Thinking's attunement to these matters is named as:

   startled dismay (*das Erschrecken*)

   reservedness (*die Verhaltenheit*)

   awe (*die Scheu*).

Startled dismay, Heidegger says, is the enaction of thinking whereby one "returns from the ease of comportment within what is familiar to the openness of the press of the self-sheltering [that which holds itself back or withdraws, but which pushes or presses forward *in* its self-sheltering/concealing]" (11/15).

But this startled dismay is not an evading. "Rather, *because* it is precisely the self-sheltering [withdrawal, concealing] of [that is part and parcel of] be-ing that opens up in this startled dismay... what is own to the 'will' of this startled dismay allies itself *to* startled dismay from within...." (11/15). This is what Heidegger calls *reservedness* (*Verhaltenheit*). The thinking relation to the withdrawal of be-ing by staying with the withdrawal by reservedness—not turning away from it, but holding it in its and thinking's hesitation (*Zögerung*). Thus, the "ground" of be-ing in Da-sein is originarily and essentially an "abground" (*Abgrund*), the staying away of ground. This is how be-ing happens or comes forth, unfolds historically. "In reservedness—and without eliminating that return—the turn into the hesitant self-refusal reigns as the deep swaying of be-ing." (12/15)

Awe goes even further than reservedness. From awe, "arises the necessity of reticence [*Verschweigung*]" (12/15); "it is the letting-sway of be-ing as enowning, which through and through attunes every bearing in the midst of beings and every comportment to beings." (12/16)

Da-sein is en-owned—and thus humans are enowned *as Da-sein.* En-owning takes place in the withdrawal or self-sheltering/concealing of be-ing, the ab-ground or staying away of ground (which is the truth of be-ing).

Gathering the crucial dimensions here, we can say: (1) "How it is" with be-ing is such that humans (here as Da-sein) participate in the "make-up" of be-ing but do not control or create be-ing. (2) The enowning throw of be-ing includes as essential to it the withdrawal, self-sheltering/concealing. (3) The participation of humans as Da-sein includes—as what is own to it—the reservedness, the reticence that mirrors the withdrawal within be-ing as enowning.

The courage to think possibility. Held within these various matters mentioned here at the beginning is perhaps the most challenging opportunity for thinking at this time in the history of thought. It is an opportunity to think and put into language what to many appears as undoable: a radical shift in how we think the way things are, how it is in the world.

Thinking this possibility—to some an impossible task—calls for ignoring the skeptics and simply getting on with the work. Right now philosophical scholarship is partially and unduly dominated by the "nominalism" of postmodernist "pluralism." Everything is equally "valid" because there is no "objective" validity. There are only texts to be interpreted unto traces and layerings of meaning (subtexts) that have no ground. Multiple contexts, pluralistic relativism, and social construction—all hold the attention of the most recent trends in continental philosophy, which has its historical roots in phenomenology, hermeneutics, and hermeneutic phenomenology. But in trying to avoid the pitfalls of metaphysical unity, presence, and objective truth (which surely need to be "gotten over"—thinking needs to be released from these "traps"), perhaps these trends fail to avoid the pitfall of becoming blind to emergence and to experience—forgetting perhaps that paradigms and constructions are not about nor sustained by the phenomenon and emergence.

If postmodernist pluralism is about expression that is determined not to claim too much, then hermeneutic phenomenology is about saying "the same old thing," which happens to be the way things are—to the eye that sees—but saying it in a slightly different way, called for by the necessity of thinking that emerges from within be-ing as enowning. But its matter is held within the sheltering of be-ing, of the other beginning.

Surely interpretation is part of all that we know. But it is also true that apples do fall, rain does happen, and there *are* cars, trees, and the heavens. Thus, the interpretation of texts is surely essential to any "true" philosophizing; but this interpretation cannot ignore emergence: the way things are, or how it is, in the world.

The dance is between emergence and interpretation, between the role of humans (the enowned throwing open of the throw of be-ing, which Da-sein does) and the emerging unfolding that throws itself (be-ing's throw) *to* Da-sein.

Language in emergence and interpretation. In traversing the path of be-ing-mindful of these matters, we are called to think along with Heidegger, unto its next possible unfolding, the emerging possibility for thinking the way things are. We see that Heidegger's philosophy has been—and will continue to be—useful in other domains of research and creative thinking: architecture, art and aesthetics, theoretical physics, environmental thinking, qualitative research in nursing and interpretive studies, among others. Given that we today recognize the need to learn how to think matters outside the reductionist forms of rationalistic inquiry and how to maintain the necessary rigor while doing qualitative research, Heidegger's contributions in the realm of interpretation/hermeneutics as well as his original and creative philosophy beyond subjectivity, i.e., beyond dualism, come in handy.

The new language that has emerged in Heidegger's thought opens out onto a fresh pathway, to what is most "own," which sheds light on what is going on on the deepest level of language, thinking, and interpreting the way things are. The finest example of this is Heidegger's use of the word *ereignen* in German—*enowning* in English. If we learn to hear what "own" means in our language, this whole dimension will open out in front of us. First, rather than the more abstract "essence" of this or that, we learn to look for and say "what is own" to something. What is own to nature, what is own to language, what is own to human beings. (What would Aristotle say is "own" to human beings? What would Descartes say is "own" to humans? What would Newton say is "own" to the physical universe? Heisenberg?)

Now we see that what is "own" to nature and what is "own" to human thinking is not separate. Thus thinking/saying goes beyond the subject-object dichotomy or dualism. Then, if we think this "owning" process itself—how nature "owns up" to what it is, how we find what is "own" to nature, how nature "owns itself over" to us or "owns" us (in a non-possessive way)—our thinking is then turned to this dynamic of "owning" itself. This is what Heidegger calls *Ereignis* or "enowning."

Central to this enowning is the dynamic connection between what is (being, emergence) and thinking's interpreting of the way things are. I have named this relation that of emergence and interpretation (more technically: hermeneutics).

Thus we need to focus on the core role that language has in any thinking on this level—including the key understanding of translation as interpretation. (This is important, in that anyone who reads Heidegger has to take into account the German original way of using language–"languaging," if you will—and how to deal with that in one's own language.)

Being enactive thinking, the words and language that I use here themselves manifest the power that words have to shape meaning—a certain way of "taking care of" language.

The place where humans, things/beings, and the dynamic by which they are (here: emergence) is thought/said in a non-dualistic manner. Normally named being, beings, and Dasein—or: emergence, what emerges, and interpretation—this threefold character of the way things are is said and thought in their coming-together or "fusion." Unearthing the hermeneutic situation in the way things are (in their appearing, emergence) is useful in several ways:

a. by delineating what philosophy is for Heidegger—enactive, transformative, with a core role played by language as saying/showing,

b. by recognizing the power of language in interpretation to say/show and by keeping this showing power of language at center stage in the enactive thinking,

c. by taking enactive thinking out of the realm of a merely human will-act—beyond merely human agency—in the way of parting and gathering that belongs to the whole dynamic of being, beings, and humans (where we humans are not in charge, but rather are vigilant participants in the unfolding of what is),

How does thinking own up to this task? What is own to humans? How can one think this enowning?

If hermeneutic phenomenology is engaged in attentive awareness of what shows itself (of the "phenomenon"), in interpreting that phenomenon (unto the matter being manifest), and in putting into words what has shown itself and has been interpreted, two things are of paramount importance. One, along with everything that is disclosed or unconcealed, the very dynamic of disclosing or emergence is manifest *along with*. Two, the interpreting and the saying (putting into words) are of one piece. That dynamic is an undivided action of thinking. That is why thinking is always saying. This notion is a bit foreign to our traditional ears.

With this interweaving of emergence and interpretation—and the further core interweaving of interpretation and saying ("language"), which is even more enigmatic to our philosophical ear—we need to think through the connection of interpretation and hermeneutics to language, saying, and the word. Whereas one could try to separate the matters of hermeneutics and of language, enactive thinking shows that the matters of language, hermeneutics, and saying are all essentially and irretrievably intertwined.

One of the texts in which Heidegger opens up this matter for thinking is the dialogue with the Japanese philosopher, published under the title "*Aus einem Gespräch von der Sprache,*" in *Unterwegs zur Sprache.*[4] This text is most useful, in that the very way of language and saying that happens *within* this dialogue enacts precisely the matter that is questioned and presented, e.g., the matter of interpretation/hermeneutics. As we handle this text mindfully, we find our *enacting* the very question that is presented—thus letting emerge in action (deed, enaction) precisely what the "matter" is—a far cry from a "theory" or a "definition" "about" language.

The German title of this dialogue is *Aus einem Gespräch von der Sprache.* Quite literally, this says: "From within a Dialogue *from* Language." This is the same *from* (*von*) that is in the title of *Beiträge zur Philosophie (Vom Ereignis)*—*Contributions to Philosophy* (From *Enowning*)—and carries a lot of significance. There, it is a matter "from" enowning. Here, it is a matter "from" language, in the sense that language itself has something to do with how the dialogue unfolds. Language "plays" with *us*, one could maybe say.... Rather than being a dialogue "about" language and herme-

---

4 Heidegger 1985. In the subsequent citations the first number refers to the original Neske edition of *Unterwegs zur Sprache* (1959), which appears in the margin of the *Gesamtausgabe* edition. The second number refers to the English translation, for orientation purposes. All translations of this text are mine.

neutics, what is happening is that language itself is having its say with us, with our thinking. We think *from* that place. Phenomenologically speaking, it is the saying/showing that language and the word itself does that we are heeding and actively engaged in. So it is not "about" language at all. Rather it is "from" language: We in our thinking are called upon to undergo an experience *with* language, *from* language. But what does "language" say here?

The full title of this dialogue in German reads: "*Aus einem Gespräch von der Sprache. Zwischen einem Japaner und einem Fragenden,* which I translate as "From within a Dialogue from Language: Between a Japanese and an Inquirer." Language is the theme, and hermeneutics is an inherent part of the matter at hand.

Hermeneutics was initially (historically, with Schleiermacher, for example) about interpretation of literary works. But for Heidegger it is not that. "In *Being and Time* hermeneutics means neither the theory nor the art of interpretation... but rather the attempt to determine first and foremost what is own to interpreting [*Auslegen,* laying-out] from within the hermeneutical [from within what hermeneutics does]" (Heidegger 1985, 97/11). Still, what the word *hermeneutics* says is enigmatic. Is it in *any* way suitable? Or was it once and is no more? Heidegger points out that in his later writings he no longer uses the word. The question then becomes: Why is it that Heidegger in his later writings no longer uses this word?

This use of and then no-longer-use of the word *hermeneutics* has something to do with how the "way" belongs to thinking. Ways of thinking have this mysterious dimension whereby they take us into what is nearest at hand, which in its turn would bring us "back" to... the beginning, to what gets thinking going. What gets thinking going reveals and holds back simultaneously.

Gathering both (a) how Heidegger's thinking did not say this matter in a full-blown way (because it did not show itself clearly at first, and even as it did reveal itself more and more, it remained veiled—and still does today) and (b) how within the matter itself there is a withdrawal, a hiddenness, a vibrant stillness—gathering all of this up in a pregnant exchange, the Japanese offers the comment: "We Japanese do not think it strange when a dialogue leaves what it really means [intends] undetermined [in the realm of the undetermined] or even shelters it back into the indeterminable." And Heidegger responds: "This [trait] belongs to every dialogue among thinkers that turns out well [works].

This [thinking dialogue] can, as if of its own accord, take care, not only that what is indeterminable does not slip away, but that its gathering force [its power to gather] unfolds ever more brilliantly in the course of the dialogue" (100/13). Notice how language and the word plays its *own* role in the unfolding of the dialogue, how the dialogue "works" from within the *saying* of language and the word.

So what *is* this indeterminable, this gathering? It shows itself, says the Japanese visitor, in "a beholding that is itself invisible, a beholding that in its gatheredness bears itself over against the empty...." And Heidegger adds: "The empty then is the same as the no-thing, that deep swaying [*jenes Wesende*] which we try to think as the other to all that is present and absent." And the response: "To us, the "empty" is the best name for what you want to say with the word *being*...." (108/19). Then Heidegger explains how, in the first steps of thinking, the word *being* led to much confusion, stemming from the word itself, because the word *being* belongs to the language of metaphysics, as its "property." On the other hand, Heidegger was using the word in an effort to bring forth *what is own* [*das Wesen*] to metaphysics and thereby to gather metaphysics into the constraints of its limits. Asked if that is what he meant by the "overcoming of metaphysics," Heidegger says: "Precisely and only that; neither a destruction nor only a denial of metaphysics...."

Given the myriad ways of its historical unfolding, the limits to what the word says in metaphysics, and the rich possibility that inheres in the words *being* and *is*, the word *being* itself draws thinking unto reticence and reservedness. Holding back the word (for *being* or for the *indeterminable* or for the *gathering* or for the *owning-to*) is called for, "not in order for the thinker to keep it to him/herself, but rather in order to carry the word out over against [toward and back from] what is worthy of thinking (what calls for thinking's response)" (108/19).[5]

---

5 If one gets a good sense of this "to and away and unto" of the beckoning here, one will also get a better sense of what happens in *Contributions*, in the section on "Time-Space as Ab-ground" (section 242, 264 ff.), where Heidegger uses the word *Ent-rückung* (shifting or removal unto) and *Be-rückung* (enchantment or charming-moving-unto). Remembering that "ab-ground" is the staying-away of ground and that thinking needs to think *unto* the staying-away, the very "unto" is that whence the onefold of time-space first gets thought. This interlocking web of unto-away and of removing-unto opens up the space for thinking enowning, thinking be-ing as enowning, thinking the deep swaying of be-ing, in its be-ing-historical sway. Another way to think this dynamic or

In section 276 of *Contributions* Heidegger asks:

> how does what is own to language arise in the deep sway of be-ing? (1989, 500/352)

> how does language hold sway in the deep swaying of be-ing? (501/352)

> how so ... does language become experienceable in its relation to be-ing? (501/353)

In "*Der Weg zur Sprache*" in *Unterwegs zur Sprache* Heidegger provides clues toward what these questions say. "The saying [*Sage*], which resides in enowning, is—as showing [*Zeigen*]—the most own way of enowning [said here in its even more enactive form, as a verb: *Ereignen*].... Saying is the way in which enowning speaks.... For the enowning saying brings forth what emerges [things, beings, *das Anwesende*] from its ownhood—from that to where it belongs as an emergent [being, things that are]—and lauds it, i.e., allows it into its own way of being [allows it into what is its own, its *Wesen*].... Saying [is] the way/manner of enowning" (1985, 266-7/135).[6]

Heidegger says that the word *hermeneutic* modifies "phenomenology," but not as a "methodology of interpretation." This leads the dialogue to move in and out of the matter of words, e.g., why Heidegger no longer uses the word *hermeneutics* and why the word still says something useful to the discussion that opens up "saying": what is own to language and from where the dialogue "from" language emerges. Language as saying.

These words point to the "site" of language, where the dichotomy between the spoken/written word and its meaning (signifier and signified) yields to the matter for thinking that the distinction "word-to-meaning" covers over. Rather the discussion is "from" what is own to language.

---

phenomenon is to think how the unfolding, opening, deep swaying is outside the realm of any "dualistic" thinking (body-soul, night-day, metaphysics-non-metaphysics, being-beings). Can one dare to think that?

6   In a marginal note to this last sentence ("Saying...the way/manner of enowning") Heidegger writes: "belongs into enowning—*in das Ereignis gehört*." One could say, then: *being* the *manner* of enowning and belonging/fitting into enowning say the same from out of the same.

What is own/owning to language (*das Wesen der Sprache*) is something else besides what we are accustomed to think. The matter of thinking *is* the saying of be-ing. Thus language in its owning reveals the "discussion that opens" this site.[7]

So Heidegger thinks the word *hermeneutics*:

> *Inquirer*: Exactly. The expression "hermeneutical" comes from the Greek verb ἑρμηνεύειν. The verb refers to the noun ἑρμηνεύς, which we can connect to the name of the god Ἑρμῆς, in a play of thinking that is more binding than the rigor of science. Hermes is the messenger of the gods. He brings the message of the sending/shaping [*Geschick*]; ἑρμηνεύειν is that laying open [*darlegen*: revealing] that brings tidings, insofar as it is capable of hearing a message. Such laying open becomes the laying-out of what was said earlier by the poets, who themselves (according to Socrates's word in Plato's dialogue *Ion* (534e)... "messengers of the gods." (1985, 121/29)

Hermeneutics here is other than interpreting texts. It must be heard phenomenologically:

> *Inquirer*. Because it was this originary sense that moved and helped me to characterize the phenomenological thinking that opened the way for me to *Being and Time*. What mattered then—and still matters—is to bring forth the being of beings; of course, no longer in the manner of metaphysics, but rather such that being itself comes to the fore. Being itself—this says: emerging of what emerges [*Anwesen des*

---

7 In the first paragraph of the lecture *Georg Trakl. Eine Erörterung seines Gedichtes*, published in *Unterwegs zur Sprache* as "*Die Sprache im Gedicht*" ("Language in the Poem"), Heidegger says: "*Opening discussion* [*discussing that opens*] means to direct something into its place/site. Then: to heed that site/place. Both—directing into and heeding the place/site—are preparatory steps in 'discussing that opens.' And yet, we already venture enough if in the following [lecture] we limit ourselves to the preparatory steps. The opening discussion ends—corresponding to any pathway of thinking—in a question. That question inquires into the location of the place/site [*nach der Ortschaft des Ortes*: into the placeness of the place, the site-hood of the site]....

"Originarily the word *place/site* means the tip of the spear. Everything comes/runs together in it. The place/site gathers to itself, in the highest degree. The gathering permeates and sways through everything. The site/place, the gathering, takes-in to itself, preserves what is taken-in—but not like a capsule that closes off, but rather such that it [the site/place] shines through the gathered, lights it up, and thereby first releases it into its own." (1985, 37/159).

Anwesenden: unfolding of what unfolds, presenc*ing* (versus presence) of what presences], i.e., the twofold of the both from within their onefold. This is what speaks to humans and calls them to what is their own (116/30).

What matters is to bring forth in language—as saying—emergence and what emerges. This twofold speaks to humans, and humans respond to its enowning. What holds in this dynamic humans-twofold (in something like a threefold: humans-emergence-the emergent thing) is language/saying. This is what is own to the hermeneutical.

Interpreting the dialogue, perhaps we are enacting the thinking *from* what is own to language in its owning. Language and hermeneutics are of one piece. They are in action as humans think/say the twofold of emerging and of what emerges (be-ing as emergence and beings as the emergent).

The dialoguing partners continue:

> *Japanese*: Thus your mindfulness of language...
>
> I: of language in its relationship to the deep sway of being, i.e., to the holding sway of the twofold.
>
> J: But if language is the basic trait in the hermeneutically determined needfulness, then from the beginning you experience what is own to language very differently, that is, from what happens in the metaphysical way of thinking. This is actually what I wanted to refer to earlier.
>
> I: But what for?
>
> J: Not for the sake of contrasting something new over against what has been up to now, but rather to remind us that—precisely in the attempted mindfulness of what is own to language—the dialogue speaks as an historical dialogue.
>
> I: From within the thinking recognition of what has been (127/34).

Returning to the question of language and hermeneutics, we listen to the partners in dialogue:

> J: ... But I believe that I now see more clearly the *full import* of the belonging-together of the hermeneutical and of language.

I: Full import in what direction?

J: Toward a transformation of thinking – a transformation, however, that cannot be brought about as readily as a ship can change course – and even less as the consequence of an accumulation of the results of philosophical research.

I: The transformation takes place as a wandering...

J: in which one site is left behind in favor of another...

I: which requires a discussion that opens up.

J: The one place is metaphysics.

I: And the other? We leave it without a name (137/42).

Now the dialoguing partners return to their earlier question: How does Japanese say "language/*Sprache*"? With some hesitation the Japanese dialoguing partner finally gives the Japanese word for language: *Koto ba*. The word *Koto* says: a graceful attraction, the coming to radiance in fullness, what gives delight, something like the bringing of a message, the "enowning of the clearing-opening message of the graceful attracting, the swaying enowning." The word *ba* says: leaves, including and especially the leaves of the blossom, the petals.

Koto ba is the Japanese word for *language*: Language, then, could be said to be the unfolding/opening/letting emerge (which is what enowning, the be-ing historical sway that is the deep sway of be-ing, is) that attracts gracefully, like the opening of the leaves and the petals of a flower. This notion of language allows for much reticence, for it names the saying power of language that says/shows without pouncing on the phenomenon (on what emerges in emergence). This way of language does not define, delimit, reduce—but rather opens up and says and points to....

> I: That [*Koto ba*, the petals that emerge from *Koto*, i.e., "language" in Japanese] is a wondrous word and thus not able to be thought through all the way. It names something different from what the metaphysically understood words like *Sprache* [language], γλῶσσα, *lingua*, *langue* and *language* represent to us. For a long time now I am hesitant to use the word *language/Sprache* when thinking the swaying of what is its own [*Wesen*].
>
> J: But can you find a more appropriate word?

I: I think that I might have found it—but I want to protect it from being used as a common [faddish, current, too familiar] label and from being corrupted [falsified] to signify a concept.

J: What word do you use?

I: The word *saying/Sage*. It means: saying and its said and the to-be-said. [read: the saying itself, the "what" of the said, and what calls for saying—what calls unto us, what turns its gaze to us, what calls for gathering in the saying. This is a very important interlocking web for understanding what it is that language does to us and what it is that grounds as well as opens up "hermeneutical phenomenology."]

J: What does "saying" [*sagen*] mean?

I: Apparently the same as *showing/zeigen* in the sense of: letting appear, letting shine [forth]—but all of this in the manner of hinting.

J: In accord with that, saying is not the name for a human speaking [languaging]...

I: but for that deep swaying which your Japanese word *Koto ba* hints at: shaped and sent in saying, essentially connected to saying, coming from saying itself [not coming from *human* saying]: *das Sagenhafte*...

J: in whose hinting I am, only now through our dialogue, at home – so that I also now see more clearly how well-guided Count Kuki was when, under your guidance, he tried to think and be mindful of the hermeneutical.

I: But you also see how meager and inadequate my guidance was bound to be; for, with the look into what is own to saying, thinking only *begins* that pathway which takes us back, from a merely metaphysical representing, into heeding the hints of that message, whose message-bearers we would really want to become.

J: The pathway thereunto is long (144/47).

The dialogue is moving around within the question of language, saying, and hermeneutics. It has become clear that it is not the usual sense of language that is at stake, that Heidegger prefers to use the word *saying/sagen* rather than *language/Sprache* or *languaging/speaking/sprechen* to name this matter for thinking. So that thinking needs to wander "into the site/place where the own/owning of saying" is [*Wanderung in die Ortschaft des Wesens der Sage*].

This does somehow distinguish between language/speaking and saying—and all that that entails. But not much is won by simply making that distinction. What is called for is: Within a certain and essential reservedness, thinking must be attentive to the "mystery" of saying, to the withdrawal that is said in the saying. So that mystery becomes mystery and shines forth as mystery, only when the matter (showing, self-showing, emergence) of mystery's holding sway within saying itself does not come transparently to the fore!

So the danger is (a) to talk too loudly about mystery, and then (b) to miss and misread its sway. We need to shelter the mystery's wellspring—and that is perhaps the most difficult. So we must speak "about" language—but when we pay this close attention to language/speaking, the question emerges: Is there such a thing as speaking/languaging "about" language?

Now the dialogue moves to the crucial matter of thinking "from" language rather than "about" language, clarifying all the interweaving dimensions of the saying and enactive thinking *from*....

I: A speaking *about* language [a languaging *about* language] almost inevitably turns language into an object.

J: Then what is its own [what belongs to it in its deep sway] disappears.[8]

I: We have positioned ourselves above [*über*] language, instead of hearing *from* it.

J: Then there would only be a speaking/languaging *from* language...

I: in such a manner that languaging would be called *out from* what is its own and be guided *to it*.

J: How can we do that?

I: A speaking *from* language could only be a dialogue.

J: Without a doubt, we are moving in a dialogue.

I: But is it a dialogue *out from* the owning of language?

---

8 The Hertz translation says "its reality vanishes"—translating *das Wesen* as "reality." This is clearly *not* what is being said here; philosophically "reality" is not at issue—leaving aside the fact that Heidegger does not use the language of "reality."

J: It seems to me that we are now moving in a circle. A dialogue from language must be called from its own. How is the dialogue capable of such without first letting itself into a hearing that, as it were, reaches into language's own/owning?

I: I used to call this estranging relationship the hermeneutic circle.

J: It prevails everywhere in the hermeneutical, that is to say—according to your explanation today—where the relation/connection between message and message-bearer holds sway.

I: The message-bearer must already come from [well up from] the message. But s/he must also have already gone to it.

J: Didn't you say earlier that this circle is inevitable—and that, instead of trying to avoid it as a seemingly logical contradiction, we must walk it [go on it, practice it]?

I: Yes. But this necessary recognition of the hermeneutic circle does not yet signify that, in the representing of the recognized circling, the hermeneutic circle has been experienced.

J: You would thus abandon your earlier position.

I: Of course—and especially insofar as the talk of a circle always remains in the foreground.

J: How would you now portray the hermeneutical relation?

I: I would like to avoid such a portrayal as decisively as I would avoid a speaking *about* language.

J: So everything would depend on achieving a co-responding saying from language.

I: Any such saying co-responding could only be a dialogue.

J: But obviously a dialogue of a very special kind.

I: Such a one that would remain originarily joined and enowned to what is own to saying.

J: But then we dare not any longer call every talking-together a dialogue...

I: in case from now on we hear this name as naming the gathering unto what is own to language [as it gathers in its owning] (149/50).

In this sense "dialogue" works in that what is own to language—i.e., saying—owns humans, unto their ownhood within and in responding to language's own/owning. This cannot happen in speaking *about* language, but only in saying *from* language, from the deep sway of what is its own.

This dynamic obviates the matter of "written" or "spoken." Rather, it involves whether or not the dialogue is poi-etic, i.e., a saying that brings forth—and this can happen in either written or spoken dialogue. Indeed, this poi-etic dynamic in the own of saying undermines any *utter* distinction between the written and the spoken.

The dialogue partners, embraced as they are by the dynamic owning that language as saying is and does, are very much aware of how difficult—and well nigh impossible—this venture in thinking/saying is. Indeed the Japanese dialogue partner says as much:

> J: Are we not attempting the impossible?

> I: Indeed, as long as that message-bearing has not been sheerly guaranteed for humans—that message-bearing that the message which speaks-to humans the disclosing of the twofold needs.

> J: To call forth this message-bearing—and still more to go it—seems to me incomparably more difficult than to discuss open what is own to *Iki*.

> I: Surely. For something would have to take place by which that vast distance, in which what is own to saying comes to the fore, is opened and illuminated to message-bearing.

> J: Something like a stilling would have to take place, a stilling that would quiet the stirring of the vastness, into the conjoining of the calling saying.

> I: The hidden relationship of message and message-bearing *plays* everywhere.

> J: In our ancient Japanese poetry an unknown poet sings the intermingling scent of cherry blossom and plum blossom, on the same branch.

> I: That is how I think the owning sway unto each other of the vastness and the stillness in the same enowning of the message of the disclosing of the twofold.

J: But who today could hear therein an echo [resonating] of what is own to language that our word *Koto ba* names, flower petals that flourish from within the clearing message of the graceful attracting that brings forth?

I: Who can find in all of this a useful clarifying of what is own to language [in its owning]?

J: One will never find that, as long as one demands information in the form of theses [theorems] and catchwords.

I: But any number of us could be drawn into the preliminary play of a measure-bearing, as soon as we get ourselves ready for a dialogue from language.

J: It seems to me as if we ourselves, right now—instead of speaking about language—might have attempted some steps on the way that is entrusted to what is the owning of saying.

I: Says itself *to* saying in its own. Let us rejoice if it not only seems so but *is* so (152/53).

What is own to language (*Sprache*) is saying (*Sage*). "Saying [*Sagen*], *sagan* means to show: to let appear, in clearing-concealing to set free as to reach out and offer what we call world. The clearing-concealing, veiling offering of world is what sways in saying" (200/93). And so, finally, "The quickening in showing of saying is owning (*Das Regende im Zeigen der Sage ist das Eignen*)" (258/126).

Here, at the rounding off, we can ask ourselves a series of questions: If language says beyond the old conceptions that postmodernism is continually keeping "deferred" or "fragmented," then how do we say this language in its freshness? If language is always inhering in all emergence, how can we think this language as showing? And what is this language as interpretation? How does thinking move from a world in which (a) "reality" is taken to be objectively true, (b) the subject is taken to be the source of all knowledge, or (c) all "reality" is interpretation, i.e., constructed in/by society? Surely language exceeds these limitations! But what new way of saying/showing is called for at this juncture?

If indeed the postmodernist critique of metaphysical unity and objective reality opens us beyond the inherited paradigms of substance-metaphysics and ego-subjectivity, is there only arbitrary "construction" or interpretation? Or is there a more refined understanding of how things are, including the converging of emergence and interpretation, convergence of what shows itself and the saying/showing of that showing?

Hermeneutics does not emerge from an independent "reality," nor does it reside within its own "mere interpretation." Hermeneutics names the ongoing dynamic that moves back and forth and in and out of emergence and any saying/showing "from" language. Indeed, hermeneutics *as* this saying/showing is always already within the convergence of what shows itself and thinking's response to that. Or: The enowning throw of be-ing (emergence) enowns Da-sein, and enowned Da-sein throws-open this emergence in an interpretation that is held within and sustained by the very emergence—and this dynamic in its convolutions makes up the originary turn of enowning. Thus: In the saying that hermeneutics does, "emergence *and* interpretation" becomes the onefold of emergence that enowns the hermeneutic of enowned Da-sein. Be-ing as emergence and thinking/saying as hermeneutics *is the originary turning of enowning.*

How dare we say *this* onefold that is not a unity, but a dynamic gathering?

> *Die im Ereignis beruhende Sage ist als das Zeigen die eigenste Weise des Ereignens.*

> *...Die Sage ist die Weise, in der das Ereignis spricht....*

> Saying, which resides in enowning, is, as showing, the ownmost way of enowning.

> ...Saying is the way in which enowning speaks (266/135).

Works cited

Aczel, Amir D. 2003. *Entanglement: The Unlikely Story of How Scientists, Mathematicians, and Philosophers Proved Einstein's Spookiest Theory.* London: Plume Books.

Heidegger, Martin. 1985. *Unterwegs zur Sprache,* GA 12. Frankfurt: Klostermann Verlag. English translation as "A Dialogue on Language," in *On the Way to Language,* trans. P. Hertz. San Francisco: Harper and Row, 1971.

—. 1989. *Beiträge zur Philosophie (Vom Ereignis),* GA 65. Frankfurt, a.M.: Klostermann Verlag. English translation: 1999. *Contributions to Philosophy (From Enowning),* trans. P. Emad and K. Maly. Bloomington: Indiana University Press.

Johnson, Stephen. 2001. *Emergence: The Connected Lives of Ants, Brains, Cities, and Software*. New York: Simon & Schuster.

Maly, Kenneth n.d. *Heidegger's Possibility: Language, Emergence—Saying Be-ing*. Madison: The University of Toronto Press, forthcoming.

Ricard, Matthieu and Trinh Xuan Thuan. 2001. *The Quantum and the Lotus*. New York: Random House.

Waldrop, M. Mitchell. 1992. *Complexity: The Emerging Science at the Edge of Order and Chaos*. New York: Simon & Schuster.

TIME, OTHERNESS, & POSSIBILITY IN THE EXPERIENCE OF HOPE[1]

ANTHONY J. STEINBOCK

Hope is incontestably a basic human experience, and because it is so basic, the experience of hope can be all the more ambiguous. There are many theorists from various disciplines who have made the theme of hope a topic of research—e.g., Ernst Bloch (1959), Gabriel Marcel (1962 and 1967), Jürgen Moltmann (1965)—just to name a few. Rather than take these or other works as the basis for research on hope, I hold their conclusions in abeyance and make an initial endeavor to discern some of the fundamental, structural features of hope. I do this by describing the experience of hope with respect to three central themes that bear on lived hope: temporality, the modality of possibility, and otherness. In particular, I describe hope as directed principally toward the future as awaiting, as engaged and sustainable, and as oriented to what is beyond myself. As such, the experience of hope is essentially distinct from other experiences such as expectation, probability, wishing, longing, desiring, and denial.

For the purposes of this paper, let me make an initial observation. It is noted here as a presupposition and in demand of further explication in a longer work. Hope in general pertains to the dimension of "spirit." It is not an anonymous function, but initiated from the dimension of "person." Whether animals other than human persons "hope" is a question that has to be left open.

---

1 This paper was first presented at the 21st Annual Symposium of the Simon Silverman Phenomenology Center on the Phenomenology of Hope. at Duquesne University (2003).

1. The Temporal Dimension of Hope as Future

One of the key features of hope is time. When we examine the temporality of hoping we notice that one temporal dimension stands out as essential, namely, the future. When I hope, I am oriented toward a futural open significance, most often (but not exhaustively) expressed in terms of some futural occurrence. Let me be more precise by beginning with some very simple examples. In drawing on instances of hope, I select mundane examples by design. I do this for two reasons. First, it is too easy to speak lightly of divine things, thereby making idols of them; and by the same token, we often give ourselves too much license to speak of things horrific, thereby fetishizing them. Second, I begin with so-called mundane examples because despair arises in a multitude of everyday events, and not only those that are only issues of life and death, and likewise, because hope, which emerges in the face of the impossible, contradicts the everyday desperate situations in ways that we often take for granted.

Let's say we are in the middle of winter and I hope that it will become sunny and warm outside; I hope to go cycling. The futural dimension is evident in such acts of hope. Notice that I cannot hope that it *was* warm or that I *went* cycling; similarly, I cannot hope that it is sunny *now* and that I am cycling *now*, when I experience it as actually sunny and warm and actually cycling. The actuality of the event in the present, and *mutatis mutandis*, the past, will either be the fulfillment or disappointment of hope, but it will not constitute the temporal orientation of the hope-act. A discussion of the structure of fulfillment and disappointment where hope is concerned would take us too far beyond the limits of this paper. Suffice it to say that the fulfillment of hope depends on the manner in which the hoped-for event arrives as corresponding to the way in which the hoped-for act was directed. Such a fulfillment of hope need not be instantaneous, but can be temporally extended or historically developed. We only need note here that if a hope is realized in the manner in which the event was hoped for, or if it does not occur at all, the hope will cease because it will have been either fulfilled in the manner appropriate to the hope, or disappointed.[2]

2　The range of fulfillment and disappointment where hope is concerned is a topic for future work. Provisionally, let me say that hoping is broader than the intention-fulfillment structure, such that the "fulfillment" of hope can overfill the bounds of any intention.

Still, one may object that there are instances in which we are oriented toward the present and the past in hope. For example, let's say that I was outside in inclement weather, and while still outside I say: "I hope I am not catching a cold now," or an hour later after returning indoors, "I hope that I had not caught a cold." Although it seems that the hoping relates to the present or the past, the hope-act actually bears on an open futural significance. This can be seen more clearly when we contrast hoping with wishing (I return to this distinction below). When I *wish* I had not caught a cold, I presuppose the pastness and accomplished reality of the event. I only wish it were not true or had not happened. By contrast, when I am living through the hope that I am not catching or had not caught a cold, the future significance of this event is experienced as open for me and not as determined or completed; it is not a fait accompli. It is such an openness that relates the hope experience to the future.

Having noted that hope pertains to the future, it remains to describe its unique kind of futural orientation. Within the phenomenological tradition, it is customary to discern temporal modes in terms of time-consciousness: either as "protention," "expectation" or as "anticipation." The question concerns the relation that obtains between these kinds of time-consciousness and hope. Let me first examine whether hope founded in expectation as a mode of time-consciousness or whether hope is a distinctive act with a different temporal structure.

Briefly put, protention is a functional, anonymous sketching out of the future that is based on a present occurrence and how that occurrence was retained as past. For example, as I take notes while reading a book, my bodily comportment is directed implicitly to what follows—from sitting on the chair, to the movement of my hands as I continue to read—all of which may be disappointed or fulfilled by the on-coming events. Now, as I interrupt my note-taking to sip a cup of coffee, I reach again for my pencil, still reading my book. The protentional threads of my hand guide me to where I last placed the pencil, and I go to grasp it, miss it, grasp it, miss it, and so forth. All this can go on implicitly while still concentrating on reading a passage. Though protention is functioning through and through taking me in this fumbling manner from one to the next, without any explicit cognition of this process—at least for the first few tries—there is no necessary engagement of hope. I may then get frustrated and turn my attention to the pencil, look around; at this point I may hope to find it again (because I need to record a thought), but the hope-act has a different orientation than that of the temporal, kinaesthetic process of protention.

Hope, however, has a closer affinity to expectation. Expectation is similar to protention insofar as it is open to a futural occurrence arriving in the present, and it is also unfurled from the present and the past. Certainly, to say that expectation is related to the present and past, does not mean that it is "caused" by the present or past. Rather, we would say that it is "motivated." To say that it is motivated means that the past and the present discharge a futural event or flow of events because of the alignment of sense the expected event has to the former, not because it has an objective connection to them on the order of rational correlations or natural occurrences.

Expectation is different from protention, however, insofar as expectation is an active comportment to the future. Expectation and hope, then, have this much in common: They both exhibit an orientation toward the future, and they are both carried out within the sphere of activity, not passivity.[3] For example, having observed the recent air currents, weather patterns and cloud formations, I both expect it to be a mild and sunny day, and I hope that it will be a mild and sunny day. Here, expectation and hope overlap in terms of object-orientation. However, even though and despite the fact that I expect a mild, sunny winter day, I can hope for a violent snow storm (I want to take out my cross-country skis).

This example gives us a clear indication that expectation and hope are distinctive. The question we have to answer, however, concerns whether hope is somehow a modification of expectation or whether it is a unique and irreducible orientation toward the future. To do this, let me describe the belief structure inherent in expectation.

Intrinsic to the act of expectation is the fact that it posits the existence of something futurally. Expectation is carried out in the mode of belief as an unbroken, straightforward relation to the future. When I see the Fed-Ex person drive up to the house, I expect him to drop off a package, and when I expect him and the package, I implicitly posit the existence of the Fed-Ex person, the package, etc.; I live in the mode of natural acceptance. This is another way of saying that when I expect something, I expect it as actual, not as possible. When I see the truck pull away and turn on its turn signal, I posit its actual turning right, not its possible turning right. Of course, we may expect that something might possibly occur; I may panic in an instant that it may go straight

3   On the distinction between passive and active, see Husserl 2001.

into oncoming traffic—which would rupture my expectation, or maybe instigate a new one—but in the expectation itself, in this instance the so-called possibility is lived as actually going to occur in the mode of belief. *Expectation is not a modalization of belief;* it is another kind of belief, a straightforward one oriented in the direction of future actuality as a mode of time-consciousness. In expectation, we "count on" the futural event as it is foreshadowed or anticipated.

Further, although expectation does not exist in a relationship of causality to the present and past, it is not completely liberated from the past or present, either. There are features of the past and the present that "demand" or "speak in favor of" something occurring. When the "demand" on the part of things is "accepted" in a straightforward, unquestioning manner, the future is posited as actual (i.e., as actually coming). When such a "demand" or "speaking in favor of" is mitigated by countervailing tendencies, expectation can become modalized. In this case, something is posited as probable or as likely to occur. Likelihood and probability are "impersonal" modifications of the act-structure that is carried out in expectation.

To sum up, expectation is a temporal belief-act that is oriented toward the future as a mode of time-consciousness, and arises as motivated on the basis of the present and past. Further, the actuality posited in straightforward expectation can be modalized, e.g., in terms of probability or likelihood. Having understood expectation in this way, it is easier to see the distinctiveness and irreducibility of the hope-act. Before I give further specificity to the temporal structure of hoping, I first examine it as a modalization of straightforward belief in terms of the structure of "possibility."

2. Hope as Engaged

Expectation remains functional as the hope is carried out, even when the hope runs contrary to the expectation; likelihood is a direct modalization of expectation. But hope is not on a continuum with likelihood, say, just "quantitatively" less.[4] When I hope it will rain, I do not necessarily believe it "will" or "may" rain. Hope is different in kind, liberated from actuality and probability because hope is a unique modalization

---

4 There are of course other modalizations: doubt, negation, reaffirmation, etc.

of belief carried out in the mode of possibility. I am not suggesting that possibility only arises with hope, but that when I hope, a unique possibility structure is in play.

Let me state here at the outset that I hesitate in using the term "possibility" to characterize the hope experience because it might fail precisely in evoking the movement of hope. "Possibility," for example, can suggest that I somehow have a predetermined object "out there" ready made ("a possibility"), for which I then choose to hope. This, however, might be a more appropriate way of speaking where imagination is concerned. When I imagine, I can posit a realm of possibilities and then entertain one of them. But in hoping, I do not "hope" a possibility. Instead, as I note below, we rely on an other-than-myself that makes something possible, internally, so to speak, but I do not posit something as a possibility in hope.

Furthermore, the discussion of possibility in this context could imply that I first encounter dire circumstances and then I hope (for a different possibility) as a way of escaping them. Nothing of the sort goes on like this in the hope experience. Hope is initiated as a way of taking up a situation and living through its meaning "spontaneously," such that there is nothing thinglike to it. This is not to say that there is no motivation for hope, which as we will see is the ground of hope itself, but only that hope is not a rationalizing activity. Hope, we must insist, is evoked in the situation itself and emerges as part of its texture. It is not an ornament dressing up the situation or an afterthought posited in the face of trouble as an addendum. It is only after the fact that one can then attempt to analyze its structure, e.g., in terms of possibility. Given these limitations of the expression "possibility," I nevertheless find it useful, at least for the time being, because it gives us a critical device—by no means the only one—of distinguishing hope from other acts like imagination, wishing, and longing, and thereby assists us in honing in on the distinctive structure of the hope-act.

With this caveat, let me continue by noting that hope lives through something implicitly as possible. It goes without saying that "possibility" covers a wide range of experiences. It is therefore necessary to specify the kind of possibility that is in question in hope. In order to discern the possibility structure of hope, let me begin by contrasting it with the possibility structure peculiar to imagination. When I imagine, say, a boat sailing in my front yard, my imagining operates in the sphere of *pure, open possibility*. Anything is possible. Here we would have a kind of arbitrary possibility since it is "motivated," in the sense described above, neither by the past nor by the present, though it may borrow from the past and the present. It is completely free; I am in no way committed personally to what I imagine; there is no subjective investment, even though it is "I" who do the imagining. Imagining is an act that is quasi-tied to reality: I do not posit the boat in my yard as real, but I do posit it in the mode of "as if" it were real.

We can hone in on the structure of possibility peculiar to hope if we take yet another example, this time by distinguishing it from wishing. Wishing operates in the sphere of a *hyper-factual, open possibility*. As such, the latter has significance not only for the future, but for the past as well. Let us take an example of cycling over broken glass. The moment I roll over the glass, I can at the same time wish that I had not been biking, I can wish that I had taken another route, I can wish that I had not hit the glass, or I can wish that I will not get a flat. Like imagining, wishing can relate both to the past and the future; and although there seems to be a more direct tie to a subjective investment in the wishing, when compared to imagining, I still do not need to have a personal involvement for the wish to be a wish; I do not have to attend to it with any personal commitment; it can be frivolous or casual and still be a wish.

In distinction to both imagining and wishing, hope has a unique structure as an *engaged possibility*. For example, when I live through the experience of hoping—where the object could range anywhere from escaping from prison to completing a hike, from being with someone I love to finding a piece of dark chocolate—I am invested or committed in the outcome of the situation. Of course, I can both wish and hope for the same things, such as peace on earth, a solar eclipse, or being a horse. Important to note is that it is neither the object that qualifies the experience of hope, nor the so-called "objective" reality and how it might be perceived by others. Peculiar to the experience of hope is my subjective disposition toward the outcome as an engaged possibility, whereas in wishing, I can live in the wishing without an actual engagement in the outcome. Hence, when I am about to undergo surgery, I do more than wish all goes well (which I could do, of course), but I hope all goes well. Accordingly, I am implicitly more at a remove, as it were, when I wish than when I hope.

Of course, there are other experiences that have an engagement, similar to the act of hope, yet are distinct from the hope-act, namely, "longing." When, for example, I long to see a friend who is in prison, it is more than a wish to see him; my orientation is an engaged one, maybe even emotionally charged. But this engagement lacks another essential element that distinguishes hope both from wishing and from longing: sustainability, which presupposes a basis of hope. Thus, I may long to see my friend literally without any hope of him ever being released.

In order to articulate this sustainability peculiar to hope's structure (belonging to the modality of possibility), let me first describe the hope-act as essentially related to an other-than-myself. I reserve the treatment of hope as sustainable until after I treat the following dimension of hope (see section 4 below).

3. Hoping as Essentially Other-Related

Hoping is a way of taking up a situation not only by being personally engaged, but by experiencing myself as not being sufficient to the situation or as not in control of the situation I live through. If we inquire even further into the structure of hope, we observe that hope is an act that is directed toward an "outside" or to an "other-than-myself." This is a structure that is essential to all acts of hope, and constitutes one of the core features of this experience. Negatively put, this feature is suggested by the fact that when I hope, the hoped-for outcome is *given as not in my control to bring it about.*

Even the most ordinary cases of hope harbor something very unordinary, namely, an orientation to an "other-than-myself," and it is this sense, even if implicit, that I want to trace back to its ultimate foundation. For example, if I am gambling, repairing a computer, or in a relationship, and if I *hope* (e.g., to win, to fix it, or to be with someone), I am implicitly directed to an other-than-myself where the hope is concerned. Alternately, if I experience myself as in control of a situation or as completely confident to bring something about, I will not hope; there is no motivation for it. Therefore, no matter what the objective circumstances are, my hope implies that I am not ultimately in control of the situation, which is to say, I rely on something else that is able to govern the situation. Accordingly, not only is the current hopeful situation not in my control, in hope I find myself in relation to an outside of myself which also is not in my control.

It may be objected, however, that there are certain cases of hope where I am not oriented to any "outside" of myself; I not only trust in my own abilities, but I hope precisely in my own abilities such that the hoped for event is in my control. I could hope, for example, that I do well in an interview, or even, that I had done well on my exam. By "in my control," I understand, in its narrowest scope, my capacity, as who I am now, to bring about something in the living-present, however broadly this be taken. If I say, for instance, "I hope to finish this book soon," I do not mean that I cannot read, but that it is not in my power to bring it about now; perhaps I am lacking in energy and time, and it is literally "beyond me" to do it. Similarly, when I hope to do well in an interview or to have done well on an exam, I am appealing implicitly to something that will make it so, "something" in my future or "something" animating my past actions that will make it so. When I hope in this way, I implicitly presuppose that I, myself, have no power to produce this situation now or any power to change what is already done, but I hope that something "in" what has happened will make it so.

These are perhaps trivial examples. I mention them because even in these everyday examples, we see that to experience a "not in my control" in hope points to a "beyond myself," to an "other-than-myself" to bring about something whereby I experience, however implicitly, a dependence upon this something other beyond myself. Hence, hope is an act that expresses an experience of some power greater than my own as a power upon which I am dependent for occasioning the hoped-for event; it evokes a relation of reliance and dependence.

So far I have considered hope primarily in terms of object relations. But these experiences point back more profoundly to the experience of myself and my finitude. For this reason, when I experience hope, in any dimension of my life, it does not only indicate a power other or greater than me or an "outside" to myself; it does not just evoke a relationship of dependence and reliance; it reveals most profoundly that I am not self-grounding. If I were self-grounding, I would be sufficient unto myself, I would be my own ground for the hope-act, which is to say, there would be no emergence of hope as a distinctive experience. The other-than-myself upon which I rely in hope is the other that "grounds" me in hope, and not just particular events that are hoped-for. The experience of hope, then, reveals the experience of an "other" who gives me to myself, and hence as not self-grounding, in terms I will suggest below, as *sustainable*, without cause or arbitrariness. That which gives me to myself is that which sustains me in my openness and my becoming as witnessed in the hope-act.

The experience of dependence and reliance on a power of some kind other than or outside of myself, and the experience of not being self-grounding that is given in the hope-act, points to a dimension of experiencing that I would call most radically "religious." Even though hope does not have its only significance in the religious dimension of experience, hope only takes on its full significance at the religious level.

By religious experiencing, I do not mean practices or rituals undertaken within a religion or cultural heritage, or a making a petition to God. To cite Otto, religious experience is the experience of being before "an overpowering, absolute might of some kind," the experience of the presence of that "Something," that "whom or what," which Otto calls the "numinous" (Otto 1958, 10).[5] Here, however, the numinous is not necessarily qualified as Personal, since in any religious experience, it may still remain undetermined. Accordingly, when I hope, I may have no specific "other" in mind. In my view, however, this other-relatedness peculiar to the religious dimension of experiencing would have to be understood most profoundly as inter-Personal. Elaborating upon the latter observation would take us beyond the confines of this paper, and would demand an appeal to the experiences of various mystics to show this fundamental dimension.

Here I want to restrict myself to four observations. First, there is a general characteristic in hoping of the essential relation to a "beyond" myself that is revealed in and through the experience of hope. It suggests that the inter-personal dimension is essential to hope, and that hope cannot be reduced to the mastery of the ego.[6] Second, the experience of not being in control and of finding myself before an other-than-myself in a relation of dependence (however implicitly) means that the attitude coeval with hope is humility, not pride; "I" cannot be the ultimate motivation for hope. This would be one reason why hope could not be reducible, e.g., to desire. Desiring, like wishing and longing, are acts rooted in the "I" or the "subject." Desire has no ground, or strictly speaking, I am the ground of desire; and when I desire, I am oriented toward a specific object as subject to myself. In desire, I am left to myself, as it were, and if I were left to myself, I would only wish-for, long-for, or desire. But by virtue of the ground of hope, which is given in and

---

5   See Otto 1958, 11-23.

6   There is thus not only an inter-Personal dependence, but an inter-personal one as well in the experience of hope.

through hoping (or loving—but this is a topic for another paper), I am not left to myself. In this way, hoping does not evolve from desire, but it can signal the eclipse of desire. In desire, the "other" is the object of my desire. In hope, the other-than-myself is sustainer of the hope act in its initiated orientation.[7]

Third, the hope experience is rooted ultimately in a religious experiencing, and this is why hope can and must point to an other-than-myself in all instances of hope, no matter what that hope pertains to or no matter how vague this "beyond" myself might be experienced in otherwise everyday acts of hope. Certainly, hope takes place in acts that are not explicitly religious. Hoping that my cell phone works after I drop it is not directly a religious act. When I take it to the repair shop, and hope the agent can fix it, I am relying upon the ability of another person to fulfill my hope. I do not have to pray to God, for example, for this to be the case. My point, however, is that these experiences are grounded in a dimension of experiencing instituted through a primordial experiencing of an outside force in terms of reliance and dependence. Without any explicit religious appeal, a hope, one as seemingly innocuous as hoping my cell phone works, is only possible on the basis of such experiencing. Accordingly, when I hope for something, my hoping is oriented precisely as a specification or delimitation trained on this or that. This is why hoping my cell phone works is not explicitly a religious act. Nevertheless, since hoping is most fully religious in character, my hoping with respect to the cell phone is simultaneously a de-limitation, that is, an opening; it opens me, implicitly, precisely to this foundational religious dimension.

Finally, because it is in the religious dimension of experience that hope receives its fullest significance, wherein modes of givenness such

---

7 Not being left to myself means that I am not self-grounding. I am given to myself as sustainable, or alternately, that I am sustained by this ground. On the one hand, being sustainable in the matter of who I become means that I am not determined in advance. If it were given as determined, neither hope nor fatalism could emerge as possible experiences (a point I will come back to below—since hopelessness presupposes hope). On the other hand, being a sustainable in the matter of who I can become means developing "my way" is sustainable on the basis of hope. If my emergence were arbitrary (say, in the case of vitalism), there would be no sustainability for "my way," no experience of a "vocation," and no "ground" for the hope of the sustainability of my way, and no basis for experience of hope to emerge.

as epiphany and revelation are operative (and not the presentation of objects), the very structure of intention-fulfillment has to be called into question where hope is concerned. Not only does the ground of hope not fit the category of object-givenness, but we would have the experience of more being given than what I hoped-for, and hence an "overflowing" beyond the intention of hope. Accordingly, we would have to distinguish between the intention of hope, which is oriented toward something, and hopefulness. Hopefulness is already an orientation to the ground of hope, without any particular object intended in the hope act. In fact, that comportment of hopefulness, which is grounded in the ground of hope, imbues and animates all I do, even when I explicitly carry out an act of hope. For this reason, hopefulness would have to be understood as foundational for the hope-act, and as oriented toward the ground of hope as no-thing in particular, could be understood most profoundly as "revelatory" of mystery.

Hoping therefore entails a basis for hope, which is a reliance on an other force for living the situation beyond its otherwise closed strictures. But this ground of hope is only given in and through the hope act itself. I do not first think "I cannot bring something about by myself; therefore, I will hope." It is not as if the ground of hope were somehow given first, and then I hope, or when I hope, the hope act somehow causes the ground of hope. When I hope, "I" do not "appeal" to the ground of hope; but in and through hoping, an appeal is made, or can be understood as having been made. It is not my hoping that is efficacious, but the other-than-myself which is the motivation in hoping. As I intimated above, hoping is a peculiar way of taking up a situation spontaneously, originally each time, such that the experience itself is the relying on another force of some kind and such that it "reveals" a ground of hope out of which hoping itself becomes possible. The ground of hope is "discovered" only in and through the experience of hoping.

4. Hope as Sustainable

Hope is the experience of an engagement. In addition, due to the other-oriented dimension of hope, which reveals a ground of hope, possibility is also *sustainable*. For this reason, hope cannot be "merely" subjective. Without this basis or ground of hope, which enables the orientation in hope to be sustainable, one would be unable to distinguish, e.g., a hope from a mere wish or hope from merely longing. Longing and wishing are differentiated by the former demanding an engagement and the latter permitting a frivolity. But both are differentiated from hope insofar as hope is, essentially, sustainable. Thus, in wishing, longing, like in hoping, there is nothing we can do; but in hope, something can be done, as it were, and this goes to the ground of hope.

When I hope, for example, that I find a piece of dark chocolate, or when I hope to become a horse, all objective criteria are held in check by the ground of hope, whatever that may be. I take the hoped-for event as sustainable. Somehow it can happen, despite what I expect, despite its probability, despite what others think, despite how it may look "objectively." Note also that the motivation with respect to hope is essentially different from that of expectation. A motivation is given for expectation "internally," as it were, from the past and present. In hope, a "beyond" motivates and sustains the hope (precisely as the ground of hope, be it the horse-people, the Holy, etc.).

Let's examine the other side of what it means for hope to be lived as sustainable. When I am engaged in the hoped-for outcome as sustainable, I simultaneously have before me the contingency of that same outcome as not occurring. Although the ground of hope is the founding moment in the sense that it makes hope sustainable, to be sustainable also entails a contingency. Otherwise, the act of hope would be immaterial. Let me give an example. I am seated in a café, waiting for a friend to arrive. We had made plans to meet for a performance; my friend is reliable, and I expect him to arrive any time now. As the hour approaches, I begin to get nervous, and I hope that he arrives soon. Here, I experience that he may not arrive on time. Expectation is still functional, and in all probability he will arrive on time, but now an act of hope is carried out that intervenes in the situation and qualifies it uniquely. If the contingency were not given along with the positive sustainability, hope would not arise as an experience.

Notice that the other-than-myself or outside-of-myself I mentioned above cannot be experienced as a pre-determining, necessitating force, be it either from laws of nature or a deity. In fact, it is in the face of such necessitating determinacy that I hope (and this means that in hope such a force has to be experienced as something other than necessitating). On the other hand, by noting that a hoped-for event is experienced as contingent, I am not suggesting that the event is experienced as impossible—that is, where it is given as ruled out in advance.

Certainly, something may be understood objectively to be impossible, or be experienced as impossible by someone else. But I cannot at the same time hope and experience what is hoped-for *as* impossible. For example, I might hope to survive an F5 tornado while standing in its path, even though for everyone else it would just be "suicide." For me, it is—by some means, and motivated by the ground of hope—experienced as possible to survive it even though I am aware that I probably will not survive it. There is at least a hairsbreadth of sustainability given in hope. If I *experience it as* impossible, I will not hope.

Thus, hope does not have the same rapport with impossibility as it does with some of the other features I have described, like expectation, probability, and improbability. But whereas hope may be at odds with expectation or probability while I live through both (possibly) contesting experiences, hope *transforms* the experience of impossibility such that the two cannot be lived through simultaneously. For example, I am on the coast when an earthquake hits offshore; an enormous tidal wave towers above me on the beach and I take any attempt to flee as futile; it is impossible to outrun the tsunami, and I give up. Now, if I were to experience hope in such an instance, which is entirely possible, I could not simultaneously experience my escape as impossible. Hope lives the situation in such a way that the "limits" are no longer definitive, and their rupture is sustainable. Hope does not merely mollify the experience of the impossible; it commutes the experience of the impossible into a sustainability.

In brief, hope operates in the sphere of engagement and sustainability; it takes place in excess of or in the face of expectation, probability, improbability, and impossibility, but in the latter case, it transforms the experience of the impossible and makes it precisely, hopeful.

5. Hope and Denial

With the commutation of the experience of impossibility through the experience of hope, questions concerning denial naturally surface. When I hope, am I not just really living in denial, in denial, that is, of an impossible situation? For the sake of simplicity, let us define denial as not accepting the "facts" as they are presented, so that when I am confronted with a situation, I posit a different reality. Objectively speaking, the reality I deny may or may not be true. At issue is the fact that when I live in denial, I do not accept the reality as presented, and I do this by positing a different one. Further, in denial, I do not explicitly experience my positing of a new reality *as* a denial. Rather, I take my position as "just the way things are." It is only to another that I am "in denial" or it is adduced as such by the outside. Finally, denial is not future oriented, but present oriented. In denial, I assert that the present situation is such and such; there is no different outcome to be awaited, and no change of a situation. I posit the state of affairs as such, now; this is the way it is and nothing anyone can say or do will change that.

In hope, however, I do not deny the present facts, for in some sense, they are already accepted. Yet, in this tacit acceptance, hope is directed toward the future and a possible transformation of the current situation. What is held in check, as I intimated above, is the expected, the likely or unlikely, or the impossible outcome of the situation. Further, in hope, I do not posit the futural outcome as real, for if it were real, I would be precisely in the experience of the fulfillment of hope, which, when fulfilled, would be the cessation of hope. But where hope is operative, it is functional "despite" or in the face of an outcome that might run counter to the hoped for event.

Let's take the example of a person missing in action (MIA), and let's begin with the case of denial. After a time, let's say, a loved one hears word from military officials that his brother has been killed in a war. Denial would imply a negation of this situation and the positing of another one. "I don't believe it" (i.e., I *believe* something else); "he is still alive"; "he will come back home soon." Or I can catch myself in denial "It can't be true," I say to myself. One could live in this belief posture for an indeterminate time. Certainly, the person who is living in actual denial of this official promulgation may actually be right; perhaps it is a case of mistaken identity; the brother is still alive and will come back. The point is that in denial a situation is negated and a different reality is accepted such that when I deny a particular "reality" there is no room for hope, since I have already asserted another reality.

Now, if we examine this example in light of hope, we see immediately how hope is distinctive from denial. In hope, there is not a direct denial of the situation; but I do not accept the finality of it, either. Against expectation as an unbroken, straightforward relation, against probability or impossibility, I *hope*, which takes up the situation as an engaged, sustainable one with at least an implicit ground for that hope. "Yes, I understand what you tell me, but still I hope he is alive." I do not imagine that he is alive; I do not expect that he is alive, I am not "optimistic" that he is alive. I hope, against all odds, that he is alive. Someone may think that I am just desperate; my family and friends may think that I am "in denial." But when I *live* through the experience of hope I do not negate a current reality by positing a different reality, I implicitly acknowledge both the negative and positive possibilities, and live the hoped-for event as sustainable. The positing of a new present reality on either side of the report (acceptance or denial), would not be the experience of hope; it might be the disappointment or fulfillment of hope as accepting a new reality, but it would not be or would no longer be hope.

6. The Temporal Structure of Hope

Hope, I have maintained, is not itself a temporal act, i.e., in the manner of protention, expectation, or anticipation, but it does have a temporal character. Its temporal character is what I call "awaiting." This awaiting is an openness and an endurance, what we could also term a patience. By "patience," I do not mean a kind of "waiting around," but a mode of comportment that is precisely in opposition to my *actively* assuming control of the situation, that is, in contrast to what we might term an "actience."[8] In hoping, I await not only the fulfillment of hope; I endure in hope not only because the hope is sustainable (by virtue of the ground of hope), but I await due to the contingency expressed in hope. Certainly, I can give up hope, even generate a new hope. My point is that in the experience of hoping, as long as the hope is functional, ongoing, *as long as we live in the hope, this awaiting is an enduring, a patience.*

Let's contrast this awaiting as endurance and patience with a similar but essentially different temporal experience of waiting-for. Waiting-for as futurally oriented is tied to expectation; more precisely, waiting-for is a modification of expectation. I cannot wait-for something that I do not also expect; but as we have seen, I can hope for something that I do not expect; I await, and while the hope is ongoing, I await enduringly. In hope, I await the return of the MIA, while I may not expect the return or even wait-for such a return.

Let's now look at a particularly complex situation involving expectation, waiting-for and awaiting. I am in a waiting room at the doctor's office. I have given my name, informed the receptionist that I have an appointment, etc. I *expect* the nurse to call my name any moment now. I look

---

8   I take this expression from Mike Smith who offered this distinction.

at the clock, a few minutes have past, and I patiently *wait-for* the nurse to call my name. Notice that as long as I expect the course of events to follow through according to how they have run in the past (if it accords with my expectation), I do not hope that the nurse will arrive; he will, it is just a matter of time; I wait-for the call with more attentiveness than merely expecting. Now 30 minutes have past and he has still not called my name, and I grow irritated and impatient. Notice also that while I could remain or could have remained patient, impatience is a possibility in waiting-for, something that is not possible in awaiting.

I can become impatient in waiting-for because I assert my wanting to be in control of the situation, and this implicitly removes the relation of dependence and reliance that is essential to hope and awaiting in hope. Waiting-for can be impatience because it allows the expression of my being in control, or negatively put, of my not wanting to be dependent or reliant on anything else, either actually or virtually. Thus, the moment I want to take over the situation, or feel it necessary to take control of the situation—and maybe well I should—is the moment I am no longer in the hope-experience.

In contrast, I remain patient in awaiting because of my dependence on the other-than-myself, the ground of hope, in hoping. In some sense, I have to let it happen. But I also hope, in patience, because in and through the hope act, the ground of hope gives the hope as sustainable. I can "await" in hope, since I am not left to myself.[9] By contrast, there are no grounds for impatience; there might be grounds for anxiousness, uncertainity, etc. due to the contingency mentioned above, but in the hope act itself, there can only be grounds for endurance in awaiting.

---

9 Lest we think that hope is always positive, even within the religious sphere of experience, let us examine an example from St. Teresa of Avila. She writes: "Look at the good remedy the devil gave me and the charming humility—the great disquiet within me. But how could I quiet my soul? It was losing its calm; it remembered favors and gifts; it saw that this world's pleasures are disgusting. How it was able to go on amazes me. I did so by means of hope because I never thought (insofar as I now recall, for this must have happened twenty-one years ago) I would cease being determined to return to prayer—but I was waiting to be very purified of sin. Oh, how wrong was the direction in which I was going with this hope! The devil would have kept me hoping until judgment day and then have led me into hell." See St. Teresa of Avila 1976, Ch. 19/11. In this case, hoping was a distraction and a false humility since according to her the devil had insidiously become the sustainer of hope.

It is true that I could become impatient with respect to something that was hoped for, but at that moment, at the moment I become impatient, the hope act has ceased. *Impatience is a sign of disappointed hope.* Hope has become something else at that point. Maybe the hope just goes away, maybe it becomes hopelessness, or even despair, maybe I just "wait-for." But, again, as long as the hoping is functional, there is patience where the fulfillment of hope is concerned.

I ask the receptionist if it will be much longer, and I am told that the doctor had an emergency, he will be back eventually, but it may take a while. Now it is not clear that I will get my appointment since I have to be somewhere. I don't expect the doctor to show up in time, but a hope arises, namely, that the doctor will get here before I have to leave. This hope is the intrusion of patience in the situation, and immediately colors it differently; the tenor of my comportment in this situation is modified precisely in terms of hope. I hope the doctor arrives in time for me, even if it runs contrary to everything I expect or wait-for; I really do not believe the doctor will arrive in time, but I hope so. As long as I hope, I will remain there in the doctor's office. I endure it, I tarry with the situation; I do not leave.

These descriptions of the hope-experience have yielded some basic structures of hope, and have also enabled us to glimpse its distinctiveness from other acts that share similar characteristics or that might be associated with hope. Hope, for example, has an irreducible futural sense, but is not a mode of time-consciousness. Its temporal structure is constituted as awaiting. It is an act that is essentially related to what is beyond myself. Similar to other acts of the emotional life, like loving, it is essentially "other-related," where this "other"—however it is given—becomes the ground or basis of hope. Further, hope introduces a dimension of possibility, precisely as sustainable and engaged. As such, it is essentially distinct from experiences like imagining, wishing, longing, or negatively, denial. Finally, one cannot simultaneously experience hope and the impossible *as* impossible; if this were the case, the latter would be precisely the experience of despair or hopelessness.

There are admittedly many other dimensions of the hope-experience that would have to be considered: a more detailed account of fulfillment and disappointment peculiar to hope, the relation between hope and hopefulness, the relation between faith and hope, desire and hope, promise and hope, optimism and hope, and the relation between despair and hopelessness. But this delimitation of the hope experience at least provides us with a few fundamental features of this unique experience that can be qualified and elaborated upon in future work.

Works Cited

Bloch, Ernst. 1959. *Daz Prinzip Hoffnung*, 3 vols. Frankfurt am Main: Suhrkamp.

Husserl, Edmund. 2001. *Analyses Concerning Passive and Active Synthesis: Lectures on Transcendental Logic*, trans. Anthony J. Steinbock. Dordrecht: Kluwer Academic Publishers, 2001.

Marcel, Gabriel. 1962. *Homo Viator: Introduction to a Metaphysic of Hope*, trans. Emma Craufurd. New York: Harper Torchbooks.

———. 1967. "Desire and Hope," trans. Nathaniel Lawrence. In *Readings in Existential Phenomenology*, eds. Nathaniel Lawrence and Daniel O'Connor. Englewood Cliffs, N.J.: Prentice Hall.

Moltmann, Jürgen. 1965. *Theologie der Hoffnung*. Munich: Christian Kaiser.

Otto, Rudolf. 1958. *The Idea of the Holy*, trans. John W. Harvey. New York: Oxford University Press.

St. Teresa of Avila. 1976. *The Collected Works of St. Teresa of Avila*, vol. 1, trans. Kieran Kavanaugh O.C.D. and Otilio Rodriguez O.C.D. Washington, D.C.: ICS Publications.

NOTES ON CONTRIBUTORS

Ronald Bruzina is Professor of Philosophy at the University of Kentucky. He is the author of *Edmund Husserl and Eugen Fink: Beginnings and Ends in Phenomenology, 1927-1938* (Yale University Press, 2005). He is preparing a four-volume edition in German of Fink's complete notes from 1926-1940 to appear in Eugen Fink's *Gesamtausgabe* (Karl Alber).

Keith D'Souza, S.J., teaches Philosophy and Religious Studies at St. Pius College, the Archdiocesan Seminary of Bombay, India. His specialized areas of teaching, research, and interest are hermeneutics, fundamental theology, and inter-religious dialogue.

Paul Gyllenhammer is Assistant Professor of Philosophy at St. John's University, Queens, NY. He has recently published "Three Dimensions of Objectivity in Husserl's Account of Passive Synthesis," *Journal of the British Society for Phenomenology*; "The Call of Literature and Sartre's Reevaluation of Bad Faith," in *Phenomenology and Literature* (forthcoming).

David Ingram is Professor of Social and Political Philosophy at Loyola University Chicago. His publications in the area of hermeneutics, philosophy of history, and critical theory include *Habermas and the Dialectic of Reason* (1987); *Critical Theory and Philosophy* (1990); and *Reason, History, and Politics* (1995).

David Koukal is Professor of Philosophy at the University of Detroit Mercy. His scholarship deals with how the work of various phenomenologists relate to imagination, media, pedagogy, politics, and technology.

Kenneth Maly is Emeritus Professor of Philosophy at the University of Wisconsin-La Crosse and lives now in Toronto. He is the co-editor of *Heidegger Studies* and *Environmental Philosophy*, the editor of two volumes on Heidegger and Heraclitus and co-translator of several books by and about Heidegger, among them *Contributions to Philosophy (From Enowning)*. His new book *Heidegger's Possibility: Language, Emergence—Saying Be-ing* will appear in 2007 (The University of Toronto Press).

Hans Rainer Sepp has held various teaching and research positions in Germany and in Europe. He is the author of *Praxis und Theoria: Husserls transzendentalphänomenologische Rekonstruktion des Lebens* (Alber, 1997); *Bildung und Politik im Spiegel der Phänomenologie* (Königshausen & Neumann, 2004). He has also edited numerous volumes on phenomenological topics.

Anthony Steinbock is Professor of Philosophy at Southern Illinois University at Carbondale. He is the author of *Verticality and Idolatry: On a Phenomenology of Religious Experience* (Indiana, forthcoming), *Home and Beyond: Generative Phenomenology after Husserl* (Northwestern, 1995; German translation, 2003), and is the translator of Edmund Husserl, *Analyses Concerning Passive and Active Synthesis: Lectures on Transcendental Logic* (Kluwer, 2001).

Jacques Taminiaux is Professor Emeritus at the University of Louvain and Boston College. He is the author, among many others, of *Heidegger and the Project of Fundamental Ontology* (SUNY, 1991; *Poetics, Speculation, and Judgment: The Shadow of the Work of Art From Kant to Phenomenology* (**SUNY, 1993**); *The Metamorphoses of the Phenomenological Reduction* (Marquette UP, 2004); *Art et Événement* (Berlin, 2005)

Pol Vandevelde is Professor of Philosophy at Marquette University. He is the author of *Etre et discours. La question du langage dans l'itinéraire de Heidegger (1927-1938)* (Académie royale de Belgique, 1994) and *The Task of the Interpreter: Text, Meaning and Negotiation* (University of Pittsburgh Press, 2005). He also co-translated into French books by Heidegger (Gallimard 1991) and Husserl (Millon, 1998).

David Vessey is a visiting scholar and lecturer at the University of Chicago. He works on twentieth-century Continental philosophy, especially hermeneutics, and on the intersection between phenomenology and American pragmatism.

Stephen Watson is Professor of Philosophy at the University of Notre Dame. His writings include *Extensions: Essays on Interpretation, Rationality, and the Closure of Modernism* (SUNY, 1992), *Tradition(s) I: Refiguring Community and Virtue in Classical German Thought* (Indiana, 1997) and *Tradition(s) II: Hermeneutics, Ethics, and the Dispensation of the Good* (Indiana, 2001). His recent scholarship includes a number of articles on philosophical interpretations of Paul Klee.

INDEX